Praise for *Core Animation*

"[This book is] a neat introduction to Core Animation. Both beginners and advanced developers will find many useful nuggets of information and techniques in this book."

—Brian Christensen

"*Core Animation* has prepared me for the future of user interface programming on Macs and iPhones—and I'm glad it's here because the future is now."

—Brent Simmons, NetNewsWire Developer

"Anyone endeavoring to undertake animation of any significance can benefit from owning a copy of this book. Marcus Zarra and Matt Long provide a much-needed guide to the basics of simple and grouped animations along with stylistic guidelines for when and how they should be used. However, it is the treatment of the book's advanced material that will keep this book relevant to the developer long after it has been used to master the basics."

—Daniel Pasco, CEO, Black Pixel

Marcus Zarra
Matt Long

Core Animation

Simplified Animation Techniques for Mac® and iPhone® Development

✦Addison-Wesley

Upper Saddle River, NJ • Boston • Indianapolis • San Francisco
New York • Toronto • Montreal • London • Munich • Paris • Madrid
Cape Town • Sydney • Tokyo • Singapore • Mexico City

The publisher offers excellent discounts on this book when ordered in quantity for bulk purchases or special sales, which may include electronic versions and/or custom covers and content particular to your business, training goals, marketing focus, and branding interests. For more information, please contact

U.S. Corporate and Government Sales
(800) 382-3419
corpsales@pearsontechgroup.com

For sales outside the United States, please contact

International Sales
international@pearson.com

Visit us on the Web: www.informit.com/aw

Library of Congress Cataloging-in-Publication Data:

Zarra, Marcus, 1970-
   Core animation : simplified animation techniques for Mac and iPhone development / Marcus Zarra, Matt Long.
       p. cm.
   Includes bibliographical references and index.
   ISBN 978-0-321-61775-0 (pbk. : alk. paper) 1. Computer animation 2. Core animation (Application development environment) 3. Application program interfaces (Computer software) 4. Mac OS. 5. iPhone OS. I. Long, Matt, 1973- II. Title.
   TR897.7.Z37 2010
   006.6'96—dc22

                                                              2009038600

ISBN-13: 978-0-321-61775-0
ISBN-10: 0-321-61775-4
Text printed in the United States on recycled paper at Courier in Kendallville, Indiana.

First printing December 2009

Editor-in-Chief
Karen Gettman

Senior Acquisitions Editor
Chuck Toporek

Senior Development Editor
Chris Zahn

Managing Editor
Kristy Hart

Project Editors
Julie Anderson
Jovana San Nicolas-Shirley

Copy Editor
Apostrophe Editing
Services

Indexer
Erika Millen

Proofreader
Sheri Cain

Editorial Assistant
Romny French

Interior Designer
Gary Adair

Cover Designer
Chuti Prasertsith

Compositor
Nonie Ratcliff

Table of Contents

Part I   Getting Started with Core Animation

1   What Is Core Animation?   3

Animation and the Cartesian Plane 3
Your Free Lunch 5
What Is a Layer? 5
    What's a Layer For? 8
Animation and Layers 9
    Animation Pacing 9
Math? I Was Told There Would Be No Math 10
Core Animation and the iPhone 11
Notes on Sample Projects 12
    Setting Up Xcode Projects for OS X (Xcode 3.1 and Earlier) 12
Summary 14

2   What Can and Should I Animate?   15

What Can I Animate? 15
    Color 16
    Motion 17
    Attributes 18
    Visibility 18
    Filters 19
    Content 19
    Masking 20
What Should I Animate? 22
    Design Principles 22
    When Should I Use Core Animation? 23
    What Shouldn't I Animate? 23
Summary 24

Part II   Core Animation Fundamentals

3   Basic Animations   27

The Simplest Animations 27
The Animation Proxy Object 28
The Differences Between Window, View, and Layer Animation 28

Window Resizing 28
View Resizing 30
Layer Resizing 31
Preparing a View to Perform Layer Animation 32
Create the Xcode Project 33
Add the Animation Layer to the Root Layer 34
Layer Allocation Considerations 35
Using CABasicAnimation 36
Animating Versus Setting Layer Properties 37
Implicit Layer Animation and the Default Timing Function 38
Visual Stickiness 39
Useful Animation Properties 40
Animation Grouping 41
Summary 44

4   **Keyframe Animation**   **45**

Changing Values Over Time 46
Two Methods to Specify Keyframe Destinations 46
From Basic Animation to Keyframe Animation 50
Keyframe Animation Timing 50
Monitoring Keyframe Destinations 52
Keyframe Animation for UI Cues 56
Implementing the Icon Shake Using Keyframe Animation 57
Summary 66

Part III   **Core Animation Layers**

5   **Layer Transforms**   **69**

Scale Transform 70
Using -rotateTransform: 72
Using -rotate3DTransform: 73
Anchor Points 74
Combining Transforms 76
Scale Versus Bounds 79
Summary 81

6   **Layer Filters**   **83**

Applying Filters to Core Animation Layers 84
Animating an Applied Filter 85
Receiving User Input 89

Making the Effect "Sticky" 91
Controlling Filter Values with Data Bindings 92
Applying Filters to Transitions 98
The Default Transitions 98
Using Custom Transitions 101
Summary 109

7   QuickTime Layers   111

Working with QTMovieLayer 111
Creating a Simple QTMovieLayer-Based Player 112
Adding Overlays 118
Overlaying a Time Code 119
QTMovieLayer and contentsRect 122
Working with QTCaptureLayer 123
Creating and Displaying the QTCaptureLayer 125
Capturing the Current Image 127
Summary 129

8   OpenGL Layer   131

Rendering Video in a CAOpenGLLayer 131
Layer Timing 133
Rendering Multiple Video Channels 138
Implementing the CAOpenGLLayer Derived
OpenGLVidGridLayer 140
Summary 148

9   Quartz Composer Layer   149

Creating a Multi-Video Stream with Quartz Composer ... 150
Creating Controllable Parameters 152
Creating the Xcode Project 152
Adding a QCCompositionLayer to the Window 153
Passing Parameters to the Quartz Composition 154
Getting Image Data from the Composition 155
Obtaining the Current Image in Code 157
The Quartz Composition Layer and OpenGL 159
Summary 160

10   Other Useful Layers   161

CAShapeLayer 161
Manipulating the Path Stroke 163
Using CAShapeLayer as a Layer Mask 165

CAGradientLayer 168
CAReplicatorLayer 171
   Building the UIView 171
   Utilizing the ReplicatorView 173
Summary 174

Part IV   Advanced Core Animation

11   User Interaction   **177**
The Click of a Mouse 177
Hit Testing CALayer Objects 177
Hit Test 179
Example Application: Color Changer 179
LZButtonLayer 179
Interface Builder 182
Building the Layers 183
Watching the Mouse 186
Keyboard Events 188
Layer-Backed Views 190
Summary 191

12   Performance   **193**
Hardware Acceleration 193
Rules of Thumb 194
   Avoid Offscreen Rendering 194
   Limit the Use of Filters and Shadows 195
   Use Transition Effects Wisely 195
   Avoid Nested Transforms 195
   Minimize Alpha Blending 196
Tiled Layers 199
   How Does This Work? 201
Multithreaded Animation 202
   Mutlithreading with Filters 204
   Threads and Run Loops 204
Summary 205

13   Core Animation on the iPhone   **207**
The (Cold Hard) Facts About Core Animation on the iPhone 207
   The Good 208
   The Bad 208

Building a Core Animation Application for Cocoa Touch 209
    Setting Up the Xcode Project 209
    Building the UIWindow 210
    Adding the QuartzCore Framework and Binding the Objects 211
Core Animation and Cocoa Touch Example 214
    Setting Up the Xcode Project 215
    Building the TouchMeViewController 216
    Implementing the TouchableView 218
Doing Animations at the UIView Level 223
    Building the Application 223
    Building the View Controller 223
Summary 226

Index   **227**

About the Authors

Marcus Zarra is the owner of Zarra Studios, LLC and the creator of seSales and iWeb Buddy. In addition, he is a coauthor of *Cocoa Is My Girlfriend*, a wildly popular blog covering all aspects of Cocoa development. Zarra has been developing software since the mid-1980s and has written software in all the major technological fields.

Matt Long has been in the software industry since 1996. He has developed software with a wide array of technologies and platforms in addition to OS X and the iPhone, including Unix, Microsoft Windows, and Microsoft .NET. His experience on these other platforms makes him uniquely qualified to help other programmers who are themselves making the transition to the Mac OS X and iPhone using Cocoa and Cocoa Touch. In addition, he writes for the *Cocoa Is My Girlfriend* blog, which demonstrates usage of not only Core Animation but many other technologies related to Mac OS X and the iPhone.

Acknowledgments

A while back, I had the pleasure of meeting a fellow developer by the name of Matt Long and helped him become more proficient with Cocoa and its related technologies. During that time, we continued to share what we were learning and teaching in the form of the blog *Cocoa Is My Girlfriend*. All that led to this book. What started out with a simple altruistic gesture has turned into the text you are about to enjoy.

First, I would like to thank Matt Long for convincing me to share what we learned in a broader space than just one-on-one. I think that discussion has changed both our lives forever.

I would also like to thank two great friends that I made along the way of learning and working with Cocoa and Objective-C. Both Mike Lee and Daniel Pasco have been great supporters of this book and have helped me when things became difficult.

Lastly, I would like to thank my wife, who puts up with the long nights, missing weekends, and all the traveling that this career path has caused. I frequently tell people that my wife rarely walks besides me; she is more often behind me, pushing me forward. Without her, I would not be where I am today. Lyndia, thank you for all your support.

—*Marcus Zarra*

An endeavor such as writing a book is one I thought I could never pursue, let alone accomplish, but here we are at the end of the project, and somehow I've proven that wrong. Along the way, some folks have helped immensely to make that a reality. And so here they are.

I will start with my beautiful wife, Elissa. We married in June 1997 and moved to Colorado four months later. She is my complement. We were made for one another. I enjoy her and am thankful for her. She always works hard to clear the path to enable me to get work done, including writing this book. She takes great care of our four kids and our home. I love her and am very blessed to have her. I would call her my best friend, but I tend to think that phrase is kind of silly. She's more than a best friend. She's my wife.

I would like to acknowledge my friends Joel Schuster and Chuck Dunn—some fellow programmers who tease me about using a Mac. Not so sure they're still laughing, but they're good friends who help me to keep going. Sorry guys, but Java still sucks and C#, well, it's moderately better. But I digress.

Dr. Gregory Plett is also a good friend who kept asking me, "How's the book coming?" I appreciate his prodding. Greg has taught me a lot over the years, and I keep learning from him—both in engineering and in life.

Thanks also go to Fraser Hess, who kept us honest by asking Core Animation questions at NSCoder Night. We just kept telling him, "It's in the book." He didn't find it amusing, but now that the book is released, we can really mean it. I hope it will be a useful reference to him and other Cocoa/Cocoa Touch programmers. There would be some glaring omissions had it not been for Fraser's questions.

I also want to thank Chuck Toporek and Chris Zahn, our editors who helped to keep us on task. Thanks for giving me some slack when I had surgery, but thanks for also pushing us forward. I'm sorry it took so long, but I hope we can do this again.

Finally, I want to acknowledge my coauthor Marcus Zarra. Marcus is a good friend and fellow programmer, but more than that he has been and continues to be a great mentor to me. We started the blog, *Cocoa Is My Girlfriend*, together. We started NSCoder Night in Colorado Springs together, and we wrote this book together. I wouldn't have been able to do any of that without his mentoring. Marcus gives his time and his voluminous programming knowledge (including his endless rattling off of facts about Objective-C internals) without expecting anything in return. He's a very giving person, and I'm thankful to have met him. Thanks for everything, Marcus. I do appreciate it. Show your gang signs my friend... [...]. Down with the dot!

—*Matt Long*

PART I

Getting Started with Core Animation

IN THIS PART

CHAPTER 1   What Is Core Animation?   3

CHAPTER 2   What Can and Should I Animate?   15

What Is Core Animation?

IN THIS CHAPTER

▶ **Animation and the Cartesian Plane**

▶ **Your Free Lunch**

▶ **What Is a Layer?**

▶ **Animation and Layers**

▶ **Math? I Was Told There Would Be No Math**

▶ **Core Animation and the iPhone**

▶ **Notes on Sample Projects**

Core Animation enables you to develop complex animations for many different types of applications. You can simply animate your views within a window, or you can create a thousand sprites represented by layers on the screen for that next killer game. In this chapter, we introduce you to the basic concepts behind Core Animation. We take a look at views and layers to ensure you understand what you can do with animation in each. We start with a discussion about animation and the coordinate plane and then move on to getting well acquainted with the Core Animation base class, CALayer, and its related protocols.

Animation and the Cartesian Plane

When you have become familiar with Core Animation and start using it in your applications, you will see that animation is easy on both Mac OS X and the iPhone. The fact is, though, that animation has not always been easy. Prior to Core Animation, you needed to understand some fairly complex subjects such as double buffering and more complicated mathematics such as plane geometry—especially if you wanted to give your animations any sense of depth. Core Animation abstracts all of that away. If you wanted to move a sprite across the screen doing it the old way, you needed to create an off-screen graphics context, draw your sprite to that context, swap out that context with one currently on the screen, move the sprite position, and then draw to the swapped out off-screen graphics context. Lather, rinse, repeat.

Although this process isn't terribly difficult, it can present some challenges to the developer that Core Animation completely eliminates. The Core Animation way to do the exact same thing is to create a layer that contains your sprite and simply call –setPosition. As you learn in chapters to come, the position of a layer is represented by a single point on the screen. By default, a layer's position is the center point of the layer within its parent's coordinate space. So what does that mean?

Core Animation uses the standard Cartesian coordinate system you remember from geometry and trigonometry. The values for *x* are on the horizontal axis, and the values for *y* are on vertical axis. When naming a point, the *x* is always the first value, so a value of 25,35 means *x* = 25 and *y* = 35. Different from a standard Cartesian coordinate plane, however, is that you are only ever using the upper-right portion of the plane where the numbers are all positive. This means that the bottom-left corner of the screen is at point 0,0. The upper-right portion of the screen then is the width (*x*) and height (*y*) depending on the resolution of the screen you use. On a 15-inch MacBook Pro, this value is 1440,900. For example, if you created a sprite on a layer and wanted to animate it from coordinate 0,0 on this MacBook Pro, you could set the position of the sprite to 0,0 when it is created and then call –setPosition(CGPointMake(1440,900)) and the sprite layer would animate to the upper-right corner of the screen. Of course, this assumes that the sprite is in a view that covers the entire screen, as layers cannot display without being backed by a view.

Differing Coordinate Systems

One thing you should keep in mind when determining where to position your layers on a view is that the coordinate system might work differently from one system to another. If you have experience drawing in a coordinate system on other platforms such as Windows, the coordinate system might feel upside down. On Windows, the origin point 0,0 is located at *the upper-left* corner of the screen instead of the bottom-left corner.

Fortunately, if you are used to using a coordinate system that works this way, Cocoa views provide a simple way to help you feel right at home. You can create your own NSView derived view and override the method called –isFlipped. In this method, simply return YES (a true value) and Quartz (the 2D drawing system) assumes you want to draw everything with your coordinate origin in the upper-left corner.

Interestingly, this coordinate system—with the origin in the upper-left corner—is the default for drawing behavior in a UIView on the iPhone, so keep that in mind if you need to duplicate drawing functionality between OS X and the iPhone. You want to override NSView and have –isFlipped return YES for OS X so that you don't need to rewrite your code for the iPhone.

Your Free Lunch

They say that there is no such thing as a free lunch, but when it comes to animating with Core Animation, you don't just get lunch, you get a drink and desert as well. For example, all the drawing going on is happening behind the scenes using OpenGL. Yet, you don't need to know anything about OpenGL to take advantage of the hardware acceleration offered by your video card. This is fully abstracted by Core Animation. If you do want to get to the more nuts-and-bolts level of OpenGL, though, you can do so by using the CAOpenGLLayer on OS X. As of this writing, things aren't quite as easy on the iPhone for OpenGL, but they are not too far off. The layers and layer-backed views on the iPhone also give you great performance benefits.

Another freebie in Core Animation is that all the animation happens on a background thread. This means that the user interface isn't blocked when the animation runs. And you don't need to be a multithreading expert to take advantage of it! In fact, if you've never worked with multiple threads, you won't notice a thing. Just set the animatable property on your layer or view and watch the action happen.

> **NOTE**
>
> To learn more about how to use Core Animation in your iPhone apps, see Chapter 13, "Core Animation on the iPhone."

What Is a Layer?

The layer, represented by the CALayer class and its derivatives, is the most basic fundamental building block you will use for your all your Core Animation-based applications. All Core Animation layers provide a lightweight layer within a view that enables you to display visual content. Here is how Apple describes a CALayer in the API documentation:[1]

> CALayer is the model class for layer-tree objects. It encapsulates the position, size, and transform of a layer, which defines its coordinate system. It also encapsulates the duration and pacing of a layer and its animations by adopting the CAMediaTiming protocol, which defines a layer's time space.

Notice how it says that it is the "model class." This might be confusing if you are familiar with the Model-View-Controller (MVC) design pattern, as you might more naturally think that because Core Animation is of a visual nature, the View part of MVC might make more sense. Ultimately, it is the NSView on the OS X side and the UIView on the iPhone side in which the layer is stored that does the drawing. The CALayer simply contains the data (model) that is relevant to all the layer's attributes such as background color, border width, position, size, transform, and such.

---

[1]From p. 7 of Apple's *CALayer Class Reference*: http://developer.apple.com/mac/library/documentation/GraphicsImaging/Reference/CALayer_class/CALayer_class.pdf.

Core Animation provides a slew of different layers that help you achieve different functions based upon your application needs. If you need to play a movie, for example, you wouldn't want to try to grab the movie frames manually and display them in the `content`

NOTE

See Chapter 2, "What Can and Should I Animate?," to see a list of the animatable properties of a layer.

field of the layer as this would create a lot of overhead, and your movie wouldn't play smoothly. Instead, you would simply want to use a `QTMovieLayer`, which abstracts movie playback very well. All you need to provide to a `QTMovieLayer` is a path to a movie file on disk, and it handles the rest. Figure 1-1 shows the hierarchy of Core Animation layers and the frameworks to which each of them belong.

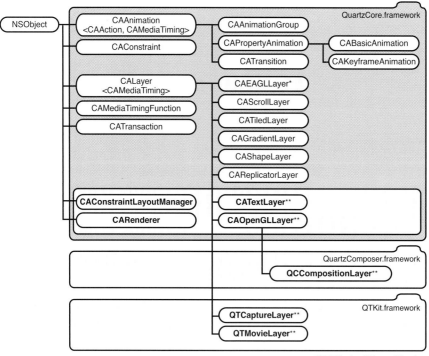

FIGURE 1-1   Core Animation Layers

As Figure 1-1 shows, there are numerous layers available in the Core Animation toolbox. Here is a brief explanation of each layer type:

▶ `CALayer`
This is the base class from which all Core Animation layers derive.

▶ `CATextLayer`

This layer provides a convenient way to display a string in your layer tree. You specify all the layout information as with any other layer, but you can also specify the text, font, font size, and foreground color that the layer uses for the text provided. If you specify an `NSAttributedString`, these other fields with be ignored. This layer is only available on OS X.

▶ `CAScrollLayer`

This layer enables you to scroll content that is larger than the viewport of the containing view.

▶ `CATiledLayer`

This layer enables zooming and panning of content that is larger than the viewport of the containing view.

▶ `CAOpenGLLayer`

This layer provides a convenient way to do OpenGL rendering in your application. We cover this layer is greater depth in Chapter 8, "OpenGL Layer." This layer is only available on OS X.

▶ `CAEAGLLayer`

This layer provides a way to perform OpenGL rendering on the iPhone. This layer is only available on the iPhone.

▶ `QTMovieLayer`

This layer enables you to simply play back QuickTime movies in your Core Animation-based application. Because it is a Core Animation layer, you can add additional layers to its `sublayers` property and composite other visuals on top of a playing movie. We cover this layer in greater depth in Chapter 7, "QuickTime Layers." This layer is only available on OS X.

▶ `QTCaptureLayer`

This layer takes advantage of a camera connected to your computer for the purpose of video capture and real-time playback. You can use your iSight camera or a muxed device such as a DV camera to capture video. The actual capturing is done via other QuickTime classes available, but the `QTCaptureLayer` enables you to see current frames from your connected camera in real time. We cover this layer in greater depth in Chapter 7. This layer is only available on OS X.

▶ `QCCompositionLayer`

This layer enables you to play back a Quartz composition as part of your Core Animation-based application. It also enables you to control the Quartz composition using key-value coding. We cover this layer in greater depth in Chapter, 9 "Quartz Composer Layer." This layer is only available on OS X.

As of Mac OS X 10.6 Snow Leopard and iPhone OS 3.0, these additional layers are also available:

- ▶ CAShapeLayer
  This layer enables you to create an arbitrary shape based upon a path that you define. We cover this layer in detail in Chapter 10, "Other Useful Layers."

- ▶ CAGradientLayer
  This layer provides a convenient way to display a linear gradient. You can define multiple colors and stops at which points the display shifts to the different colors you have specified. We cover this layer in detail in Chapter 10.

- ▶ CAReplicatorLayer
  This layer replicates the sublayers you add to it according to the parameters you specify. We cover this layer in detail in Chapter 10.

What's a Layer For?

Layers provide a discreet component or building block for creating complex animations. There are actually two basic categories for animation:

- ▶ View animation, which is primarily used when you want to give your user interface some visual cues.

- ▶ Layer animation, which is more commonly used for application content and functionality.

You will at times want to use layers for your user interface. However, it is not as common to use it that way because layers do not receive events such as clicks and key presses. You need to capture the event at the backing view level and then pass it on to the layer if you want to do something with that information in the layer.

Imagine a *Space Invaders* game for the iPhone. You create a ship sprite that moves along the bottom of the view when you tilt the device side to side. This sprite is drawn on its own layer. When an accelerometer event is received in the backing view, you pass along the event to the layer and call -setPosition on the layer to move it where it should be according to the accelerometer event. You might also want to receive tap events, so you can fire the ship's photon torpedoes at the invaders; these are also sprites, each in their own discreet layers.

You can see how quickly the number of layers you would need for a game would accumulate. Layers are the right choice in this kind of application as they are lightweight and perform well. Views also perform well, and you could certainly use them instead of layers; however, you gain performance when using layers over views when the number of items (either layers or views) on the screen reaches a certain count. This is less of an issue on OS X than on the iPhone of course, but keeping your application lean and efficient is always a good idea.

1

Animation and Layers

In Core Animation, timing is everything. When you animate a layer property, you have to decide how long the animation should take, how it should move (easing), whether it should return to its starting value, and how many different values the property should have during its run (basic animation versus keyframe animation). You specify each of these attributes by setting values for the animation properties. However, these values are not specified in the layer itself, but rather in the CAAnimation animation object and its derivatives, CABasicAnimation and CAKeyframeAnimation.

Once again, the layer is a model object, *not* a view object in the MVC design pattern. The layer contains attributes that describe the layer: position, frame, colors, and so on. Similarly, an animation describes the animation itself, but the properties you set relate to the layer

> **NOTE**
>
> Basic animation and keyframe animation are covered in great detail in their respective chapters: Chapter 3, "Basic Animations," and Chapter 4, "Keyframe Animation."

you are animating. You cause a layer to animate by adding the animation object to the layer object with a call to -addAnimation:forKeyPath. Similarly, you stop a layer from animating by removing the animation from the layer with a call to -removeAnimation: forKeyPath, although the default behavior is for an animation to be removed automatically after it has run.

Animation Pacing

As previously mentioned, Core Animation gives you a lot of functionality for free. When you perform animation without Core Animation, you iterate a property value using a loop. Doing so produces an animation that changes in a linear fashion. This is to say that the animation animates at a constant rate. Each step in the animation is reached in an exactly subdivided increment of the total duration. In Core Animation, however, the default animating functionality causes an animation to ease in and ease out. This means that the animation starts out slow, speeds up in the middle, and then slows again when it gets close to its destination value. This concept of easing causes an animation to appear more natural and organic—whereas a linear animation has a more static feel because the property changes at an exact and rigid constant rate.

Core Animation gives you a great level of flexibility when it comes to animation pacing. For the vast majority of applications, you will be satisfied with the built-in pacing functions. These include

▶ Linear, for when you do want that more static feel.

> **NOTE**
>
> The default animating functionality is ease in/ease out, but this is not obvious because if you check the value of the timingFunction parameter of your animation, you will find that it is set to nil, which might indicate to you that the animation is using linear animation as the default. This is not the case.

▶ Ease in, where your animation starts out slowly and then reaches full speed.

▶ Ease out, where your animation starts out at full speed and then slows as it reaches its destination value.

▶ Ease in, ease out, where your animation starts out slow, speeds up in the middle, and then slows down again as it reaches its destination value; this is the default behavior.

All the calculations are done for you automatically, you simply specify which pacing function you want to use. If you decide, however, that you want to have more control over the pacing of your animation, you can specify an array of timing functions and times in a keyframe animation that will give you the control you are looking for. You learn more about animation pacing in Chapter 4.

Math? I Was Told There Would Be No Math

When you first start using Core Animation, you might assume you need to use trigonometric equations to do complex calculations for effects such as scaling and rotation. Fortunately, this is not the case. The scale and rotation, and a slew of other properties, are animatable with little code. You simply specify start and stop values along with the property you want to animate, and Core Animation handles the rest.

In one of our earliest blog posts[2] on Core Animation, we explain how to scale a cluster of layers. We referred to the effect as the Dashboard Effect. We later realized that when people think of an effect in Dashboard, they are usually thinking of the ripple effect you see when you add a new widget to the Dashboard. What we mean by Dashboard Effect, however, is the effect you see when you initiate the Dashboard with a key-press or a hot corner, depending on how you have it configured in the Mac OS. The widgets appear to fade and fly in from outside of your screen when you open Dashboard. And when you close it, they fade and fly out.

At first, we tried to figure out the equations for scaling each layer manually, but then it became clear that Core Animation layers use a tree hierarchy and automatically cascade effects to child layers. What this means in essence is that all you need to do is add the cluster of layers to one large parent layer and simply scale that parent layer, and all the child layers will automatically scale with it. You can achieve this effect with the code in Listing 1-1.

LISTING 1-1   Scaling Layers

```
- (void)doItIn:(float)duration
    {
        // Set the animation duration
        [[NSAnimationContext currentContext] setDuration:duration];
```

[2]*Core Animation Tutorial: Dashboard Effect* http://www.cimgf.com/2008/03/15/core-animation-tutorial-dashboard-effect/.

LISTING 1-1   Continued

```
if( scaleUp )
{
    // Scale everything (x, y, and z) by a factor of
    // factor (static variable) and reduce the opacity
    CATransform3D transform = CATransform3DMakeScale(factor,
                                                     factor,
                                                     factor);
    [mainLayer setTransform:transform];
    mainLayer.opacity = 0.0f;
    scaleUp = NO;
}
else
{
    // Scale the rect back down to the original and bring up
    // the opacity
    CATransform3D transform = CATransform3DMakeScale(1.0f,
                                                     1.0f,
                                                     1.0f);
    [mainLayer setTransform:transform];
    mainLayer.opacity = 1.0f;
    scaleUp = YES;
}
}
```

Listing 1-1 shows only the transform of the main parent layer. Adding the child layers is fairly simple, and we have provided the code from that blog post as a resource for this chapter, so take a look at it to see the complete code and how to implement this effect.

> **NOTE**
>
> The sample project that demonstrates this effect is called, simply, Dashboard Effect.

For many people, using more complex mathematics is daunting, but again, as part of your free lunch from Apple, you don't *need* to know much in the way of mathematics to effectively use Core Animation. Basic arithmetic is really all you need to know. It is that simple.

Core Animation and the iPhone

You might be reading this book because you want to use Core Animation for an iPhone app you're working on. We have dedicated an entire chapter to using Core Animation on the iPhone to help you understand some of the basic differences. The differences are small, and often you can use the exact same code on the iPhone that you would use on the desktop. In subsequent chapters, you learn about all the different aspects of Core Animation, and we try to discuss the differences that are relevant to the iPhone where it makes sense to do so. In some of the layer-specific chapters, we don't discuss the iPhone because these layers are not yet available for the iPhone.

Notes on Sample Projects

All the sample projects we provide in this book have a main application delegate class. In the case of sample code on OS X, we create an application delegate class that we always name AppDelegate. In iPhone projects, the project template automatically creates an application delegate class named using the format <project_name>AppDelegate, in which <project_name> is the name you give your project.

> **NOTE**
>
> If you use Xcode 3.2 or later, the project template automatically creates an application delegate for OS X projects the same way it does for iPhone projects. If you use anything earlier, however, you need to use the steps in the next section to set up your own AppDelegate class.

On OS X, the majority of the code is placed in the AppDelegate class. On the iPhone, the majority of the code is placed in the view controller class for the view being developed, whereas the application delegate class provides basic setup and boostrapping of the application. It's a subtle difference, although an important one.

Setting Up Xcode Projects for OS X (Xcode 3.1 and Earlier)

When you create a new project in Xcode 3.1 or earlier for OS X development, the project template does not automatically create the application delegate class for you as it does in iPhone projects or OS X projects in Xcode 3.2 and later. Adding one is not difficult, but you need to know how to do it if you set up your own projects from scratch rather than simply relying on the sample code. When you create a project for OS X development, use the following steps to add an application delegate and the QuartzCore framework, the framework that provides the Core Animation classes.

1. In Xcode, press Shift-⌘-N and select **Cocoa Application** in the Project Templates dialog.

2. Name the project and click Save.

3. Expand the Frameworks group, Control-click the Linked Frameworks subgroup, and select **Add > Existing Frameworks**.

4. In the resulting dialog, navigate to */System/Library/Frameworks* and select **QuartzCore.framework**. Click Add and then Add again when prompted.

5. Control-click the Classes group and select **Add > New File**.

6. In the New File template dialog, select **Objective-C class** under the Cocoa group and click Next.

7. Name the file *AppDelegate.m* and make sure Also Create "AppDelegate.h" is checked. Click Finish.

8. Select **AppDelegate.h** to open the file in the code editor and add the following code to import the `QuartzCore` framework and to create an outlet to the window in your XIB:

```
#import <QuartzCore/QuartzCore.h>
@interface AppDelegate : NSObject
{
    IBOutlet NSWindow *window;
}
```

9. Select **AppDelegate.m** to open the file in the code editor and add the following code to turn on layer backing for your window's `contentView`:

```
@implementation AppDelegate
(void)awakeFromNib;
{
    [[window contentView] setWantsLayer:YES];
}
@end
```

10. Under the Resources group in your project, double-click *MainMenu.xib* to open the XIB in Interface Builder.

11. From the Library palette, drag an `NSObject` object into *MainMenu.xib* and rename it `AppDelegate`. You need to be in icon view to rename the object. Click once to select the object. Pause and then click it again to place it in edit mode. Then you can rename the object.

12. Make sure your `AppDelegate` object is selected. In the object inspector, click the Identity tab and change the Class field to `AppDelegate`.

13. In *MainMenu.xib*, control-click on File's Owner and drag the connection to the `AppDelegate` object. Select `delegate` in the ensuing context menu.

14. In the *MainMenu.xib*, control-click on `AppDelegate` and drag the connection to the Window object. Select window in the ensuing context menu.

15. Save the XIB file and return to Xcode.

This setup is the foundation for all the projects we create on OS X. From this template, you can add actions and outlets that connect your controls in the XIB to a reference in your `AppDelegate` class. We refer to these steps for setting up your OS X-based projects throughout this book.

Summary

Core Animation is a huge evolutionary step for the Mac OS. Other OSs will continue to try to mimic what Apple has done but will likely continue to fall short. The Core Animation framework is quite amazing for all it provides for free. With just a little effort and some good ideas, you can produce some incredibly compelling and useful applications. Core Animation gives you more than you might expect, and we would bet that in each subsequent version we will see even more exciting capabilities.

What Can and Should I Animate?

IN THIS CHAPTER

▶ **What Can I Animate?**

▶ **What Should I Animate?**

Core Animation provides a wide array of properties that you can animate on both Core Animation layers and Cocoa windows and views. But just because you have Core Animation in your toolkit, though, doesn't mean it should be used for everything in your app. This chapter looks at the properties you can animate and discusses whether you should animate them.

Core Animation is a great technology, but every great technology can be overused or downright abused. We make some suggestions to help you avoid the pitfalls that lead to such abuse. You'll be thankful you took our advice and so will your users.

What Can I Animate?

Animation is something that you apply to visual things: windows, views, and layers. Animation doesn't make sense unless there is something being changed visibly on the screen. This is why although you can use a layer as a key-value coding container for custom properties, you might not animate those properties. Animatable properties are only those properties that provide visual feedback when changed and are the only properties that are animatable according to the Core Animation specification.

The categories covered in this section help you get a better understanding of what properties are available for you to animate.

Color

Core Animation uses an internal algorithm to calculate animation of color changes. When you specify a fromValue and a toValue or byValue in a CABasicAnimation or an array of CGColorRef values in an array that you provide to the values field of a CAKeyframeAnimation, Core Animation determines and fills in all the in between colors to be used over the duration of the animation.

Listing 2-1 demonstrates how to create a basic animation that changes the background color of a layer from red to green over a period of 5 seconds.

> **NOTE**
>
> **Tweening**
>
> In the world of animation, this is known as *tweening*; where the code looks at the start and end values and automatically calculates and runs the values in between.

LISTING 2-1   Animating the Background Color from Red to Green

```
- (CABasicAnimation*)backgroundColorAnimation;
{
    CABasicAnimation *anim =
    [CABasicAnimation
    animationWithKeyPath:@"backgroundColor"];

    [anim setDuration:5.0];

    CGColorRef red =
    CGColorCreateGenericRGB(1.0, 0.0, 0.0, 1.0);
    CGColorRef green =
    CGColorCreateGenericRGB(0.0, 1.0, 0.0, 1.0);

    [anim setFromValue:(id)red];
    [anim setToValue:(id)green];

    CFRelease(red);
    CFRelease(green);

    return anim;
}
```

The example code creates a basic animation object, CABasicAnimation, using the keypath backgroundColor and sets a starting value and ending value using the -setFromValue and -setToValue parameters. It sets the duration to 5 seconds by calling -setDuration:5.0. When this animation is added to a layer, the layer's background color starts to animate immediately.

On the iPhone, this code changes slightly as colors are manipulated using the UIColor class. Listing 2-2 demonstrates how to create the same animation for the iPhone.

LISTING 2-2   Animating the Background Color from Red to Green on iPhone

```
- (CABasicAnimation*)backgroundColorAnimation;
{
    CABasicAnimation *anim =
    [CABasicAnimation
    animationWithKeyPath:@"backgroundColor"];

    [anim setDuration:5.0];

    [anim setFromValue:(id)[[UIColor redColor] CGColor]];
    [anim setToValue:(id)[[UIColor greenColor] CGColor]];

    return anim;
}
```

Color fields that you can animate include

▶ `backgroundColor`
  The layer's background color.

▶ `borderColor`
  The color of the layer's border.

▶ `shadowColor`
  The color of the layer's shadow. At the time of this writing, the `shadowColor` property is not available on the iPhone.

Motion

When you want motion on the screen, Core Animation provides rectangles and points in each layer that you can animate. Motion fields you can animate include

▶ `anchorPoint`
  The default `anchorPoint` of a layer is `0.5,0.5`, which indicates the center of the layer is the `anchorPoint`. If you change the `anchorPoint` to `0.0,0.0`, it will be located at the bottom-left corner.

▶ `bounds`
  The `bounds` property animates the shape of the bounding rectangle. It does not affect the layer's position.

▶ `frame`
  The `frame` property is not animated in a layer. You can set this parameter and the layer's internal value with change; however, you won't see the actual animation. If you want to animate a layer's bounds, that is, its bounding rectangle, use the `bounds` property. If you want to change the position, use the `position` property. On views and windows, setting `frame` causes the bounding frame to animate.

▶ position
Use the `position` property to move a layer's position. The `position` is dependant upon the `anchorPoint` property. If you want to center a layer in its parent view, leave the `anchorPoint` at the default of `0.5,0.5` and then calculate the center of the parent view. Listing 2-3 demonstrates how to center the layer.

LISTING 2-3   Center the Layer in Its Parent View

```
NSRect parentViewRect = [[window contentView] frame];
[layer setPosition:
    CGPointMake(parentView.size.width/2.0,
    parentView.size.height/2)];
```

▶ zPosition
The `zPosition` property controls the *z*-index of the layer. This determines the layer's position from front to back. It can be animated to transition one layer on top of another.

Attributes

Each visible characteristic of a layer can also be animated. These are referred to as *attributes* because they are the fields that affect the visible attributes of the layer.

Attribute fields that you can animate include

▶ borderWidth
The `borderWidth` property sets the width of the border that surrounds the layer.

▶ cornerRadius
The `cornerRadius` property sets the radius of the corners of the layer giving the layer a rounded rectangle look.

Visibility

Layer's are visible components, but you can determine how visible. Sometimes, you need to see through partially or completely. You control this with the visibility fields.

Visibility fields that you can animate include the following:

▶ opacity
The `opacity` property determines the layer's opacity. A value of `1.0` sets the layer to fully opaque, and a value of `0.0` sets the layer to fully transparent. Use values in between to set just how opaque you want your layer to be.

▶ hidden
In theory, the `hidden` property is animatable; however, it's actually just an On or Off switch. If you want to animate the visibility of a layer, use the `opacity` property instead of `hidden`.

Filters

When used in conjunction with Core Image, Core Animation layers can have complex filters applied to them by setting one or more of the filter fields. Core Image filters are not, at the time of this writing, available on the iPhone.

Filter fields that you can animate include the following:

- `filters`
  The `filters` property is an array of filters that you can apply directly to the layer's content. It affects the entire layer, including the border and background.

- `compositingFilter`
  Different from the `filters` property, the `compositingFilter` property uses a single filter as its parameter.

- `backgroundFilters`
  The `backgroundFilters` property provides a way for you to apply filters to the layer's background only.

Content

The content field of a layer is set using an image, specifically a `CGImageRef`. If you use a `CAKeyframeAnimation` to animate this field, you can create a simple slideshow application with a minimal amount of code. You can create an array of `CGImageRef` objects and set that array as your animation's `values` field. When the animation is added to the layer, it transitions between each image in the order they are found in the array. You can alter the order of the images by changing the order of the array. You can also change the type of transition you use. We cover transitions in great depth in Chapter 6, "Layer Filters."

Content fields that you can animate include

- `contents`
  The `contents` property expects a `CGImageRef` object to display an image.

- `contentsRect`
  Think of the `contentsRect` property as a view port of the layer contents. The contents rectangle values (x, y, width, and height), are tied to the size of the layer bounds. The four values of the `contentsRect` rectangle, however, are proportions rather than actual points on the screen. The default is 0.0, 0.0, 1.0, 1.0. When you change the x, for example, the value is between 0.0 and 1.0. If you set x to 0.25, the view port of the content's rect displays at pixel 100.0 of a 400.0-pixel wide layer (400.0 × 0.25), or 25 percent of the layer's original width. If you set the width to 0.25, the width of the view port is be 100.0 pixels on a 400.0-pixel wide layer (400.0 × 0.25), or 25 percent of the layer's original width. Figures 2-1 and 2-2 demonstrate how `contentsRect` works by showing what portion of the original image layer is displayed in the `contentsRect`.

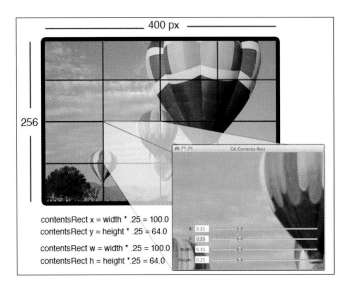

FIGURE 2-1   One Quarter Width and One Quarter Pixel Position

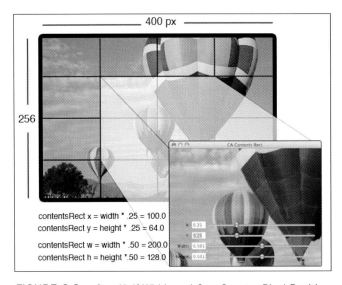

FIGURE 2-2   One Half Width and One Quarter Pixel Position

Masking

Layers provide a way to mask their contents using masking fields. Masking fields that you can manipulate include

▶ mask

The mask property is itself a layer. The opacity of the mask layer determines how the effect renders. When you specify a mask, keep in mind that that the mask bounds determine what is allowed to show through rather than what is blocked from view. In other words, if you specify the width and height of the mask layer to be 300 × 300 pixels and specify the center of the window as the mask layer's position property, you see a 300 × 300 portion of the containing layer show through in the center of the window. The surrounding part of the 300 × 300 square is what is actually masked, as illustrated in Figure 2-3.

FIGURE 2-3   A Simple Mask Layer

▶ masksToBounds

The masksToBounds property ensures that content is clipped to the bounding rectangle. It is particularly useful when you have set a corner radius on a layer with content and want to ensure that the content doesn't spill to the outside of the content rectangle where the rounded corners are.

NOTE

At the time of this writing, there is no way to simply invert the mask. If you want to mask the surrounding area instead, you must draw and fill the appropriate path in the mask layer with –drawInContext in a derived layer or use -drawLayer:inContext if you use a delegate.

What Should I Animate?

Core Animation gives you a lot of power and flexibility enabling you to enhance your application's user interface with ease. There are, however, principles that you should adhere to when you use Core Animation. In other words, just because you can animate something doesn't mean you should. In this section, we talk about some overarching principles that should guide your designs, and some suggestions of things you should animate and things you should not.

Design Principles

Let's face it; developers are not designers. There are a few exceptions to that statement, but for the majority, it is a rule. If you are a designer and you take offense to that statement, be thankful for your abilities and forgive the sentiment. For the rest of us, however, here are some helpful guidelines.

Keep It Simple

You've heard this one a thousand times, but you still ignore it. Most developers have to be reminded on a regular basis that just because you can add all the controls you need to a tiny little iPhone view to perform some task doesn't mean you should. When you think of simplicity, don't think of what will make it simplest for you to implement but what will make it simplest for your user to use. Keeping it simple is all about them—not you.

Don't Design, Borrow

You are likely in the nondesigner engineer camp as that label applies to the majority. You should probably never, therefore, try to design a user interface from scratch. Instead, look at the other applications out there that you admire most and borrow ideas from the ones you like.

Pay a Graphic Artist

If you can afford good graphic artists, use them. I've seen some amazing designs that scoped out the project so well that it left little room for feature creep. Getting a proper design done is well worth the money. Build that cost into project estimates when freelancing and be prepared to pay that up front in your own applications that you intend to sell.

By the Book

When it comes to design, you should adhere to Apple's Human Interface Guidelines (HIG). This is especially true for iPhone development where designing things another way will likely not only look bad but will also create usability issues for your end users. For example, if you try to load your views on top of the current view by adding them as subviews instead of using a navigation controller stack, your design will be difficult to maintain from a coding standpoint, and the flow of the application will disorient your end user. Instead, when you create new views, use view controllers and push and pop them on and off of the navigation stack as specified in the iPhone HIG.

When Should I Use Core Animation?

On certain online discussion forums, people often ask questions like, "I've heard this Core Animation thing is something I should use, but I'm not sure when to use it and when to just use standard views." I would summarize the answer this way. Use views for user input elements and use Core Animation for design elements. In some cases, however, it makes sense to use a hybrid.

User Input

If you need to capture input from the user, use a standard control—which is based on either an NSView on the Mac or a UIView on the iPhone. If you have design skills, Core Animation layers can provide a simpler path to changing the look of your controls to suit your design, but for the rest of us, leave the views alone. Your users will recognize them and will know how to use them instinctively.

Design Elements

If your application requires some sort of animation to adorn the view, use Core Animation layers. For example, if you want to rotate a sunburst image in the background of your carnival game for the iPhone, use a Core Animation layer. Or if you want to animate an image within your view, load the image and set the layer's contents field to display the image. Then move its position with either implicit or explicit animation.

Hybrid

Sometimes, you want to adorn your control views with layers because this visually enhances the view. For example, if you want to display an indeterminate progress indicator in a view while some data is downloading from a website, you can design the view and place the progress indicator in its center in Interface Builder. Then you can make the containing view have a border and a rounded rectangle by accessing the view's layer and setting the cornerRadius and borderWidth properties (see Figure 2-4).

FIGURE 2-4   Activity Indicator View with Rounded Corners

What Shouldn't I Animate?

There are no hard and fast rules, so if you have gotten this far into this chapter and are still uncertain what you should animate, you should review the principles we discussed so far. These can guide your efforts.

After months of working closely with Core Animation and learning all the ins and outs, however, it is clear that there are no absolute rules about what you should not animate. You can make a case in favor of animating nearly anything. You should not make using your interface difficult because of all the animation you add to it. For instance, don't animate controls your user is going to need to click on or type text into. It's fine to animate an entire view into or out of view to draw attention to it, especially on the iPhone, but don't move buttons and text fields around on the screen for visual effect. This is just annoying and will seem more like a practical joke to your user than anything. But in the end, you need to decide what you shouldn't animate in your application. If you are not certain whether an animation makes sense, have someone use it and see how she reacts to the animation. That will get you much farther than any design rule this book offers.

Summary

What you can animate is limited to what Core Animation provides. Fortunately, it provides everything you need and probably nearly everything you would want. What you should animate, well, let's face it—that is entirely up to you. We hope that you'll adhere to the simple principles we've discussed, but we trust that whatever you build you'll build because you're inspired to make beautiful and useful software.

PART II

Core Animation Fundamentals

IN THIS PART

CHAPTER 3   Basic Animations   27
CHAPTER 4   Keyframe Animation   45

CHAPTER 3

Basic Animations

IN THIS CHAPTER

▶ **The Simplest Animations**

▶ **The Animation Proxy Object**

▶ **The Differences Between Window, View, and Layer Animation**

▶ **Preparing a View to Perform Layer Animation**

▶ **Using CABasicAnimation**

▶ **Useful Animation Properties**

▶ **Animation Grouping**

Core Animation is a powerful and mature technology that enables you to create animations that are as simple as you like or as complex as you need. To perform simple animations on windows and views, Apple provides the animation proxy object that, when called, causes an implicit animation to play when some visual component such as the view frame, opacity, or location is changed. For basic layer animation, the CABasicAnimation class provides a way to animate between two values, a starting value and an ending value. In this chapter, we look at these most basic methods for implementing animation in your application.

The Simplest Animations

With Core Animation integrated into Cocoa, you can animate windows, views, and layers implicitly by simply setting the value of the parameter you are interested in animating to some new value. When using a layer (CALayer), all you need to do is set the value with a direct call. For example, if you want to change the bounds of a layer, you simply call [layer setBounds:newFrame] where layer is the CALayer object you've created and added to your layer tree and newFrame is a CGRect containing the values of the new bound's size and origin. When this code is run, the change to the bounds of the layer is animated using the default animation for the keypath "bounds."

Similarly, when using a window (NSWindow) or view (NSView), all you need to do is set the value of the window or view property using the animation proxy object. This means that instead of calling [view setFrame:newFrame] to set the view frame, for example, you instead call `[[view animator] setFrame:newFrame]`. The difference is that we have instructed the view's animator proxy object to set the property for us—which implicitly animates the value from the current value to the value specified in `newFrame`.

The Animation Proxy Object

So what is the animator proxy object? The animator proxy object is available in both `NSView` and `NSWindow`. It implements the protocol `NSAnimatablePropertyContainer`. This container uses Key-Value Coding to set the actual value of whatever parameter was specified while doing the value interpolation and animation behind the scenes.

As the name implies, the animator proxy acts as an agent that takes the value you give it and handles animating the property from the starting or current value to the value specified. It then sets the property as if you had called set on the property explicitly.

The Differences Between Window, View, and Layer Animation

The idea behind animation in windows, views, and layers is the same; however, the implementation differs. In this section, we discuss one of the most common animations you will likely want to implement—frame resizing.

Window Resizing

Since the first version of Mac OS X, the ability to animate a window's frame has been available to developers in the method `-(void)setFrame:(NSRect)windowFrame display:(BOOL)displayViews animate:(BOOL)performAnimation`. The first parameter is the new frame you are animating to. The second parameter tells the window to call `-displayIfNeeded` on all of its subviews, and the third parameter tells the window to animate the transition from its current frame to the frame specified in the first parameter. If this last parameter is set to `NO`, the change to the new frame happens immediately rather than progressively with animation.

> **NOTE**
>
> This call is different than what you use for changing the frame in both `NSViews` and `CALayers`. They both have a method called `-setFrame`. We discuss that more in moment.

With this built-in window frame resizing capability, why would you need to use Core Animation for changing a window's frame? The answer is, simply, you don't. For many cases when resizing, you can use the built-in functionality and you probably should. There may be times, however, when you want more control over animating windows. Keep several things in mind when doing so. `NSWindow` has an animator proxy just like `NSView`. When you call the animator, it animates the parameter you specified, but the parameter is the catch. If you want to move the window to a different position on the screen, for instance, you can either call `- (void)setFrame:(NSRect)windowFrame display:(BOOL)displayViews` (notice the missing third parameter) on the animator proxy object, or you can add an animation to the animations dictionary of the window itself.

First, let's look at how to use the animator proxy. Take a look at the following.

```
[[window animator] setFrame:newFrame display:YES];
```

This makes it simple to animate the frame.

By default, the animation plays back over the course of 0.25 seconds. If you want to change the duration, use an `NSAnimationContext` object, which is the `NSView/NSWindow` counterpart to the `CATransaction`. If we wrap the call to `-setFrame` in an `NSAnimationContext`, the animation runs at the duration we specify. Listing 3-1 demonstrates how to do this.

LISTING 3-1   Wrap Frame Change in an NSAnimationContext

```
[NSAnimationContext beginGrouping];
[[NSAnimationContext currentContext] setDuration:5.0f];
[[window animator] setFrame:newFrame display:YES];
[NSAnimationContext endGrouping];
```

This causes the frame to change over the course of 5 seconds rather than the default of 0.25 seconds. As you see in the next section, this grouping mechanism is also what you use when you want to change the duration of an animation for an `NSView`.

Basic animation using Core Animation can also be used on windows and views, but there is a slight difference in how the animation is set up. As an alternative to calling `-setFrame` on the window animator proxy, we can create a `CABasicAnimation` and animate the `frame` property. Take a look at Listing 3-2 to see how to create, add, and run a basic animation on a window.

LISTING 3-2   Adding an Animation to the Window Animations Dictionary

```
CABasicAnimation *animation =
        [CABasicAnimation animationWithKeyPath:@"frame"];
[animation setFromValue:[NSValue valueWithRect:oldFrame]];
[animation setToValue:[NSValue valueWithRect:newFrame]];
[animation setDuration:5.0f];
[window setAnimations:[NSDictionary animation forKey:@"frame"]];
[[window animator] setFrame:newFrame display:YES];
```

The visual effect is identical to what you see occur when running the code in Listing 3-1.

View Resizing

Views can be resized the same as windows can, but the keypath you use differs. You can call -setFrame on a view using the same code you used for a window, as shown in Listing 3-3.

LISTING 3-3   Animate View Frame Change in an NSAnimationContext

```
[NSAnimationContext beginGrouping];
[[NSAnimationContext currentContext] setDuration:5.0f];
[[view animator] setFrame:newFrame display:YES];
[NSAnimationContext endGrouping];
```

The only difference between this code and the code in Listing 3-1 is the object we're calling –setFrame on—a view in this case.

If you want to use explicit animation, instead of animating the frame, animate the frameOrigin and the frameSize. Listing 3-4 shows how to animate both of these properties.

LISTING 3-4   Explicitly Animating Frame Origin and Size

```
CABasicAnimation *originAnimation = [CABasicAnimation
                    animationWithKeyPath:@"frameOrigin"];
[originAnimation setFromValue:[NSValue
 valueWithPoint:oldImageFrame.origin]];
[originAnimation setToValue:[NSValue valueWithPoint:newFrame.origin]];
[originAnimation setDuration:5.0];

CABasicAnimation *sizeAnimation = [CABasicAnimation
          animationWithKeyPath:@"frameSize"];
[sizeAnimation setFromValue:
[NSValue valueWithSize:oldImageFrame.size]];
[sizeAnimation setToValue:[NSValue valueWithSize:newFrame.size]];
[sizeAnimation setDuration:5.0];

[[view animator] setAnimations:[NSDictionary
                    dictionaryWithObjectsAndKeys:originAnimation,
                    @"frameOrigin",
                    sizeAnimation,
                    @"frameSize",
                    nil]];

[[view animator] setFrame:newFrame];
```

Layer Resizing

Animating a layer's frame is a bit different from doing the same in windows and views. There is no animator proxy available in a CALayer object, but rather animation is always used when you make an explicit change to a property. In fact, if you don't want animation used, you have to explicitly turn animation off. Listing 3-5 demonstrates how to do this.

LISTING 3-5   Explicitly Disabling Layer Animation

```
[CATransaction begin]
[CATransaction setValue:[NSNumber numberWithBool:YES]
                forKey: kCATransactionDisableActions]
[layer setBounds:bounds];
[CATransaction commit];
```

> ### NOTE
>
> **Notes on Disabling Animations**
>
> Alternatively, you can disable animations in a layer based on a keypath by using the delegate method:
>
> `- (id<CAAction>)actionForLayer:(CALayer *)layer forKey :(NSString *)key`
>
> It returns an object that implements the CAAction protocol. It might also return NSNull, which in effect disables the animation for the key specified in the key parameter of the delegate method. When you implement this delegate method, simply check to see if the layer passed in is the one you are working with, and then check to see if the key field is the same as the keypath for which you want to disable animation. If it is, return NSNull.

The CATransaction class is the Core Animation analogue to AppKit's NSAnimationContext object we used in Listing 3-2 and 3-4 for windows and views. Just like NSAnimationContext, CATransaction enables us to set the animation duration. Listing 3-6 demonstrates how to do this.

LISTING 3-6   Setting Animation Duration in a Layer

```
[CATransaction begin]
[CATransaction setValue:[NSNumber numberWithFloat:5.0f]
                forKey: kCATransactionAnimationDuration]
[layer setBounds:bounds];
[CATransaction commit];
```

As you might suspect, we can also animate properties of a layer explicitly. To achieve the exact same effect as we did with the code in Listing 3-6, we can instead use the code in Listing 3-7.

LISTING 3-7   Explicitly Animating the Layer Bounds Property

```
CABasicAnimation *boundsAnimation = [CABasicAnimation
                    animationWithKeyPath:@"bounds"];
[boundsAnimation setFromValue:[NSValue valueWithRect:oldRect]];
[boundsAnimation setToValue:[NSValue valueWithRect:newRect]];
[boundsAnimation setDuration:5.0f];

[layer setBounds:NSRectToCGRect(newRect)];

[layer addAnimation:boundsAnimation forKey:@"bounds"];
```

> **NOTE**
>
> **Notes on Frame Animation**
>
> You might have noticed in the layer example code, we are calling –setBounds rather than –setFrame. It is common to want to move a layer around its containing view, which causes many first-time Core Animation programmers to attempt to use frame as the keypath for layer resizing. As you will quickly learn, however, animating the frame itself won't work. The frame field of the layer is a derived value—calculated from the position, bounds, anchorPoint, and transform properties. This means that although you can set the frame explicitly, it will not animate. This is not a problem though. You just need to determine whether you want to *move* the frame or *resize* the frame. If you want to animate the size of the layer's rectangle, use bounds as your keypath. If you want to move the frame, use position as your keypath. If you want to move *and* resize the layer at the same time, create two animations, one to animate the bounds and one to animate the position.

In Listing 3-6, we used the CABasicAnimation class, the primary animation object for basic animation. We take a deeper look at it shortly, but first we are going to set up a simple Xcode project to demonstrate basic layer animation.

Preparing a View to Perform Layer Animation

The first thing you want to do when you create a Core Animation based project is to make sure the root layer of your view is layer backed. Let's walk through creating a Core Animation-based project and set up the root layer on OS X.

Create the Xcode Project

To create our application, follow these steps:

1. In Xcode, press Shift-⌘-N and select Cocoa Application in the Project Templates dialog.

2. Name the project **CA Basics** and click Save.

3. Expand the Frameworks group, Control-click the Linked Frameworks subgroup, and select **Add > Existing Frameworks**.

4. In the resulting dialog, navigate to */System/Library/Frameworks* and select *QuartzCore.framework*. Click Add twice, as prompted.

5. Control-click the Classes group and select **Add > New File**.

6. In the New File template dialog, select **Objective-C class** under the Cocoa group and click Next.

7. Name the file *AppDelegate.m* and make sure Also Create "AppDelegate.h" is checked; click Finish.

8. Select *AppDelegate.h* to open the file in the code editor and add the following code:

```
@interface AppDelegate : NSObject {
    IBOutlet NSWindow *window;
}
```

9. Select *AppDelegate.m* to open the file in the code editor and add the following code:

```
@implementation AppDelegate
- (void)awakeFromNib;
{
    [[window contentView] setWantsLayer:YES];
}
@end
```

10. Under the Resources group in your project, double-click *MainMenu.xib* to open the XIB in Interface Builder.

11. From the Library palette in Interface Builder, drag an NSObject object into *MainMenu.xib* and rename it to AppDelegate.

12. Make sure the AppDelegate object is selected. In the object inspector, click the Identity tab and change the Class field to AppDelegate.

13. In the *MainMenu.xib*, Control-click on File's Owner and drag the connection to the AppDelegate object. Select delegate in ensuing context menu.

14. In the *MainMenu.xib*, Control-click on AppDelegate and drag the connection to the Window object. Select window in the ensuing context menu.

15. Save the xib file and return to Xcode.

The project is now set up. In the preceding steps, we created an application delegate that we use to provide control to our layer, window, and view.

Add the Animation Layer to the Root Layer

To add a layer that we will be animating, do the following:

1. Open *AppDelegate.h* and add a CALayer instance variable:

```
@interface AppDelegate : NSObject
{
    IBOutlet NSWindow *window;
    CALayer *layer;
}
```

2. Open *AppDelegate.m* and add the layer initialization code in -awakeFromNib:

```
@implementation AppDelegate
- (void)awakeFromNib;
{
    [[window contentView] setWantsLayer:YES];

    layer = [CALayer layer];
    [layer setBounds:CGRectMake(0.0, 0.0, 100.0, 100.0)];

    // Center the animation layer
    [layer setPosition:CGPointMake([[window contentView]
                        frame].size.width/2,
                        [[window contentView]
                        frame].size.height/2)];

    CGColorRef color = CGColorCreateGenericRGB(0.4, 0.3, 0.2, 1);
    [layer setBackgroundColor:color];
    CFRelease(color);

    [layer setOpacity:0.75];
    [layer setBorderWidth:5.0f];

    [[[window contentView] layer] addSublayer:layer];
}
@end
```

Note About Centering the Layer

We could call –setFrame on the layer before adding it to the root layer of our window's contentView layer tree. However, we have decided instead to set the bounds of the layer first and then set the position. (Remember frame is a derived value based on position, bounds, anchorPoint, and transform.) Setting the bounds and position properties like this makes it simpler to center the layer in the containing view. We simply obtain the parent view's width and divide it in half, and then we take the parent view's height and divide it in half. We then call –setPosition on the layer, which perfectly centers our layer in the contentView. This works because the layer's anchorPoint defaults to 0.5,0.5—the center of the containing view. If we were to change the anchorPoint to 0.0, 0.0 the bottom left of the layer would then display at the center of the contentView. Figure 3-1 shows the values for the different anchor points you can use on your layer.

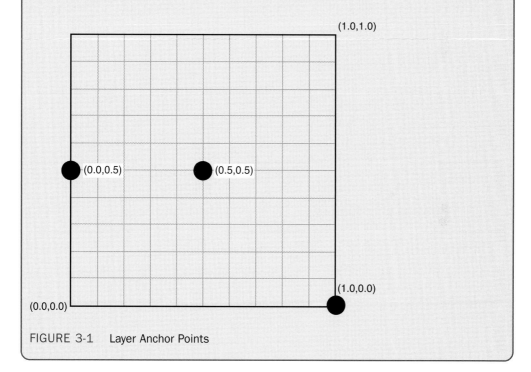

FIGURE 3-1   Layer Anchor Points

Layer Allocation Considerations

Another consideration of which you should be aware when you set up your layers is that even though you have an instance variable (ivar) of your CALayer, it is not retained unless you explicitly retain it. In the world of memory management in Objective-C, the rule of thumb is that you retain only that which you need to retain. You should not retain objects you don't need to hold onto, and you should retain objects that you do need.

It sounds simple, but in practice it tends to be more elusive. In our code in the previous steps, you see we allocate our layer by using the convenience initializer `layer = [CALayer layer];`. This allocates an auto-released `CALayer` object. When the layer object goes out of scope in the `-awakeFromNib`, it will be auto-released unless it is retained. In our case, we are adding it to the `contentView` layer `sublayers` array, which is retaining the layer for us. If, however, we wanted to wait until later to actually add the layer that we initialized in `-awakeFromNib` to the `sublayers` array, we need to allocate the layer by using `layer = [[CALayer alloc] init]`. Then we need to release the layer in the `dealloc` method with a call to `[layer release];`.

The first time you go to use the `CALayer` method called `-removeFromSuperlayer`, you will find that if you try to add the layer to the sublayer array again, it will crash your application. This is because the layer will be released in the call to `-removeFromSuperlayer`. You must retain the layer yourself if you want to remove it from its superlayer but keep it around in memory.

Using CABasicAnimation

At this point, you have already seen the `CABasicAnimaion` object in action. In this section, however, we consider in detail how to take advantage of this class and basic animations.

Basic animation as implemented using the `CABasicAnimation` class animates a layer property between two values, a starting and an ending value. To move a layer from one point to another in its containing window, for example, we can create a basic animation using the keypath `position`. We give the animation a start value and an ending value and add the animation to the layer. The animation begins immediately in the next run loop. Listing 3-8 demonstrates how to animate the position of a layer.

LISTING 3-8   Animate the Layer Position

```
- (IBAction)animate:(id)sender;
    {
        CABasicAnimation *animation =
            [CABasicAnimation animationWithKeyPath:@"position"];
        [animation setFromValue:[NSValue valueWithPoint:startPoint]];
        [animation setToValue:[NSValue valueWithPoint:endPoint]];
        [animation setDuration:5.0];

        [layer addAnimation:animation forKey:@"position"];
}
```

This code moves the `position` of a layer from `startPoint` to `endPoint`. These two values are `NSPoint` objects. The `position` property is the center point of the layer. It is set relative to its containing layer.

If you add this listing to your project we created in the previous section, you simply connect a button to the action in Interface Builder. To do so, follow these steps:

1. Open *AppDelegate.h* and add an action declaration, as follows:

```
@interface AppDelegate : NSObject
{
    IBOutlet NSWindow *window;
    CALayer *layer;
}
- (IBAction)animate:(id)sender;
```

2. Open *AppDelegate.m* and add the animate implementation code provided in Listing 3-8.

3. Open Interface Builder. From the Objects Library, drag a button onto the main window.

4. Control-click the button you just dragged on the main window and drag a connection to the AppDelegate object. Select the animate action.

5. Return to Xcode and Build and Go to see this animation run.

That's it. That is really all there is to animating a layer. You create the animation, set the to and from values, set a duration (which is optional as the default 0.25 seconds will be used if you don't specify a duration explicitly), and add the animation to the layer you want to animate.

That being said, you will not likely leave it at that because the details of implementation add nuance and complexity. For example, the first time you run the animation from Listing 3-8, you notice that while your layer animates to the correct position in the parent view using the duration you specified, when the animation completes, it jumps right back to its starting position. Is this a bug? How can we fix it? We get to that next.

Animating Versus Setting Layer Properties

When you create your CABasicAnimation, you need to specify a start and stop value for the animation using the calls to –setFromValue and –setToValue respectively. When you add your basic animation to a layer, it runs. However, when the property animation finishes, in the case of animating the position property, the layer snaps right back to its starting position.

Remember that when animating, you use at least two objects. These objects are the layer itself, a CALayer or CALayer-derived object, and the animation that you assign to it—the CABasicAnimation object in our previous examples. Just because you have set a final value (destination) for your animation object does not mean that the layer property being animated assumes this value when the animation has finished. You must explicitly set the layer's property so that when the animation has finished, the property you animated will actually be set in the layer to the to-value you specified.

You can simply cause your animation to stop at the end point you specify, but this is only a visible stickiness, if you will. The internal value is still the same. To actually change the internal model value, you have to explicitly set the property in question. For example, to explicitly set the position property, you need to call –setPosition on the layer. This creates a little problem, though.

If you set the value of a property by calling -set on that property explicitly, the default animation will be used rather than one you might set for the property you are animating. Listing 3-9 demonstrates one way you might try to set the position. Notice that we have created a basic animation to use for the position property; however, the explicit call to –setPosition on the layer overrides the animation we set in the line that follows it, making the basic animation completely useless. If you try this code, you see that although our layer ends up in the right position, it uses the default duration of 0.25 seconds rather than the 5 seconds we have explicitly set in the animation.

LISTING 3-9   Animating and Updating the Position Property

```
CABasicAnimation *animation =
        [CABasicAnimation animationWithKeyPath:@"position"];
[animation setFromValue:[NSValue valueWithPoint:startPoint]];
[animation setToValue:[NSValue valueWithPoint:endPoint]];
[animation setDuration:5.0];

[layer setPosition:endpoint];

[layer addAnimation:animation forKey:nil];
```

So now the question becomes, how can you get the animation to use the specified duration? Take a look at the last line in Listing 3-9. Notice that the forKey: parameter of the call is set to nil. This is the reason why the animation is not overriding the default. If you change the last line to [layer addAnimation:animation forKey:@"position"], the animation will work using the duration as expected. This tells the layer to use the new animation we have specified for this keypath whenever it needs to be animated.

Implicit Layer Animation and the Default Timing Function

We can use the CATransaction class to override the default duration as we previously did in this chapter, and it does make it simple to animate the layer using the duration we specify. If we use the code in Listing 3-10, the position property is set in the layer and the property is animated on its way there as you might expect.

Listing 3-10   Overriding the Default Duration for Implicit Animation

```
[CATransaction begin];
[CATransaction setValue:[NSNumber numberWithFloat:5.0]
                forKey:kCATransactionAnimationDuration];


[layer setPosition:endPoint];
[CATransaction commit];
```

However, when you run this code, you see that although it animates the position over a five second duration, it also applies the default media timing function that is kCAMediaTimingFunctionEaseInEaseOut. This function causes the animation to start slowly and then speed up only to slow down again as it approaches its destination. This functionality is fine if that is the media timing function you want, but if you want it to be linear (kCAMediaTimingFunctionLinear), for example, you need to consider another way. And there is no apparent way to set the default media timing function for implicit animations.

This means that if you want to use any other timing function than the default, you have to use explicit animation, as shown in Listing 3-9.

Visual Stickiness

Another approach we might take is to set several properties in our animation object that cause the animation to be sticky when it finishes. In other words, the layer will appear to be at the destination value. The stickiness in this scenario, however, is visual only, which is to say that the underlying value of the layer property, position continues to be the value the position was when the animation started. This is a fine approach if you don't need the internal value to be updated. Listing 3-11 shows how to implement this method, making the layer stick at the end of its duration.

LISTING 3-11   Making the Layer Position Sticky

```
CABasicAnimation *animation = [CABasicAnimation
                animationWithKeyPath:@"position"];
[animation setToValue:[NSValue valueWithPoint:endPoint]];
[animation setDuration:5.0];
[animation setFillMode:kCAFillModeForwards];
[animation setRemovedOnCompletion:NO];


[layer addAnimation:animation forKey:@"position"];
```

We need to set two animation properties for the layer to stay at the destination position. First is the fill mode. We tell it to anchor the animation value to the final value by calling –setFillMode, passing it the constant kCAFillModeForwards. Then we must tell the animation not to remove itself from the layer's array of animations when the animation completes by calling –setRemovedOnCompletion passing it NO.

> **NOTE**
>
> This code effectively causes the animation to finish at the destination, but remember it is only a visible effect. The internal position value of the layer is still at the start value. This becomes problematic if you need to obtain the current value after your animation has run.

Useful Animation Properties

You have already discovered all the properties that you can animate in a layer. However, there are numerous properties available in the animation (CABasicAnimation) object that can give you greater control and enhance your animations.

▶ Autoreverses
By setting autoreverses to YES, the animated property returns to its starting value after it has reached its destination value, but instead of snapping back to the start value, it animates there.

▶ Duration
Duration is a parameter you are quite familiar with at this point. It sets the amount of time to be taken between the fromValue and toValue of the animation. Duration is also affected by the speed property.

▶ RemovedOnCompletion
The default value for this property is YES, which means that when the animation has finished its specified duration, the animation is automatically removed from the layer. This might not be desirable. If you want to animate the property you've specified again, for example, you want to set this property to NO. That way, the next time you call –set on the property being animated in the animation, it will use your animation again rather than the default.

▶ Speed
The default value for this property is 1.0. This means that the animation plays back at its default speed. If you change the value to 2.0, the animation plays back at twice the default speed. This in effect splits the duration in half. If you specify a duration of 6 seconds and a speed of 2.0, the animation actually plays back in three seconds—half the duration specified.

▶ BeginTime

This property is useful in an animation group. It specifies a time for the animation to begin playing in relation to the time of the parent group animation's duration. The default is 0.0. Animation grouping is discussed in the next section, "Animation Grouping."

▶ TimeOffset

If a time offset is set, the animation won't actually become visible until this amount of time has elapsed in relation to the time of the parent group animation's duration.

▶ RepeatCount

The default is zero, which means that the animation will only play back once. To specify an infinite repeat count, use 1e100f. This property should not be used with repeatDuration.

▶ RepeatDuration

This property specifies how long the animation should repeat. The animation repeats until this amount of time has elapsed. It should not be used with repeatCount.

Animation Grouping

In the previous section, "Useful Animation Properties," we defined two particular properties that are only pertinent to animation grouping: beginTime and timeOffset. Before discussing those, however, let's consider why you might want to use an animation group rather than just adding a list of animations to the layer.

In Listing 3-12, you can see that we build up a list of basic animations and simply add them to the layer. If you want all your animations to begin at the same time and each of them have the same duration, this method is perfectly adequate.

LISTING 3-12   Adding a List of Animations to the Layer

```
- (IBAction)animate:(id)sender;
{
    NSRect oldRect = NSMakeRect(0.0, 0.0, 100.0, 100.0);
    NSRect newRect = NSMakeRect(0.0, 0.0, 300.0, 300.0);

    CABasicAnimation *boundsAnimation =
    [CABasicAnimation animationWithKeyPath:@"bounds"];
    [boundsAnimation setFromValue:[NSValue valueWithRect:oldRect]];
    [boundsAnimation setToValue:[NSValue valueWithRect:newRect]];
    [boundsAnimation setDuration:5.0f];

    CABasicAnimation *positionAnimation =
    [CABasicAnimation animationWithKeyPath:@"position"];
```

LISTING 3-12   Continued

```
    [positionAnimation setFromValue:
    [NSValue valueWithPoint:
    NSPointFromCGPoint([layer position])]];
    [positionAnimation setToValue:
    [NSValue valueWithPoint:NSMakePoint(0.0, 0.0)]];
    [positionAnimation setDuration:5.0f];

    CABasicAnimation *borderWidthAnimation =
    [CABasicAnimation animationWithKeyPath:@"borderWidth"];
    [borderWidthAnimation setFromValue:[NSNumber numberWithFloat:5.0f]];
    [borderWidthAnimation setToValue:[NSNumber numberWithFloat:30.0f]];
    [borderWidthAnimation setDuration:5.0f];

    [layer addAnimation:boundsAnimation forKey:@"bounds"];
    [layer addAnimation:positionAnimation forKey:@"position"];
    [layer addAnimation:borderWidthAnimation forKey:@"borderWidth"];
}
```

Each animation has a duration of 5 seconds, and they begin to play back simultaneously in the next run loop and they end at the same time. The position of the layer moves to the bottom left corner, the border width grows to 30 pixels, and size of the layer grows from 100×100 pixels to 300×300 pixels.

Let's say that we would prefer that, rather than having all our animations play simultaneously, we want them to play back sequentially—one following the previous. We can achieve this by using a group animation and setting the beginTime field. I should mention now that in this case it might make more sense to use a keyframe animation instead, but you need to read Chapter 4, "Keyframe Animation," to see how that works.

We must explicitly specify the duration of our animation group so that the time for each individual animation can be split up accordingly. In our example, we set our duration of the animation group to last 15 seconds and get each of our individual animations to play back for 5 seconds. Listing 3-13 shows how we can take a previous example and instead use animation grouping for greater control over animation playback.

LISTING 3-13   Using Animation Grouping

```
- (IBAction)animate:(id)sender;
{
    NSRect oldRect = NSMakeRect(0.0, 0.0, 100.0, 100.0);
    NSRect newRect = NSMakeRect(0.0, 0.0, 300.0, 300.0);

    CABasicAnimation *boundsAnimation =
    [CABasicAnimation animationWithKeyPath:@"bounds"];
```

LISTING 3-13   Continued

```
[boundsAnimation setFromValue:[NSValue valueWithRect:oldRect]];
[boundsAnimation setToValue:[NSValue valueWithRect:newRect]];
[boundsAnimation setDuration:15.0f];
[boundsAnimation setBeginTime:0.0f];

CABasicAnimation *positionAnimation =
[CABasicAnimation animationWithKeyPath:@"position"];
[positionAnimation setFromValue:
[NSValue valueWithPoint:
NSPointFromCGPoint([layer position])]];
[positionAnimation setToValue:
[NSValue valueWithPoint:NSMakePoint(0.0, 0.0)]];
[positionAnimation setDuration:15.0f];
[positionAnimation setBeginTime:5.0f];

CABasicAnimation *borderWidthAnimation =
[CABasicAnimation animationWithKeyPath:@"borderWidth"];
[borderWidthAnimation setFromValue:[NSNumber numberWithFloat:5.0f]];
[borderWidthAnimation setToValue:[NSNumber numberWithFloat:30.0f]];
[borderWidthAnimation setDuration:15.0f];
[borderWidthAnimation setBeginTime:10.0f];

CAAnimationGroup *group = [CAAnimationGroup animation];
[group setDuration:15];
[group setAnimations:
[NSArray arrayWithObjects:boundsAnimation,
positionAnimation,
borderWidthAnimation, nil]];

[layer addAnimation:group forKey:nil];
}
```

Notice that we have set the duration for each of the individual animations to the full fifteen seconds, but each of the animations have their begin times set to start one after the other at 0.0, 5.0, and 10.0.

You also notice that the only thing we add to the layer is the group animation. The animation objects in the group have been added with a call to -setAnimations.

You can see that there is a good bit of flexibility provided through grouping. You just need to tweak your durations and begin times to suit your needs. If you want the animations to overlap, you just change the begin times to reflect when you want them to start playing back. You want to keep your duration times all the same; otherwise each keypath value (that is, bounds, position, and borderWidth) in the layer snaps back to its original value when its duration has completed, which gives predictable, yet seemingly sporadic, behavior. Keeping all the durations the same makes them wait the full duration before they snap back. If you don't want them to snap back, you need to explicitly set their values when the animation finishes, which we previously discussed in the section, "Using CABasicAnimation."

Summary

Basic animation is powerful. You have a lot of flexibility in the way you can achieve your application animation goals. Often you won't need to go beyond what is provided for you in basic animation. Keep it simple. If all you need is the animator proxy, use it. If all you need is to set a layer property, call that property's set method and let Core Animation handle the rest. If you need to have more flexibility over the animation parameters, use a CABasicAnimation object and set all the animation properties yourself. Just remember that probably more often than not, you only need basic animation.

CHAPTER 4

Keyframe Animation

IN THIS CHAPTER

▶ Changing Values Over Time

▶ Two Methods to Specify
  Keyframe Destinations

▶ From Basic Animation to
  Keyframe Animation

▶ Keyframe Animation Timing

▶ Keyframe Animation for
  UI Cues

Core Animation provides a way for you to have complete control over your animations. This control comes in the form of what is called *keyframe animation*. Keyframe animation enables you to specify the values for each of the major steps in your animation and then fills in the rest for you.

The terminology used to describe keyframe animation is rooted in the film industry. As film animation moved to computers, this concept of filling in between the keyframes has remained a necessary part of creating smooth animations using a process called *tweening*. Core Animation is no different. You specify the keyframes in your animation, and Core Animation handles the tweening process for you. It calculates what needs to be done in between each keyframe based on the property you have specified in your animation and interpolates all the intermediary values. It's quite convenient and makes animation coding tasks much simpler.

Cheap Film Standard

The term *keyframe animation* comes from film animation. Before the advent of rendering farms and green screens, artists would use old-fashioned pencil and paper to draw the primary or key frames of an animation. Artists could then flip between the different frames to ensure that the basic animation was occurring the way they had envisioned it. Next the keyframes would be handed off to another artist to do the grunt work of drawing the frames that would come in between and enable the animation to be played back at the industry standard 24 frames per second (fps).

This standard of 24fps came about in the motion picture industry because the cost of film was so expensive studio producers ran tests to determine how to maintain a smooth look while using the fewest frames (and therefore the least amount of film) possible. Twenty-four fps became the standard, and it is this rate that moviegoers have come to expect whether they realize it. That's why you see many video camera manufacturers touting "film" or "frame" mode in their cameras as this mimics film's vaunted 24fps. Have you ever watched a feature film or something by the BBC? It probably feels strange to you, because these films are most commonly shot at 60fps interlaced or 30fps, progressive scan. A movie buff will notice the difference immediately.

In this chapter, we discuss how to move from basic animation to keyframe animation. It is similar, so the transition should be smooth. We also introduce you to layer rotation and how to add some content to your layer by drawing a path.

Changing Values Over Time

Core Animation offers a wide range of properties that you can animate. Keyframe anima-tion is the process of changing one of these properties over time. You can think of a keyframe animation as a group of basic animations strung together and run in sequence.

In the context of Core Animation, interpolation (which is analogous to tweening in film) uses the value of a property between each keyframe to calculate the starting and stopping values of the surrounding keyframes. Another way to think about this is to imagine the bases of a baseball diamond. Each base is a key frame. The runner knows that when he hits the ball, he must run to first base, then second base, third, and then home if he wants to score a run (and doesn't get thrown out in the process). The steps between each base don't concern him though he must run to get to each of those destinations. Similarly, the animation in a keyframe animation runs to each destination point (keyframe) in sequence until all destinations have been reached.

Of course, in the case of a baseball diamond shape, your last keyframe value would be the same as your first.

Two Methods to Specify Keyframe Destinations

When you want to animate a property, you can either specify an array of values that the property will reach in sequence, or you can specify a Core Graphics path:

> ► An array of values is more readily used to specify things like color changes to backgrounds and borders or border widths and rectangle sizes or even CGImage(s) for the content key path. You can also animate the transform property by specifying a list of CATransform3D objects to the values array.

▶ Core Graphics paths are used for moving objects from point-to-point around the screen on a path. Whenever a `CGPoint` is the type of the property, a Core Graphics path is likely the right choice. You will use the `anchorPoint` and `position` properties to animate paths.

In terms of precedence, a path overrides an array of values. This means that if you specify a path with a call to `-setPath`, anything specified in the values field with a call to `-setValues` will be ignored. The code in Listing 4-1 and Listing 4-2 demonstrates how to use a Core Graphics path and an array of values, respectively. The listings are functionally the same, yet the result is quite different. The animation in Listing 4-1 causes the layer to bounce across the screen in an arcing parabolic pattern. Listing 4-2 causes the layer to bounce across the screen in more of a square tooth pattern.

LISTING 4-1   Path Animation

```
- (CAAnimation*)pathAnimation;
{
    CGMutablePathRef path = CGPathCreateMutable();
    CGPathMoveToPoint(path,NULL,50.0,120.0);

    CGPathAddCurveToPoint(path,NULL,50.0,275.0,150.0,275.0,150.0,120.0);
    CGPathAddCurveToPoint(path,NULL,150.0,275.0,250.0,275.0,250.0,120.0);
    CGPathAddCurveToPoint(path,NULL,250.0,275.0,350.0,275.0,350.0,120.0);
    CGPathAddCurveToPoint(path,NULL,350.0,275.0,450.0,275.0,450.0,120.0);

    CAKeyframeAnimation *
    animation = [CAKeyframeAnimation
            animationWithKeyPath:@"position"];

    [animation setPath:path];
    [animation setDuration:3.0];

    [animation setAutoreverses:YES];

    CFRelease(path);

    return animation;
}
```

LISTING 4-2   Values Animation

```objc
- (CAAnimation*)valuesAnimation;
{
    NSPoint pt0 = NSMakePoint(50.0, 120.0);
    NSPoint pt1 = NSMakePoint(50.0, 275.0);
    NSPoint pt2 = NSMakePoint(150.0, 275.0);
    NSPoint pt3 = NSMakePoint(150.0, 120.0);
    NSPoint pt4 = NSMakePoint(150.0, 275.0);
    NSPoint pt5 = NSMakePoint(250.0, 275.0);
    NSPoint pt6 = NSMakePoint(250.0, 120.0);
    NSPoint pt7 = NSMakePoint(250.0, 275.0);
    NSPoint pt8 = NSMakePoint(350.0, 275.0);
    NSPoint pt9 = NSMakePoint(350.0, 120.0);
    NSPoint pt10 = NSMakePoint(350.0, 275.0);
    NSPoint pt11 = NSMakePoint(450.0, 275.0);
    NSPoint pt12 = NSMakePoint(450.0, 120.0);

    NSArray *values = [NSArray arrayWithObjects:
                [NSValue valueWithPoint:pt0],
                [NSValue valueWithPoint:pt1],
                [NSValue valueWithPoint:pt2],
                [NSValue valueWithPoint:pt3],
                [NSValue valueWithPoint:pt4],
                [NSValue valueWithPoint:pt5],
                [NSValue valueWithPoint:pt6],
                [NSValue valueWithPoint:pt7],
                [NSValue valueWithPoint:pt8],
                [NSValue valueWithPoint:pt9],
                [NSValue valueWithPoint:pt10],
                [NSValue valueWithPoint:pt11],
                [NSValue valueWithPoint:pt12],
                nil];

    CAKeyframeAnimation
    *animation = [CAKeyframeAnimation
            animationWithKeyPath:@"position"];

    [animation setValues:values];
    [animation setDuration:3.0];

    [animation setAutoreverses:YES];

    return animation;
}
```

You can see both patterns in Figure 4-1. You could add many more points to the values array to more closely mimic the pattern you get using a path, but using a path is much more convenient.

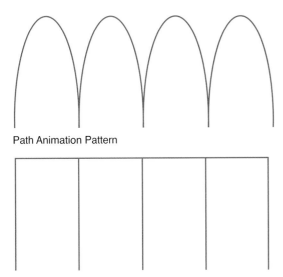

Path Animation Pattern

Values Animation Pattern

FIGURE 4-1   Animation Patterns, Path Versus Values

Figure 4-2 shows the animation of two layers running in tandem: a parabolic pattern with the green layer running along the path as specified in Listing 4-1, and the square-toothed pattern in the red layer running to each value as specified in Listing 4-2.

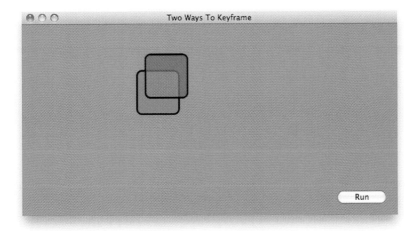

FIGURE 4-2   Two Ways to Keyframe Demo Application

From Basic Animation to Keyframe Animation

Although a basic animation requires you to specify only the start and stop value and/or by value, keyframe animation enables you specify

- An array of values for each keyframe. For example, you could use an array of CGColorRef objects to animate a background color change.

- An array of values between 0.0 and 1.0 used specify the percentage of the total time spent between each keyframe.

- An array of timing function objects (CAMediaTimingFunction) used to specify the pace of each animation process between key frames. These fields specify with one of the predefined functions, such as kCAMediaTimingFunctionEaseIn, that the animation should start off slowly and then speed up over time.

Keyframe animation is actually quite simple. First, consider the basic steps you need to successfully animate a property using keyframe animation:

1. Decide which property you want to animate (for example, frame, background color, anchor point, position, border width, and so on).

2. In the values field of the animation object, specify the start value, the end value, and all values in between. These are your keyframes. (See Listing 4-2 for an example).

3. Specify the full duration of the animation using the duration field.

4. Optionally, specify time durations for the animation that will occur between each keyframe using the times field. If you don't specify these, Core Animation evenly divides the duration by the number of values provided in the values field, minus one.

5. Optionally, specify the timing functions to control animation pacing.

That is all you need to do. You create your animations and add them to your layer. The -addAnimation call starts the animation.

Keyframe Animation Timing

Core Animation provides a high level of granularity for specifying how your animation will play. By default, a keyframe animation plays back evenly, dividing the time specified in the animation's duration field by the total number of keyframes minus one. You can use the following formula to determine how much time each keyframe of the animation gets

$$duration/(number\ of\ keyframes - 1)$$

For example, if we specified a 10-second animation with five keyframes, the time given to each keyframe is 2.5 seconds:

$$10 / (5 - 1) = 2.5$$

You can gain further control of your animation timing with the `keyTimes` field, which you can use to specify a percentage for each keyframe from the animation's total duration. With five keyframes specified in an animation, each `keyTime` takes up 25 percent of the total time. If we were to explicitly set up our animation to use the `keyTimes` field in a way that would essentially do the same as the default, the code would look like Listing 4-3.

LISTING 4-3   Explicitly Setting Key Times to Mimic the Default

```
[animation setCalculationMode:kCAAnimationLinear];
[animation setKeyTimes:
 [NSArray arrayWithObjects:
 [NSNumber numberWithFloat:0.0],
 [NSNumber numberWithFloat:0.25],
 [NSNumber numberWithFloat:0.50],
 [NSNumber numberWithFloat:0.75],
 [NSNumber numberWithFloat:1.0], nil]];
```

You might have noticed that we specified five values in Listing 4-3, which might not seem to match our default formula. However, when you realize that the first value (`0.0`) is simply a starting value, it becomes clear that we are only specifying four destination times, which matches the formula discussed earlier.

The animation in Listing 4-3 is identical to what you see if you didn't specify key times at all; this simply shows you how to specify the key times should you need to do that in your animation. You can alter these values to lengthen or shorten the amount of time spent between the keyframes. Just remember that each subsequent value must be greater than the previous and must not exceed `1.0`. The duration and number of keyframes provide enough information for Core Animation to interpolate the values in the exact same way by simply dividing the duration by the number of keyframes minus one.

The key times are used according to the `calculationMode` field, as shown in Listing 4-3. When specified as paced (`kCAAnimationPaced`), the key times are ignored. This is the same as if you didn't specify key times at all. When specified as linear (`kCAAnimationLinear`) the times in between keyframes are interpolated, which means that you see every step of the animation between keyframes. This is the process of tweening that we discussed at the beginning of this chapter. When specified as discrete (`kCAAnimationDiscrete`), the keyframes are the only frames displayed, with no interpolation between frames. If you moved a layer to random points on a window, for instance, you would not see the layer move to each point. Instead, you would see the layer *jump* to each point when the time for that keyframe was reached.

Monitoring Keyframe Destinations

To further understand how to apply the key times formula, go to the companion website at informit.com/coreframeworks and open the demo project called Keyframe Steps. You notice we have added timers that fire at various stages of the animation to show which point we have reached in the animation. In the Keyframe Steps example code, we animate a dot around the window in the path of a five-pointed star, as shown in Figure 4-3. As the animation reaches each point, we draw the segment of the path from the previous point to the next; this is done with timers. First, however, we had to determine how many keyframes we needed and then determined how many timers we would need.

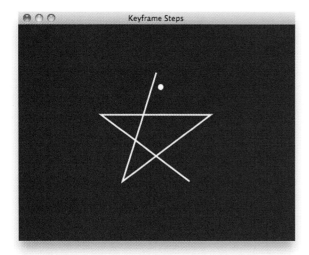

FIGURE 4-3   Keyframe Steps Demo Application

In the sample code, we have specified 10 seconds as the animation's duration. To determine how much time the animation would spend between each destination point, we applied the formula based on the duration and the number of keyframes. Including the animation's starting and ending points, there are a total of 6 keyframes. We then apply the animation timing formula as follows:

$$\text{Duration} / (\text{keyframes} - 1) = \text{time per keyframe}$$
$$10 / (6-1) = 2.0 \text{ seconds per keyframe}$$

Notice in Listing 4-4 that NSTimer is used to schedule a selector to run every 2 seconds during the animation. This causes the path to be updated and redrawn to show the star path as each destination is reached.

LISTING 4-4 Set Up the Animation and Create Timers to Monitor Animation Progress

```objc
- (IBAction)startAnimation:(id)sender;
{
    if( starPath )
    {
        // Reset our starPath CGMutablePathRef if
        // it has already run before
        CFRelease(starPath);
        [self createPath];
        [[[window contentView] layer] setNeedsDisplay];
    }

    // Define a path for the star shape.
    CGMutablePathRef path = CGPathCreateMutable();

    CGPathMoveToPoint(path,NULL,240.0, 280.0);

    CGPathAddLineToPoint(path, NULL, 181.0, 99.0);
    CGPathAddLineToPoint(path, NULL, 335.0, 210.0);
    CGPathAddLineToPoint(path, NULL, 144.0, 210.0);
    CGPathAddLineToPoint(path, NULL, 298.0, 99.0);
    CGPathCloseSubpath(path);

        CAKeyframeAnimation *animation =
    [CAKeyframeAnimation
     animationWithKeyPath:@"position"];
        [animation setDuration:10.0f];
        [animation setDelegate:self];

    // Set the animation's path
    [animation setPath:path];
    // Release the path
    CFRelease(path);

        [dotLayer addAnimation:animation forKey:@"position"];


        [NSTimer scheduledTimerWithTimeInterval:2.0
                     target:self
                     selector:@selector(legOne:)
                     userInfo:nil
                      repeats:NO];

        [NSTimer scheduledTimerWithTimeInterval:4.0
```

LISTING 4-4   Continued

```
                        target:self
                        selector:@selector(legTwo:)
                        userInfo:nil
                         repeats:NO];

        [NSTimer scheduledTimerWithTimeInterval:6.0
                        target:self
                        selector:@selector(legThree:)
                        userInfo:nil
                         repeats:NO];

        [NSTimer scheduledTimerWithTimeInterval:8.0
                        target:self
                        selector:@selector(legFour:)
                        userInfo:nil
                         repeats:NO];

        [NSTimer scheduledTimerWithTimeInterval:10.0
                        target:self
                        selector:@selector(legFive:)
                        userInfo:nil
                         repeats:NO];

    // Tell the root layer to call drawLayer
    [[[window contentView] layer] setNeedsDisplay];
}
```

As each time is reached, another point is added to the starPath path, and the root layer updates its display, as shown in Listing 4-5. The final call, legFive, closes the path.

LISTING 4-5   Selector Methods for Each Timer Add a New Point to the Path

```
- (void)legOne:(id)sender
{
    CGPathAddLineToPoint(starPath, NULL, 181.0, 99.0);
    [[[window contentView] layer] setNeedsDisplay];
}
- (void)legTwo:(id)sender
{
    CGPathAddLineToPoint(starPath, NULL, 335.0, 210.0);
    [[[window contentView] layer] setNeedsDisplay];
}
```

LISTING 4-5   Continued

```
- (void)legThree:(id)sender
{
    CGPathAddLineToPoint(starPath, NULL, 144.0, 210.0);
    [[[window contentView] layer] setNeedsDisplay];
}
- (void)legFour:(id)sender
{
    CGPathAddLineToPoint(starPath, NULL, 298.0, 99.0);
    [[[window contentView] layer] setNeedsDisplay];
}

- (void)legFive:(id)sender
{
    CGPathCloseSubpath(starPath);
    [[[window contentView] layer] setNeedsDisplay];
}
```

When we call –setNeedsDisplay on the root layer, -drawLayer gets called and the path in
its current state gets drawn to the layer, as shown in Listing 4-6.

LISTING 4-6   Draw the Path We Have Been Building at Each Timer Call

```
- (void)drawLayer:(CALayer *)layer
      inContext:(CGContextRef)context
{

    if( layer == [[window contentView] layer] )
    {
        CGColorRef white =
        CGColorCreateGenericRGB(1.0, 1.0, 1.0, 1.0);
        CGContextSetStrokeColorWithColor(context, white);
        CFRelease(white);

        CGContextBeginPath(context);
        CGContextAddPath(context, starPath);

        CGContextSetLineWidth(context, 3.0);

        CGContextStrokePath(context);
    }
}
```

Listing 4-6 is drawing the same path on each call, but the path has been extended each time the timer fired causing the lines extending from one point to the next to be drawn in succession.

> **NOTE**
>
> **Keyframe Steps Animation for iPhone**
>
> There are two version of this example application available: one for OS X and one for the iPhone. Notice that there are some differences between them in implementation. Here are the things you need to watch for:
>
> ▶ **Colors:** On OS X, use `CGColorCreateGenericRBG`; while on the iPhone, use `[[UIColor colorName] CGColor]`.
>
> ▶ **Positions:** When we set the `position` of a layer, the two coordinate systems are opposite by default, which means that the star drawing is inverted on the iPhone version. The easiest way to make them match is to set the OS X view to override the `–isFlipped` method and return yes. Then they will both use the same coordinate system.
>
> ▶ **Root Layer:** In the iPhone version, we couldn't set the root layer of the view to use the view controller as it's delegate because this would cause the button that starts the animation to stop working. Instead we created another layer called `starLayer` that we add to the root layer.

Keyframe Animation for UI Cues

Core Animation was originally written for Apple's iPhone platform and then made available to Mac OS X Leopard. If you have ever seen an iPhone or the iPod touch in action, you have witnessed Core Animation because nearly every UI action has some animation feature on these platforms. Whether you use a simple drill down menu (which slides the views in and out from the sides), or if you close your current application and return to the Home screen where the icons animate in from both sides at the same time, you see the effects of Core Animation.

One such interesting animation on the iPhone/iPod touch is what you see when you touch and hold your finger down on an icon on the Home screen. This causes all the application icons to wriggle and twist, like they're trying to get away. In this editable state, you can move the application icons around on the screen so that you can organize them to suit your needs (see Figure 4-4). Another thing you notice is a close box in the upper-left corner of the icons to indicate which applications can be deleted from your iPhone/iPod touch. If you press the Home button, all the icons stop shaking and return to their normal state.

> **NOTE**
>
> **Nondeletable iPhone/iPod Touch Applications**
>
> When you press and hold your finger on the application icons on your iPhone/iPod touch, you notice that certain applications won't have the little close box in the upper-left corner. One quick glance tells you that these are the default applications that ship with the device (for example, Camera, Clock, Photos, Settings, Safari, Weather, and so on). If you have found better third-party applications for these (well, maybe with the exception of Settings), you might consider dumping the unused default applications onto their own screen.

FIGURE 4-4   The iPhone/iPod Touch in Edit Mode

This user interface cue helps the user know that the iPhone/iPod touch is now in a different state, and you can now make changes to something. It might not be immediately obvious what that something is; however, once you start tap-dragging, it becomes apparent what you are supposed to do. Cues like this enhance the user experience and make applications incredibly intuitive. This is one of Core Animation's most useful features, so let's see how it is done.

Implementing the Icon Shake Using Keyframe Animation

We implement this icon shaking animation with Cocoa on OS X, though the implementation on the iPhone is similar. We begin by creating the animation and playing it over a longer duration to show how each parameter of the animation affects what it looks like when run. Then we set the duration to run at a time that is more on par with what you actually see on the iPhone/iPod touch.

You might want to open the sample project to see what the effect looks like. We have provided an example project for both OS X and the iPhone. They are called Icon Dance for OS X and Icon Dance iPhone for the iPhone.

Certain aspects of the Icon Dance application are going to be different than what you see on the iPhone home screen. Because Cocoa Touch currently isn't available for use with desktop applications, you can't touch your screen to start or stop the icon animation, or drag the icons around using your finger. However, the methods and associated code demonstrate how we can implement the icon shake, and it works on either platform, as you will soon see.

Figures 4-5 and 4-6 show what our application looks like when run on OS X. Figure 4-5 shows what it looks like before we add the close box, and 4-6 shows what it looks like after the close box has been added.

FIGURE 4-5   Icon Dance Demo Application

FIGURE 4-6   Icon Dance with Close Box

Using the steps to implement a keyframe animation (see the previous section "From Basic Animation to Keyframe Animation," in this chapter), let's map out the steps to implement the Icon Dance, as shown in Table 4-1.

TABLE 4-1   Icon Shake Animation Implementation Steps

Implementation Step	Value Used
1. Specify the property to animate.	`transform.rotation.x`
2. Specify the values to use for each keyframe.	`-2, 2, -2`
3. Specify the total time duration for the animation.	2 seconds
4. Specify time durations.	Not used. We allow core animation to split the time automatically between each keyframe.
5. Specify timing functions (pacing).	Use `kCAMediaTimingFunctionLinear` for all keyframes.

We are only going to specify three keyframe values to keep this example pretty simple. (Plus, that's all this animation really needs.) We simply set a large repeat number on the animation and it loops indefinitely.

Take a look at the animation creation code in Listing 4-7. Notice that the three keyframes are specified as NSNumber objects as indicated by a call to the utility function, DegreesToNumber. You can see the declaration of this function in Listing 4-8. DegreesToNumber takes a CGFloat value for its parameter and returns an NSNumber with degrees converted to radians, which is done by a second utility function called DegreesToRadians.

LISTING 4-7   Shake Animation for Rotating Each Layer Around the Center Axis

```
- (CAAnimation*)shakeAnimation;
{
    CAKeyframeAnimation * animation;
    animation = [CAKeyframeAnimation
                animationWithKeyPath:@"transform.rotation.z"];
    [animation setDuration:0.5];
    [animation setRepeatCount:10000];

    // Try to get the animation to begin to start with a small offset
    // that makes it shake out of sync with other layers.
    srand([[NSDate date] timeIntervalSince1970]);
    float rand = (float)random();
    [animation setBeginTime:
     CACurrentMediaTime() + rand * .0000000001];
```

LISTING 4-7   Continued

```
    NSMutableArray *values = [NSMutableArray array];

    // Turn right
    [values addObject:DegreesToNumber(-2)];

    // Turn left
    [values addObject:DegreesToNumber(2)];

    // Turn right
    [values addObject:DegreesToNumber(-2)];

    // Set the values for the animation
    [animation setValues:values];

    return animation;
}
```

LISTING 4-8   Utility Functions for Converting Degrees to Radians

```
NSNumber* DegreesToNumber(CGFloat degrees)
{
    return [NSNumber numberWithFloat:
        DegreesToRadians(degrees)];
}

CGFloat DegreesToRadians(CGFloat degrees)
{
    return degrees * M_PI / 180;
}
```

The first keyframe in Listing 4-7 turns the icon two degrees to the right, the second turns it two degrees to the left, and the third turns it two degrees to the right again. When the animation has completed, it starts over again and runs 10,000 times as indicated by our call to –setRepeatCount:10000. This gives the visual impression of the image shaking on a center axis. To stop the animation, remove it from the layer with a call to –removeAnimationForKey:@"rotate".

NOTE

Random Shaking

You might have noticed in Listing 4-7 that we set the begin time for the animation using a small random offset. If we don't do this, all the icons shake in sync with each other. To achieve the same effect as what you see on the iPhone, having this random offset is necessary. We use the current time in seconds to seed the random number generator. Then we grab that next random number and multiply it by .0000000001 to get a small offset. We set the animation start time to this value and return the animation. When it gets added to the layer, it plays back starting at that offset from the time it was actually added to the layer.

Rotation Axis and Layer Geometry

In this example, the rotation of our layer revolves around the center of the layer. This is the default anchor point for layers (0.5, 0.5). If you want to rotate around a different axis, for example the bottom left corner, you need to specify in the layer itself a new anchor point with a call to -setAnchorPoint:CGPointMake(0.0, 0.0). For this example, though, the default is appropriate. Layer geometry is discussed in greater detail in Chapter 6, "Layer Filters."

Perfecting the Effect

With some minor changes to the duration parameter and each of the keyframe values, we can get it to look just right. If you run the code in Listing 4-7, you notice that the shaking effect seems to run a little too slow. To make this run faster, simply change the duration field to something more appropriate. We are currently telling the animation to complete within half of a second, 0.5. If you change it to instead be finished within one-fifteenth of a second (changing setDuration:0.5 to setDuration:0.15), the animation gives you more of the desired effect.

NOTE

If you have an iPhone or iPod touch, from the Home menu, tap and hold any icon and you can see the animation run. Now run the Icon Dance example in Xcode to see how similar the effect looks.

Adding the Close Box

This part of the project is not related in particular to keyframe animation, but it will show you how to complete this effect and introduce you to drawing in layer contents.

While the animation is running, you notice a circular close box with an X inside. This is intended to indicate that an application can be deleted on the

NOTE

Close Box User Interaction

If you want to receive an event when the close box is clicked, you need to obtain the click position from the backing view and then do a hit test on the layer to see if it is in range because Core Animation layers don't themselves receive events. See Chapter 11, "User Interaction," for more details.

iPhone/iPod touch. In the Icon Dance application, the close box doesn't do anything, but it enables you to see the effect.

For this example, we will do the following:

- Set the border width for the close box layer to 3 pixels.
- Set the frame to 30 × 30 pixels.
- Set the corner radius to 15 (half the frame size) to make it look like a circle.
- Set the background color to black.
- Set the drop shadow color to black.
- Set the shadow radius to 5 pixels.
- Set the shadow opacity to 1.0 (opaque).

The code in Listing 4-9 implements each of these items. Notice that we set the delegate for the layer to self. This enables us to call - (void)drawLayer:(CALayer *)theLayer inContext:(CGContextRef) theContext (see the beginning of Listing 4-10), which enables us to add the code that draws the X in the middle of the close box layer. The code used to draw the X (shown in Listing 4-10) uses a Core Graphics path that sets a point and draws the first leg, and then sets another point and draws the second leg.

LISTING 4-9   Define the Close Box Layer

```
-(CALayer*)closeBoxLayer;
{
    CGColorRef white =
    CGColorCreateGenericRGB(1.0, 1.0, 1.0, 1.0);
    CGColorRef black =
    CGColorCreateGenericRGB(0.0, 0.0, 0.0, 1.0);

    CALayer *layer = [CALayer layer];
    [layer setFrame:CGRectMake(0.0,
                               kCompositeIconHeight - 30.0,
                               30.0, 30.0)];

    [layer setBackgroundColor:black];
    [layer setShadowColor:black];
    [layer setShadowOpacity:1.0];
    [layer setShadowRadius:5.0];
    [layer setBorderColor:white];
    [layer setBorderWidth:3];
    [layer setCornerRadius:15];
    [layer setDelegate:self];
    // Release the color refs
```

LISTING 4-9   Continued

```
    CFRelease(white);
    CFRelease(black);

    return layer;
}
```

> **NOTE**
>
> **Use an Image as Layer Content**
>
> If you prefer, you can instead use an image for the close box layer contents. Just load the image in an NSImage for OS X or a UIImage for the iPhone and get a CGImageRef object. Then set the layer's contents to that CGImageRef. Preferring an image over explicitly drawing is mostly a matter of preference; however, for our purposes, Listings 4-9 and 4-10 demonstrate how to achieve the desired look by drawing explicitly.

LISTING 4-10   Draw an X In the Close Box Layer

```
- (void)drawLayer:(CALayer *)layer
         inContext:(CGContextRef)context
{
    // Make sure the call is applied to the close
    // box layer
    if( layer == closeLayer )
    {
        // Create the path ref
        CGMutablePathRef path = CGPathCreateMutable();

        // Set the first point and add a line
        CGPathMoveToPoint(path,NULL,10.0f,10.f);
        CGPathAddLineToPoint(path, NULL, 20.0, 20.0);

        // Set the second point and add a line
        CGPathMoveToPoint(path,NULL,10.0f,20.f);
        CGPathAddLineToPoint(path, NULL, 20.0, 10.0);

        // Set the stroke color to white
        CGColorRef white =
                CGColorCreateGenericRGB(1.0, 1.0, 1.0, 1.0);
        CGContextSetStrokeColorWithColor(context, white);
        CGColorRelease(white);
```

LISTING 4-10   Continued

```
        // Start drawing the path
        CGContextBeginPath(context);
        CGContextAddPath(context, path);

        // Set the line width to 3 pixels
        CGContextSetLineWidth(context, 3.0);

        // Draw the path
        CGContextStrokePath(context);

        // Release the path
        CGPathRelease(path);
    }
}
```

Starting and Stopping the Animation

Core Animation doesn't directly provide start and stop methods. However, the animation starts when you add an animation to a layer, and the animation stops when you remove an animation from a layer. To determine if an animation is currently running, query the animation's dictionary to determine if the animation is still there. If it is, the animation is still running. If it is not, the animation has stopped.

Listing 4-11 demonstrates how you start and stop the shake animation. When the animation starts, add the close box layer first and then add the animation for key rotate. This key is important because it is used to refer to the animation when you want to stop it and to see if it is still running.

LISTING 4-11   Controlling Animation Start and Stop

```
- (void)toggleShake;
{
    if( [self isRunning] )
    {
        [self stopShake];
    }
    else
    {
        [self startShake];
    }
}

- (BOOL)isRunning;
{
    return ([self animationForKey:@"rotate"] != nil);
```

LISTING 4-11   Continued

```
}

- (void)startShake;
{
    [self addSublayer:closeLayer];
    // Tell the closeLayer to draw its contents which is
    // an 'X' to indicate a close box.
    [closeLayer setNeedsDisplay];
    [self addAnimation:[self shakeAnimation] forKey:@"rotate"];
}

- (void)stopShake;
{
    [closeLayer removeFromSuperlayer];
    [self removeAnimationForKey:@"rotate"];
}
```

When-stopShake is called, the close box layer is first removed from its parent layer and then we remove the animation from the layer. To determine whether the animation is still running, -isRunning checks to see if the animation is still in the animations dictionary. If it is there, the animation is running, otherwise, it is not.

NOTE

Icon Dance Animation for iPhone

Two version of this example application are available: one for OS X and one for the iPhone. Notice some differences between them in implementation. Here are the things you need to watch for:

▶ **Colors:** On OS X, use CGColorCreateGenericRBG. On the iPhone, use [[UIColor colorName] CGColor].

▶ **Positions:** When the position of a layer or its frame is set, the two coordinate systems are opposite by default. This means that the close box and the image are both drawn at the bottom of the frame instead of the top on the iPhone version if you used the same code. The easiest way to make them match is to set the OS X view to override the –isFlipped method and return YES, and then use the iPhone version of the code. Then they will both use the same coordinate system. In the sample code, however, we just changed the positions so you can see the differences.

▶ **CATextLayer:** At the time of this writing, CATextLayer is not available on the iPhone, so we stripped that out of the ImageLayer class on the iPhone version.

Summary

Basic animation is known as *single keyframe animation*. This definition helps to explain what keyframe animation provides. The keyframes in an animation are like a list of what `CABasicAnimation` refers to as its `toValue` field: the destination value. A list of these values can be supplied to the keyframe animation using either the animation's `values` field or its `path` field. Each of these values are destinations that the animation reaches at some point in its duration.

Keyframe animation provides a powerful way to animate any animatable layer property using a simple list of values, making it easy for the developer because the in-between values are automatically interpolated. This simplicity makes it a snap to create animation-based user interfaces informative, intuitive, and easy to implement.

PART III

Core Animation Layers

IN THIS PART

CHAPTER 5	Layer Transforms	69
CHAPTER 6	Layer Filters	83
CHAPTER 7	QuickTime Layers	111
CHAPTER 8	OpenGL Layer	131
CHAPTER 9	Quartz Composer Layer	149
CHAPTER 10	Other Useful Layers	161

CHAPTER 5

Layer Transforms

IN THIS CHAPTER

▶ Scale Transform

▶ Using -rotateTransform:

▶ Using -rotate3DTransform:

▶ Anchor Points

▶ Combining Transforms

▶ Scale Versus Bounds

Up to this point, we have discussed how to move elements around the screen, change their color, and various other interesting effects. In this chapter, we take that quite a bit further. Transforms is a catchall to describe applying a matrix transform to a layer for some startling results.

What is a transform? A transform is a term used to include any function that alters the size, position, or rotation of an object, in our case a layer. Transforms scale a layer up or down and rotate a layer along one or more planes. Transforms are applied using a matrix function that fortunately we do not need to interact with directly. Whenever we want to rotate or scale a layer, we must use a transform to accomplish the desired effect.

The topic of matrix transforms can quickly turn into a deeply mathematical conversation that is beyond the scope of this chapter. Instead, this chapter touches on a few of the more common and interesting transforms, such as rotating a layer in 3D space or creating interesting zoom effects, and how to bring them about.

> **NOTE**
>
> **Cocoa Touch**
>
> Unless otherwise specified, all the transforms discussed in this chapter can be performed both on the desktop and on any device that uses Cocoa Touch. However, it should be noted that transforms can be computationally-intensive, and on a device running Cocoa Touch, it is wise to test the performance of the animation to confirm that it is within acceptable boundaries.

Scale Transform

To demonstrate some of the capabilities of matrix transforms we take a simple layer and perform several different transforms on it. The first transform scales the layer from one size to another. To start this example, build the layers shown in Listing 5-1.

LISTING 5-1   applicationDidFinishLaunching

```objc
- (void)applicationDidFinishLaunching:(NSNotification*)notification
{
  NSView *contentView = [[self window] contentView];
  CALayer *layer = [CALayer layer];
  CGColorRef color;
  color = CGColorCreateGenericRGB(0.0f, 0.0f, 0.0f, 1.0f);
  [layer setBackgroundColor:color];
  [contentView setLayer:layer];
  [contentView setWantsLayer:YES];

  workLayer = [CALayer layer];
  color = CGColorCreateGenericRGB(0.5f, 0.5f, 0.5f, 1.0f);
  [workLayer setBackgroundColor:color];

  [workLayer setCornerRadius:5.0f];

  color = CGColorCreateGenericRGB(0.0f, 1.0f, 0.0f, 1.0f);
  [workLayer setBorderColor:color];
  [workLayer setBorderWidth:2.0f];

  CGRect workFrame = [layer bounds];
  workFrame.origin.x = workFrame.size.width / 4;
  workFrame.origin.y = workFrame.size.height / 4;
  workFrame.size.width /= 2;
  workFrame.size.height /= 2;
  [workLayer setAnchorPoint:CGPointMake(0, 0)];
  [workLayer setFrame:workFrame];
  [layer addSublayer:workLayer];
}
```

In the -applicationDidFinishLaunching: method, we grab a reference to the contentView, set its layer and flag it as layer backed. By setting the layer, we are guaranteeing what type of layer the view uses for its backing.

When the contentView is set up properly, we next construct the layer that will be manipulated. Its background color is set to gray, and the corners are rounded using setCornerRadius:. Next, the border color is set to green with a width of 2 pixels. Finally, the layer's frame is set to be a quarter the size of the contentView and centered onscreen.

In Interface Builder, add three buttons to the window; one for each transform that we perform: Scale, Rotate, and 3D Rotate. The resulting window is shown in Figure 5-1.

NOTE

On the iPhone, the layer is already in place. You need to override the class method +layerClass instead to control the layer that is used.

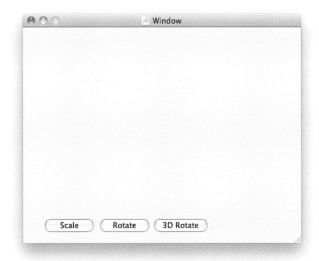

FIGURE 5-1   Interface Builder Window

The Scale button is bound to the method -scaleTransform:, implemented as shown in Listing 5-2.

LISTING 5-2   -scaleTransform:

```
- (IBAction)scaleTransform:(id)sender
{
  NSValue *value = nil;
  CABasicAnimation *animation = nil;
  CATransform3D transform;

  [[self workLayer] removeAllAnimations];
  animation = [CABasicAnimation animationWithKeyPath:@"transform"];
  transform = CATransform3DMakeScale(0.5f, 0.5f, 1.0f);
  value = [NSValue valueWithCATransform3D:transform];
  [animation setToValue:value];
  transform = CATransform3DMakeScale(1.0f, 1.0f, 1.0f);
```

LISTING 5-2   Continued

```
value = [NSValue valueWithCATransform3D:transform];
[animation setFromValue:value];

[animation setAutoreverses:YES];
[animation setDuration:1.0f];
[animation setRepeatCount:100];

[workLayer addAnimation:animation forKey:kScaleKey];
}
```

This method removes any existing animations, which keeps the animations from piling up if the user clicks on several of the buttons. Next, we want to construct an animation object that can instruct the layer on how to animate/transform. To do this, construct a CABasicAnimation with a path of transform, which tells the animation that it will be modifying the transform property of whatever layer it is applied to, and then start applying the matrix transforms to the animation. You can use several methods to construct matrix transforms. In this method, we use the CATransform3DMakeScale method and pass it the x-, y-, and z-axis for the transform. As you can see in Listing 5.2, we've set the value of CATransform3DMakeScale to 0.5 for both the x- and y-axes, and we've left the z-axis alone. To create the shrink effect, set the x and y values of the next CATransform3DMakeScale to 1.0; by setting the values of the x and y to 1.0, we cause the zoom effect to reverse.

> **NOTE**
>
> The returned CATransform3D is wrapped in an NSValue so that it can be used by CABasicAnimation. Core Animation handles pulling the CATransform3D back out of the NSValue for us.

When CATransform3DMakeScale's values are set, set the autoReverse flag to YES, give it a nice slow duration of 1 second, and set a large repeat count; here we use 100. Finally, we add the newly created animation back to the layer using a key specific to this animation. We want to use a large repeat count here so that we can give the illusion that the animation is going to continue forever. If we actually hit 100 iterations of the animation, it would finally stop.

Using -rotateTransform:

The next transform that we apply rotates the layer. The layer rotates along one axis, and then we auto-reverse the rotation, as shown in Listing 5-3.

LISTING 5-3   -rotateTransform:

```
- (IBAction)rotateTransform:(id)sender;
{
  NSValue *value = nil;
```

LISTING 5-3   Continued

```
CABasicAnimation *animation = nil;
CATransform3D transform;

[[self workLayer] removeAllAnimations];
animation = [CABasicAnimation animationWithKeyPath:@"transform"];
transform = CATransform3DMakeRotation(1.57f, 0.0f, 0.0f, 1.0f);
value = [NSValue valueWithCATransform3D:transform];
[animation setToValue:value];
transform = CATransform3DMakeRotation(0.0f, 0.0f, 0.0f, 1.0f);
value = [NSValue valueWithCATransform3D:transform];
[animation setFromValue:value];
[animation setAutoreverses:YES];
[animation setDuration:1.0f];
[animation setRepeatCount:100];
[workLayer addAnimation:animation forKey:kScaleKey];
}
```

In this example, CATransform3DMakeRotation is applied to the single axis rotation to the layer. Unlike the transform method shown in Listing 5-2, this example uses four parameters: the first parameter is the angle, expressed in radians, and the next three are the x-, y-, and z-axes. The layer is rotated by 1.57 radians (that is, 90 degrees) on the x-axis. The values for the x-, y-, and z-axes are a bit unusual. These values refer to the *magnitude* of the rotation and accept a value between -1.0 and 1.0. The rotation is set to be a full positive magnitude along the z-axis, which produces what appears to be a 2D rotation in a clockwise direction.

> **NOTE**
>
> What you see when we walk through these examples is that they all follow the same basic flow. We build a CATransform3D using one of the numerous foundation methods and then apply it to the layer.

> **NOTE**
>
> The value 1.57 used in Listing 5-2 represents the radian value of the angle. To translate degrees into radians, use the formula $X\pi/180$. For example:
>
> $90\pi/ 180 = 45(3.1415) / 180 = 0.7853$

Using -rotate3DTransform:

The next example takes the previous one a step further by rotating the layer along two axes; see Listing 5-4.

LISTING 5-4   -rotate3DTransform:

```
- (IBAction)rotate3DTransform:(id)sender;
{
  NSValue *value = nil;
  CABasicAnimation *animation = nil;
  CATransform3D transform;

  [[self workLayer] removeAllAnimations];
  animation = [CABasicAnimation animationWithKeyPath:@"transform"];
  transform = CATransform3DMakeRotation(1.57f, 1.0f, 1.0f, 0.0f);
  value = [NSValue valueWithCATransform3D:transform];
  [animation setToValue:value];
  transform = CATransform3DMakeRotation(0.0f, 1.0f, 1.0f, 0.0f);
  value = [NSValue valueWithCATransform3D:transform];
  [animation setFromValue:value];
  [animation setAutoreverses:YES];
  [animation setDuration:1.0f];
  [animation setRepeatCount:100];
  [workLayer addAnimation:animation forKey:kScaleKey];
}
```

Listing 5-4 is nearly identical to Listing 5-3 except for the values passed into the CATransform3DMakeRotation method. This example sets both the *x*- and *y*-axes to 1.0, which produces a rotation on both axes and gives the illusion that the layer is flipping diagonally.

Because we rotate the layer by 90 degrees and auto-reversing, this example appears to be flipping all the way around on two axes. This would be useful when you have a two-sided layer (such as a coin or a poker chip) and want to flip between its sides.

Anchor Points

As previously mentioned in the discussion about layers, anchor points become extremely important when dealing with transforms. When you apply a transform to a layer, the transform uses the anchor point to determine where to rotate, scale, and so on.

With the examples so far, the scale transform (shown earlier in Listing 5-2) causes the layer to appear to shrink into the middle of the window, as shown in Figure 5-2. This is because the default position of the anchor point of any layer is the center.

However, if we alter -applicationDidFinishLaunching: and move the anchor point to the lower-left corner of the layer, as shown in Listing 5-5, we get a dramatically different effect.

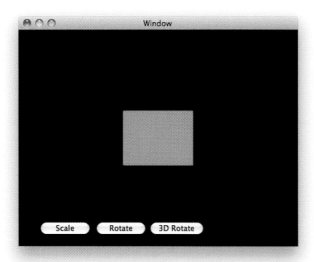

FIGURE 5-2   Center Anchor Point

LISTING 5-5   Updated Anchor Point

```
CGRect workFrame = [layer bounds];
workFrame.origin.x = workFrame.size.width / 4;
workFrame.origin.y = workFrame.size.height / 4;
workFrame.size.width /= 2;
workFrame.size.height /= 2;
[workLayer setAnchorPoint:CGPointMake(0, 0)];
[workLayer setFrame:workFrame];
[layer addSublayer:workLayer];
```

In Listing 5-5, we added the line [workLayer setAnchorPoint:CGPointMake(0, 0)];. This relocates the anchor point to the lower-left corner of the layer. When the scale transform is run, you can see that the layer appears to shrink to the lower-left corner, as shown in Figure 5-3.

By combining transforms along with anchor point manipulation, you can produce some interesting results. For example, we could cause the layer to rotate along the z-axis with a single corner remaining stationary. By moving the anchor point to the desired corner and rotating only along the z-axis, the layer appears to rotate as if it were attached to some object. If we then placed another layer that matches that same corner, it would be a very convincing effect.

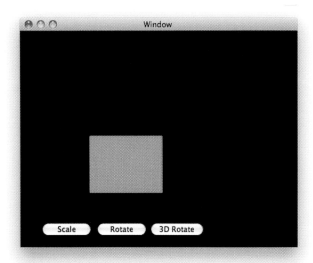

FIGURE 5-3   Lower Left Anchor Point

Combining Transforms

So far, we have covered single transforms, either rotating or scaling the layer. But what if you want to perform more than one transform at the same time? Fortunately for you, we're about to show you how.

To demonstrate how to combine transformations, we do a slightly different project. We start with a standard Cocoa application from the Xcode template and add an AppDelegate. The AppDelegate retains a reference to the NSWindow so that it can be manipulated. Then, within the -applicationDidFinsihLaunching: method, we set up the layers, as shown in Listing 5-6.

LISTING 5-6   applicationDidFinishLaunching

```
- (void)applicationDidFinishLaunching:(NSNotification*)notification
{
  CGColorRef color;

  NSView *contentView = [[self window] contentView];
  CALayer *rootLayer = [CALayer layer];
  color = CGColorCreateGenericRGB(0.0, 0.0, 0.0, 1.0);
  [rootLayer setBackgroundColor:color];
  [contentView setLayer:rootLayer];
  [contentView setWantsLayer:YES];

  layer = [CALayer layer];
  color = CGColorCreateGenericRGB(0.5f, 0.5f, 0.5f, 1.0f);
```

LISTING 5-6   Continued

```
[layer setBackgroundColor:color];

[layer setCornerRadius:5.0f];

color = CGColorCreateGenericRGB(0.0f, 1.0f, 0.0f, 1.0f);
[layer setBorderColor:color];
[layer setBorderWidth:2.0f];

[layer setBounds:CGRectMake(0, 0, 100, 100)];
[layer setPosition:CGPointMake(55, 55)];

[rootLayer addSublayer:layer];
}
```

The -applicationDidFinsihLaunching: method grabs a reference to the contentView and adds a CALayer to it before turning on layer backing. The rootLayer's background color is also black.

Next, create the layer we are going to manipulate and set its color to gray with a green, 2-pixel border and a 5-pixel corner radius. Unlike Listing 5-1, this layer will be 100 × 100 pixels and positioned in the lower-left corner of the contentView.

There's also one additional change to make in Interface Builder. Add a square NSButton to the contentView, make it transparent, and resize the button to the same dimensions as the window. This enables the user to click anywhere within the window and trigger the action, which we get to next.

Bind the large button's action to the AppDelegate and its -(IBAction)action:(id)sender method that we are about to declare.

When the user clicks on the window, we want to take the workingLayer and move it to the upper-right corner. While doing that, we want to both rotate the layer 180 degrees and scale it down to one-tenth its current size. The first possible solution to this problem can be found in Listing 5-7.

LISTING 5-7   -action:

```
- (IBAction)action:(id)sender;
{
  NSRect frame = [[[self window] contentView] frame];
  float x = frame.origin.x + frame.size.width - 30;
  float y = frame.origin.y + frame.size.height - 30;
  CATransform3D rotate;
  CATransform3D scale;
```

LISTING 5-7   Continued

```
[CATransaction begin];
[CATransaction setValue:[NSNumber numberWithFloat:5.0f]
                forKey:kCATransactionAnimationDuration];

[layer setPosition:CGPointMake(x, y)];
scale = CATransform3DMakeScale(0.1f, 0.1f, 1.0f);
rotate = CATransform3DMakeRotation(1.57f, 0.0f, 0.0f, 1.0f);
[layer setTransform:rotate];
[layer setTransform:scale];

[CATransaction commit];
}
```

However, when this code is run, the layer moves and rotates, but it does not scale. This is because calling -setTransform: is only a property, and the last value we set into it wins and discards any previous values that have been set. Although this can be useful in some situations—as both the removal of the old transform and the setting of the new transform are both animated—it is not the effect we look for in this example.

Because the transforms override each other, the transforms need to be combined before applying them to the layer. This is accomplished with the CATransform3DConcat method, which takes two CATransform3D references and returns a single combined CATransform3D, as shown in Listing 5-8.

LISTING 5-8   -action:

```
- (IBAction)action:(id)sender;
{
  NSRect frame = [[[self window] contentView] frame];
  float x = frame.origin.x + frame.size.width - 30;
  float y = frame.origin.y + frame.size.height - 30;
  CATransform3D rotate;
  CATransform3D scale;
  CATransform3D combine;

  [CATransaction begin];
  [CATransaction setValue:[NSNumber numberWithFloat:5.0f]
                  forKey:kCATransactionAnimationDuration];

  [layer setPosition:CGPointMake(x, y)];
  scale = CATransform3DMakeScale(0.1f, 0.1f, 1.0f);
  rotate = CATransform3DMakeRotation(1.57f, 0.0f, 0.0f, 1.0f);
  combine = CATransform3DConcat(rotate, scale);
```

LISTING 5-8   Continued

```
    [layer setTransform:combine];

    [CATransaction commit];
}
```

In this completed -action: method, the final resting position of the CALayer is calculated before beginning a CATransaction block. This ensures that the changes animate together and at the same duration. We then set the duration for the CATransaction using its +setValue:forKey: method, passing in the kCATransactionAnimationDuration key.

After the CATransaction has begun, we can set any animatable property on the layer that we want, and it automatically animates for us using CATransaction's duration. Instead of constructing several CABasicAnimation objects and applying them to the layer, you can just set the properties directly.

The first property to set is the position. Because the anchor point is at the center of the layer, you can easily calculate the position 5 pixels away from the upper-right corner of the window and set the position property of the layer. The layer is moved from its original position in the lower-left corner to the upper-right corner over a period of 5 seconds.

Next, you need to construct the transform that gets applied to the layer. To begin, build the two subtransforms, as such:

▶ Create a scale transform, which scales the layer to one-tenth its original size.

▶ Construct a rotation transform, which rotates the layer 1.57 radians (180 degrees).

With both transforms in place, the next step is to combine them using the CATransform3DConcat method.

When the two transforms are combined, apply them to the layer and commit the CATransaction. The result is a layer that gracefully slides from the lower-left corner to the upper-right corner, scaling down to one-tenth its original size and rotating 180 degrees while moving. This gives you the impression that the layer is zooming from nothing while it is sliding into position.

> **WARNING**
>
> The order in which you pass the subtransforms to the CATransform3DConcat is important. If you do not get the expected effect from CATransform3DConcat, try reversing the parameters and then build and run the project again.

Scale Versus Bounds

In the "Combining Transforms" example, we combined the scale and rotation transforms to produce the desired effect. You might ask: Why not just change the bounds of the layer instead and avoid the overhead of combining the transforms?

The reason is because there is a significant difference between *scaling* a layer and *changing its bounds*. When a layer is scaled, the layer still thinks it is the original size and draws itself at the original size before the scale is applied. However, if we change the bounds and then scale the layer, the layer won't look quite right because it *knows* it is a different size.

For example, if we changed the layer's bounds in the "Combining Transforms" example instead of doing a scale transform, the end result of the animation would look like Figure 5-4.

FIGURE 5-4   Bounds and Rotation Animation

Notice that the end layer looks like a circle. This is because we changed the bounds of the layer but did not change the corner radius or the border width. However, when a scale transform is used, the result has the effect we're looking for, as shown in Figure 5-5.

This gives you a square. One thing you notice when looking at Figure 5-5 is that the border isn't visible; this is because the scaled border is less than 0.5 pixels. Also, because the corner radius (originally 5 pixels) is less than 1 pixel, it also is no longer visible. When working with a complex layer tree, the difference between changing the bounds and the scale can be quite dramatic. If we had scaled this layer *up* by 100 percent, the border would be 50 pixels wide!

FIGURE 5-5   Scale and Rotation Animation

5

Summary

Transforms can be extremely daunting when you first start working with them. Worse, if you decide to research them online, it can be even more confusing. This walk-through of the concepts has hopefully helped you to realize their usefulness and flexibility.

CHAPTER 6

Layer Filters

IN THIS CHAPTER

▶ Applying Filters to Core
   Animation Layers

▶ Controlling Filter Values with
   Data Bindings

▶ Applying Filters to Transitions

As with most Apple technologies, Core Animation provides a means to bridge into other core capabilities. One such bridge enables the developer to interface directly with Core Image—Apple's image manipulation and processing framework. This means that as a Core Animation programmer, you have at your disposal all the Core Image filtering capabilities.

Practically, this means that you can apply, for example, a Gaussian blur to a layer's contents. You set the blur radius on the filter and apply it, or you can animate the blur radius and cause it to blur and then resolve to clear over a duration that you specify. Or say you want to apply a glass distortion effect on an image. You can create a Core Image filter specifying the name CIGlassDistorion and provide the input parameters that filter needs according to the Core Image Filter Reference.[1]

In this chapter, we explore in depth how to effectively apply filters to Core Animation layers, how to control filter parameters using key-value coding, and how to use filters for transitions.

At the time of this writing, Core Image filters are not supported on the iPhone, so this chapter covers only what is available on OS X. You can perform graphic manipulations on the iPhone, however, such capabilities are not yet available as part of Core Animation, making that information beyond the scope of this book.

---

[1]http://developer.apple.com/documentation/graphicsimaging/
   Reference/CoreImageFilterReference/Reference/reference.html.

Applying Filters to Core Animation Layers

Apple's *Core Image Programming Guide*[2] and related *Core Image Filter Reference*[3] provide the full API specification for effectively using filters in layers and views. You need to access those references to see a full list of all the filters available to you.

To add a Core Image filter to a layer, simply create a `CIFilter` object and add it to the layer's `filters` array parameter, as shown in Listing 6-1.

LISTING 6-1   Adding a Gaussian Blur Filter to a Layer

```
CIFilter *blurFilter =
    [CIFilter filterWithName:@"CIGaussianBlur"];


[blurFilter setDefaults];
[blurFilter setValue:[NSNumber numberWithFloat:5.0f]
              forKey:@"inputRadius"];


[layer setFilters:[NSArray arrayWithObject:blurFilter]];
```

When you run the code in Listing 6-1, the filter is applied to the `layer` when it is added to the layer tree for whatever view contains it. In this example, the layer's view has a Gaussian blur with a 5-pixel radius applied to it. You can see what the output of this code looks like in Figure 6-1. From the companion website (informit.com/coreframeworks), open the sample project called GaussianBlurLayer if you want to see the complete code listing.

Many of the filters available don't require anything except specifying the default parameters through a call to –setDefaults. Simply change the name of the filter to one of the others in the filter reference, and you can see what we mean.

Applying filters to a layer in this way is not terribly useful. As with most technical subjects, the details of mastering filters are more involved. Because this is a book about Core Animation, what we more likely want is a way to apply the filter within the context of animation. What you might want in a real-world application is to animate the filter on the layer rather than simply applying it and leaving it as a static layer with a filter applied. We cover that next.

[2]http://developer.apple.com/documentation/GraphicsImaging/Conceptual/CoreImaging/CoreImage.pdf.

[3]http://developer.apple.com/documentation/GraphicsImaging/Reference/CoreImageFilterReference/CoreImageFilterReference.pdf.

FIGURE 6-1   Gaussian Blur Filter Applied to Image

Animating an Applied Filter

You likely want to apply a filter to a layer in response to user input. For example, you might want to create a Core Animation layer-based button that has a 5-pixel Gaussian blur applied to it when clicked. To do so, create a layer-backed `NSView` derived view to contain the layer that will be animated. When you add the filter to the layer in your view initialization, set its `inputRadius` field with an initial value of 0.0 so that no evidence of the effect is visible when the layer first displays. Then, in response to a click, you can animate the `inputRadius` property to a value that makes the button blur and return to clear. On the companion website, the demo application Click to Blur demonstrates this capability. Open that project now to see this capability in action.

Each image you see in Figure 6-2 represents one view; each view contains a Core Animation layer. The image you see is the contents of the view's layer. Behind each layer is a view called BlurView that does the following:

▶ Holds the `CALayer`-derived layer, called `BlurLayer`, upon which the animation gets performed

▶ Receives the mouse-down event we use to trigger the animation

Every layer has a `filters` field that holds an `NSArray` of Core Image filter objects. Think of this array as an array of filters that might or might not be used. You can build up a list of filters that you might use, and then you can enable them through key-value coding when you receive user input, such as a button click. We get to the key-value coding in a moment. The Click to Blur demo application causes the icon image to blur and become clear again when the view receives a mouse click.

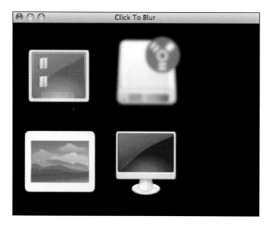

FIGURE 6-2   Gaussian Blur Filter Applied to Image

Key-value coding manipulates the values of the filter, but to do so we first need to name each filter we plan to use. The name of the filter is important because it will be used in the key-path to the filter parameters such as `inputRadius`. For further discussion, take a look at the sidebar, "Key-Paths in Key-Value Coding." We also need to change the initial input radius (the `inputRadius` parameter on the `CIFilter` object) value to `0.0f`. This is the starting value for the input radius of the blur. We start at zero, so the blur effect is not initially visible.

Key-Paths in Key-Value Coding

Key-Value Coding (KVC) is a useful feature of the Objective-C language. If you have had any experience writing code in Objective-C, you are likely already familiar with the concept. KVC enables member or instance variables (commonly referred to as *ivars*) of an Objective-C class to be accessed by name rather than by direct reference by using a call to `–setValue:forKey` and `–valueForKey` to set and retrieve values for your ivars. KVC is what enables bindings to work.

Key-paths are important to understand. In this chapter, we demonstrate an example of using KVC to bind filter parameters to Cocoa controls such as `NSSliders`. When the user slides the slider in the app, the slider looks up the object it is bound to and then attempts to access the ivar variable specified in the key-path. Say we have a Core Animation layer object in our `AppDelegate` class called `blurLayer` to which we have added a Gaussian blur `CIFilter` object named `blur`. To access this filter's `inputRadius` value, the key-path we use in an `NSSlider` control is `blurLayer.filters.blur.inputRadius`. Say instead of binding to the control, however, we would rather animate the blur in code. In this case our key-path changes relative to the object that contains the filter to be animated. The key-path becomes `filters.blur.inputRadius` as the base object, `blurLayer`, rather than the `AppDelegate`. In either case, notice we have employed the name we gave to our filter, `blur`, in the key-path. Look ahead to Listing 6-6 that demonstrates how this is used when creating an animation.

Listing 6-2 reflects the code changes. A change is made to the line where we set the inputRadius initial value to 0.0f and we add the line to name the filter so that it can be called later. The complete view initialization code is in Listing 6-3.

LISTING 6-2   Adding Filter Name and Setting inputRadius

```
CIFilter *blurFilter =
    [CIFilter filterWithName:@"CIGaussianBlur"];

[blurFilter setDefaults];

[blurFilter setValue:[NSNumber numberWithFloat:0.0f]
            forKey:@"inputRadius"];
[blurFilter setName:@"blur"];

[layer setFilters:[NSArray arrayWithObject:blurFilter]];
```

LISTING 6-3   BlurView Initialization Code

```
- (void)awakeFromNib;
{
    [self setWantsLayer:YES];

    // Initialize the layer
    blurLayer = [[[BlurLayer alloc]init] retain];

    [blurLayer setMasksToBounds:YES];

    // Set the layer to fill the entire frame
    [blurLayer setFrame:CGRectMake(0.0,
                    0.0,
                    [self frame].size.width,
                    [self frame].size.height)];

    [[self layer] addSublayer:blurLayer];

    // Initialize the Gaussian blur filter
    CIFilter *blurFilter =
        [CIFilter filterWithName:@"CIGaussianBlur"];

    [blurFilter setDefaults];
    [blurFilter setValue:[NSNumber numberWithFloat:0.0]
            forKey:@"inputRadius"];
```

LISTING 6-3   Continued

```
    // Give the Gaussian blur filter a name
    [blurFilter setName:@"blur"];

    [blurLayer setFilters:[NSArray arrayWithObject:blurFilter]];
}
```

We have created a CALayer-derived class called BlurLayer that we add to the BlurView
view object. The BlurLayer class simply manages the image content of the layer. The
image for each instance of the view is set in the –applicationDidFinishLaunching
method, found in the application delegate class, as shown in Listing 6-4.

LISTING 6-4   Initialization of BlurView Objects

```
- (void)applicationDidFinishLaunching:(NSNotification *)aNotification;
{
    NSString *iconPath1 = [[NSBundle mainBundle]
                    pathForResource:@"desktop"
                    ofType:@"png"];
    NSString *iconPath2 = [[NSBundle mainBundle]
                    pathForResource:@"fwdrive"
                    ofType:@"png"];
    NSString *iconPath3 = [[NSBundle mainBundle]
                    pathForResource:@"pictures"
                    ofType:@"png"];
    NSString *iconPath4 = [[NSBundle mainBundle]
                    pathForResource:@"computer"
                    ofType:@"png"];

    NSImage *image1 = [[NSImage alloc]
            initWithContentsOfFile:iconPath1];
    NSImage *image2 = [[NSImage alloc]
            initWithContentsOfFile:iconPath2];
    NSImage *image3 = [[NSImage alloc]
            initWithContentsOfFile:iconPath3];
    NSImage *image4 = [[NSImage alloc]
            initWithContentsOfFile:iconPath4];

    [blurView1 setLayerImage:image1];
    [blurView2 setLayerImage:image2];
    [blurView3 setLayerImage:image3];
    [blurView4 setLayerImage:image4];
}
```

The instance variables `blurView1`, `blurView2`, `blurView3`, and `blurView4` are `BlurView` instances, and each one has been connected to custom views in Interface Builder. You can see what these custom views look like in Figure 6-3.

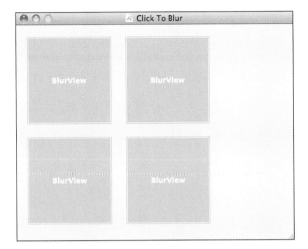

FIGURE 6-3   Custom Views in Interface Builder

Receiving User Input

Core Animation layers cannot receive mouse events; however, their backing views do. In the view initialization code (Listing 6-4), we applied the layer's filter(s) for later use when the view receives a click.

To receive a click, tell `BlurView` to accept mouse clicks by adding to the view the code in Listing 6-5.

LISTING 6-5   Enable View to Receive Events

```
-(BOOL)acceptsFirstResponder;
{
    return YES;
}
```

A first responder is a responder in the responder chain that is given the first chance to respond to an event such as a mouse click or key press. With this code in Listing 6-5, we are informing the event system that our window should be given a chance to respond to events sent to it. In this case, these are simply mouse clicks. After we have established that our view should handle its own events in this way, we can implement the code that we want to run when we receive the event. In the –mouseDown view delegate, set up a basic animation for changing the value of the blur filter's input radius, as shown in Listing 6-6.

LISTING 6-6   Add Blur Animation to the mouseDown Event

```
- (void)mouseDown:(NSEvent *)theEvent;
{
    CABasicAnimation *anim =
    [CABasicAnimation animationWithKeyPath:
        @"filters.blur.inputRadius"];

    // Set the filter's start value
    [anim setFromValue:[NSNumber numberWithFloat:0.0f]];
    // Set the filter's ending value
    [anim setToValue:[NSNumber numberWithFloat:5.0f]];
    [anim setDuration:0.2f];
    [anim setAutoreverses:YES];
    [anim setRemovedOnCompletion:YES];

    [blurLayer addAnimation:anim forKey:@"filters.blur.inputRadius"];
}
```

As shown in Listing 6-6, we create a basic animation using the key-path `filters.blur.inputRadius`. You might have already noticed, but this is where the name of the filter we added in Listing 6-2 becomes important. The `filters` field is being accessed here, and we are querying for a filter named `blur` (the name of the Gaussian blur filter we added in Listing 6-2), so we can animate its `inputRadius`.

The starting and ending values for the blur filter's `inputRadius` are set using the `-setFromValue:` and `-setToValue:` methods, as shown in the next two lines. We are going to animate the input radius from 0.0 to 5.0. Next, we set the duration of the animation to run quickly; approximately one-fifth of a second, as noted with `-setDuration:0.2f`.

The `-setAutoreverses:YES` call tells the animation to loop backward to its original value. If we left this to its default (`NO`), when the animation finished we would see the layer instantly snap back to its original value, which makes it look jerky. In this situation, it is ideal to have it *animate* back to the original value to give the animation a much smoother, polished look.

Finally, the animation is automatically set to be removed (`-setRemovedOnCompletion:YES`) from the animation when it has finished one iteration. This is actually the default behavior so this is a superfluous call. However, we include it here so you understand that this is the desired action.

Now, when the button is clicked, it blurs the entire button layer to a 5.0 pixel radius and returns to its clear state within one-fifth of a second.

Making the Effect "Sticky"

There might be times when you want the animation effect to be sticky, where rather than resetting the animated property back to its original value, you want its new value to "stick." To see an example of this, go to the companion website and launch the Click to Blur Sticky project in Xcode and click Build and Go. When you click on one of the icons, you notice that the icon stays blurred until you click it a second time, as shown in Figure 6-3.

To create this effect, so the clicked icon stays blurred and then returns to its normal state when clicked a second time, you need to keep track of the button state. This is accomplished using a BOOL value, which for this example is named toggle. The –mouseDown code now looks like what we see in Listing 6-7.

LISTING 6-7   Implementing Toggle Functionality

```
- (void)mouseDown:(NSEvent *)theEvent;
{
    CABasicAnimation *anim =
    [CABasicAnimation
       animationWithKeyPath:@"filters.blur.inputRadius"];

    if(toggle)
    {
        [anim setFromValue:[NSNumber numberWithFloat:0.0f]];
        [anim setToValue:[NSNumber numberWithFloat:5.0f]];
    }
    else
    {
        [anim setFromValue:[NSNumber numberWithFloat:5.0f]];
        [anim setToValue:[NSNumber numberWithFloat:0.0f]];
    }

    [anim setDuration:0.2f];
    [anim setRemovedOnCompletion:NO];
    [anim setFillMode:kCAFillModeForwards];
    [blurLayer addAnimation:anim
                    forKey:@"filters.blur.inputRadius"];
    toggle = !toggle;
}
```

So what changed? The first thing you notice is that depending on the current state of the toggle variable, we determine whether the start value is 0.0 or 5.0 before setting -setToValue: to the opposite value. If our toggle is not yet set, we want to animate to blurry so our starting value, fromValue, is set to 0.0 and our ending value, toValue, is set to 5.0. However, if the toggle is set, we want to animate to clear so the starting value is 5.0 and our ending value is 0.0.

Notice also that Listing 6-7 doesn't contain the -setAutoreverses call that's found in Listing 6-6. This call must be removed or set to NO for the effect to be "sticky"; otherwise it returns to its starting value and overrides -setFillMode:.

Next, we have changed the -setRemovedOnCompletion call to NO. This tells the layer not to remove the animation when it has completed.

Finally, we have added a call to -setFillMode:kCAFillModeForwards that tells the animation to leave the resulting value at whatever we specified in the -setToValue field.

Each icon now retains the blur on the first click and returns to its original value on a second click, making the Core Animation layer-based-button "sticky." In Figure 6-4, you can see that two of the icons are blurry because they have each been clicked once and retain their sticky state.

FIGURE 6-4   Sticky Blur

Controlling Filter Values with Data Bindings

Filter parameters are accessible and modifiable using KVC. This enables you to use data bindings to create layers with complex filtering and control those filters using standard Cocoa controls, such as sliders.

You might recall from the previous section that when we instantiated the CABasic Animation object on a mouse down event, we used the key-path filters.blur. inputRadius on the layer. filters represents the NSArray of filters available, blur is the name we provided to the filter upon instantiation for later identification, and `inputRadius` is the name of the filter field we wanted to manipulate. This same key path can be used when setting up bindings in Interface Builder. The difference is that we must first make the `CALayer` accessible to Interface Builder by making it a property of the `AppDelegate` class, as shown in Listing 6-8.

LISTING 6-8   AppDelegate Declaration

```
@interface AppDelegate : NSObject
{
    IBOutlet NSView *displayView;
    CALayer *imageLayer;
}

@property (retain)CALayer *imageLayer;

@end
```

In the `AppDelegate` implementation, we have to @synthensize the `imageLayer` object. Prior to Objective-C 2.0, you had to explicitly create setters and getters for your instance variables and you had to wrap changes you made to your instance variables in calls to –willChangeValueForKey and –didChangeValueForKey for your object to be KVC–compliant, which is required for bindings to work. Now, with Objective-C 2.0, this is done automatically when you make your ivar a @property and use the @synthesize keyword. The implementation code to synthesize the `imageLayer` object is in Listing 6-9.

LISTING 6-9   AppDelegate Implementation

```
@implementation AppDelegate
@synthesize imageLayer;
…
```

Switch to Interface Builder and add a slider for each of the filters we want to apply to the `imageLayer` object. In Figure 6-5, you can see that we have added sliders for a Gaussian Blur, Hue, Saturation, Contrast, and Brightness.

Before we can data bind the sliders, the filters need to be added to the `imageLayer`. For this, call –setFilters on the layer, as shown in Listing 6-10.

FIGURE 6-5   Image Adjustment Filter Sliders

LISTING 6-10   The Filters Method

```
- (NSArray*)filters;
{
    CIFilter *blurFilter =
        [CIFilter filterWithName:@"CIGaussianBlur"];

    [blurFilter setDefaults];
    [blurFilter setValue:[NSNumber numberWithFloat:0.0]
                  forKey:@"inputRadius"];
    [blurFilter setName:@"blur"];

    CIFilter *hueFilter =
    [CIFilter filterWithName:@"CIHueAdjust"];

    [hueFilter setDefaults];
    [hueFilter setValue:[NSNumber numberWithFloat:0.0]
                 forKey:@"inputAngle"];
    [hueFilter setName:@"hue"];

    CIFilter *colorFilter =
        [CIFilter filterWithName:@"CIColorControls"];
    [colorFilter setDefaults];
    [colorFilter setName:@"color"];
```

LISTING 6-10   Continued

```
return [NSArray arrayWithObjects:
    blurFilter,
    hueFilter,
    colorFilter,
    nil];
}
```

This code creates three filters: blurFilter, hueFilter, and colorFilter. The latter, colorFilter, enables us to alter three different values: saturation, contrast, and brightness. Each filter has a set of default values that we can take advantage of by calling –setDefaults. Notice also that we have given each filter a name; these names are used to access filter values with bindings and KVC.

With the filters added to the layer, we can access each filter's parameters using a key-path. The full key-paths for each slider are shown in Table 6-1.

TABLE 6-1   Filter Key-Paths

Filter Name	Filter Parameter Name	Key-Path
blur	inputRadius	imageLayer.filters.blur.inputRadius
hue	inputAngle	imageLayer.filters.hue.inputAngle
color	inputSaturation	imageLayer.filters.color.inputSaturation
color	inputContrast	imageLayer.filters.color.inputContrast
color	inputBrightness	imageLayer.filters.color.inputBrightnes

If you look at the bindings menu in the slider inspector in Interface Builder, you can see how these key-paths are applied. Figure 6-6 shows the key path for the hue filter.

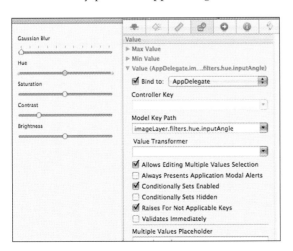

FIGURE 6-6   Bindings for the Hue Filter Slider

The remaining sliders are connected in the same way as specified by the key-paths in Table 6-1.

The complete application has a minimal number of lines of code, largely due to the power of data bindings. The complete AppDelegate implementation is shown in Listing 6-11.

LISTING 6-11   Complete AppDelegate Code

```objectivec
@interface AppDelegate : NSObject {
    IBOutlet NSView *displayView;
    CALayer *imageLayer;
}

@property (retain)CALayer *imageLayer;

- (NSArray*)filters;
- (CGImageRef)nsImageToCGImageRef:(NSImage*)image;

@end



@implementation AppDelegate

@synthesize imageLayer;

- (void)awakeFromNib;
{
    [displayView setWantsLayer:YES];

    imageLayer = [[CALayer layer] retain];

    CGRect frame = CGRectMake(0.0f,
                    0.0f,
                    [displayView frame].size.width,
                    [displayView frame].size.height);

    [imageLayer setFrame:frame];
    [imageLayer setCornerRadius:15.0f];
    [imageLayer setBorderWidth:3.0f];
    [imageLayer setMasksToBounds:YES];

    NSString *imagePath = [[NSBundle mainBundle]
                    pathForResource:@"balloon"
                            ofType:@"jpg"];
```

LISTING 6-11   Continued

```
    [imageLayer setContents:
     (id)[self nsImageToCGImageRef:
        [[NSImage alloc] initWithContentsOfFile:imagePath]]];


    [imageLayer setFilters:[self filters]];

    [[displayView layer] addSublayer:imageLayer];

}

- (NSArray*)filters;
{
    CIFilter *blurFilter =
        [CIFilter filterWithName:@"CIGaussianBlur"];

    [blurFilter setDefaults];
    [blurFilter setValue:[NSNumber numberWithFloat:0.0]
                forKey:@"inputRadius"];
    [blurFilter setName:@"blur"];

    CIFilter *hueFilter =
        [CIFilter filterWithName:@"CIHueAdjust"];

    [hueFilter setDefaults];
    [hueFilter setValue:[NSNumber numberWithFloat:0.0]
                forKey:@"inputAngle"];
    [hueFilter setName:@"hue"];

    CIFilter *colorFilter =
        [CIFilter filterWithName:@"CIColorControls"];
    [colorFilter setDefaults];
    [colorFilter setName:@"color"];

    return [NSArray arrayWithObjects:
        blurFilter,
        hueFilter,
        colorFilter,
        nil];
}

- (CGImageRef)nsImageToCGImageRef:(NSImage*)image;
{
```

9

LISTING 6-11   Continued

```
    NSData * imageData = [image TIFFRepresentation];
    CGImageRef imageRef;
    if(imageData)
    {
        CGImageSourceRef imageSource =
        CGImageSourceCreateWithData((CFDataRef)imageData,  NULL);

        imageRef =
        CGImageSourceCreateImageAtIndex(imageSource, 0, NULL);
    }
    return imageRef;
}

- (void)dealloc;
{
    if( imageLayer )
        [imageLayer release];

    [super dealloc];
    }

@end
```

Applying Filters to Transitions

The easiest way to start animating properties with Core Animation is by employing the animator proxy object on the view you want to animate. When you apply the animator proxy object, it invokes a number of default transitions that you might or might not notice. If you set the opacity of a layer, for instance, the transition fades by default. (Fade in is for increasing the opacity, and fade out is for decreasing it.) To see this default transition, you call –setOpacity on the animator instead of the view, and the fade transition will animate automatically with no extra coding effort on your part. The true power of transitions, though, comes in when you can specify your own transitions, and this is easily done using filters.

The Default Transitions

Core Animation provides a set of default transitions (see Table 6-2), which you can specify to use when a property change occurs.

TABLE 6-2   Default Transition Types and Their Functions

Field	Function
Fade	The constant `kCATransitionFade` indicates that the layer's contents should fade in when the transition occurs.
Move In	The constant `kCATransitionMoveIn` indicates that the layer's contents should slide in from some direction. The direction used is determined by a transition's subtype (see "Transition Subtypes" in the next section). The default transition subtype, if none is specified when `kCATransitionMoveIn` is used as the main type, is `kCATransitionFromLeft`, which specifies the contents should slide in from the left.
Push	The constant `kCATransitionPush` indicates that the layer's contents should push any existing content from some direction. The direction used is determined by a transition's subtype (see "Transition Subtypes" in the next section). The default transition subtype, if none is specified when `kCATransitionPush` is used as the main type, is `kCATransitionFromLeft`, which specifies the contents should slide in from the left.
Reveal	The constant `kCATransitionReveal` indicates that the layer's contents should be revealed from some direction. The direction used is determined by a transition's subtype (see "Transition Subtypes" in the next section). The default transition subtype, if none is specified when `kCATransitionReveal` is used as the main type, is `kCATransitionFromLeft`, which specifies the contents should slide in from the left.

The default transition subtypes are listing in Table 6-3.

TABLE 6-3   Default Transition Subtypes and Their Functions

Field	Function
From Right	The constant `kCATransitionFromRight` indicates that the animation will come in from the right.
From Left	The constant `kCATransitionFromLeft` indicates that the animation will come in from the left.
From Top	The constant `kCATransitionFromTop` indicates that the animation will come in from the top.
From Bottom	The constant `kCATransitionFromBottom` indicates that the animation will come in from the bottom.

If you want to tweak a default transition, simply add the transition to your layer's `actions` field, which is an `NSDictionary`. Specify the property you want to use for your transition by specifying its name as a key-path when you add your `CATransition` object to the layer's `actions` field. When you create the layer that you want to perform the transition on, you can simply set it up there. In the next section, we get into details of returning a specific action for property transitions, but here are the basic steps and the code to alter the transition for a given property change using the default transitions during layer instantiation:

1. Select the property you want to animate, in this case, we use opacity.

2. Create a new dictionary from the layer's current actions property.

3. Add the transition to the new actions dictionary for the key opacity.

4. Set the layer's actions property to the newly created dictionary.

The code to set the default transition for the opacity field is in Listing 6-12.

LISTING 6-12   Set the Default Transition for Opacity

```
CATransition *transition=[CATransition animation];
[transition setType:kCATransitionMoveIn];
[transition setSubtype:kCATransitionFromTop];
[transition setDuration:1.0f];

// Get the current list of actions
NSMutableDictionary *actions = [NSMutableDictionary
                          dictionaryWithDictionary:[transitionLayer actions]];
[actions setObject:transition forKey:@"opacity"];


[transitionLayer setActions:actions];
```

First, you need to instantiate the CATransition object. Using the default transitions as specified in the Tables 6-2 and Table 6-3, set the type to kCATransitionMoveIn, which causes the transition to move in from some direction. Then, in the subtype field, specify the direction from which the transition should move in; in this example, we move in from the top (kCATransitionFromTop). Next, specify the duration for the transition; in this case, a full second.

At this point, we need to add the transition to the layer's list of actions. The layer knows to use this transition rather than the default fade because of the key-path. We specify in the dictionary that our key-path is opacity. Any time the layer's opacity changes, it uses the specified transition rather than the default fade transition.

To make this work, we first instantiate a new dictionary using the original actions field from transitionLayer. We do this just in case some other actions have been specified in the collection.

We know that there isn't anything else in the dictionary; however, I mention it for clarity. You just need to understand that if you create a new dictionary and set the layer's actions to it without first grabbing what might have been there previously, you might be confused as to why other transitions are not working correctly.

Finally, set the layer's actions dictionary to point to the newly created dictionary that contains the CATransition object.

Using Custom Transitions

It is simple to specify the CIFilter you want to use for a transition. To apply the transition, use the CATransition object's filter parameter to specify the action you want to use on a particular key. When used, the filter parameter overrides the CATransition object's type and subtype parameters. If you have specified one of the default transitions using these other two parameters, they will be ignored when the filter parameter has been set.

To Delegate or Encapsulate

For most applications, you should encapsulate your custom transition functionality by implementing it in your own CALayer-derived class. You can, however, use a delegate method of the CALayer if that is more convenient. That is the only reason to prefer delegation over encapsulation—convenience. For organization and reduced code clutter, choose encapsulation over delegation, but for the quick and dirty approach, delegation is sometimes the way to go. There are two different techniques, and therefore function calls, you can implement, as shown in Table 6-4.

TABLE 6-4   Methods to Use to Encapsulate or Delegate

If you Want To:	Then:
Encapsulate	Override the following method in your CALayer-derived class:
	`+ (id<CAAction>)defaultActionForKey:(NSString *)aKey`
Delegate	Set the layer delegate to point to your controller and implement the following delegate method:
	`- (id<CAAction>)actionForLayer:(CALayer *)layer` `                          forKey:(NSString *)key;`

It is sometimes quicker and more convenient to simply use a delegate to specify the transition filter you want to use. If you are implementing a custom transition with a delegate, first set the delegate for the layer in question in the application's delegate code; for example:

```
[layer setDelegate:self];
```

Then you implement the delegate method for setting an action for a particular key and layer:

```
- (id<CAAction>)actionForLayer:(CALayer *)layer
                          forKey:(NSString *)key;
```

In this delegate method, you are provided two items that enable you to specify what kind of filter to apply to perform your transition: the layer and the key-path string. You have two options:

▶ You simply check to see if the layer object passed in is the one you want to work with by comparing memory addresses with the == operator.

▶ If you've assigned the layer a name, you can compare the name string. Then you
check to see if the key passed in is the key-path you want to work with.

If you prefer to encapsulate the code in your own CALayer-derived class, you override
-defaultActionForKey so that it returns an action for a particular key. The layer is already
known because we have encapsulated it; for example:

```
+ (id<CAAction>)defaultActionForKey:(NSString *)aKey
```

The Ripple Transition

We have included two sample projects
to demonstrate how to implement the
ripple transition in this section. One
shows how to implement it using delegation, the other using encapsulation.
You might want to open one or both
projects now to see the complete
solution.

For this example, we change the layer's
transition to use Core Image's ripple
effect filter, CIRippleTransition. It
requires the fields shown in Table 6-5 to
be specified.

> **NOTE**
>
> For more information about
> CIRippleTransition, refer to the *Core
> Image Filter Reference* document from Apple.
> This can be found on your system in the
> Core Reference Library, which you can
> launch by going to *http://developer.apple.
> com/mac/library/documentation/Graphics
> Imaging/Reference/CoreImageFilterReference
> /Reference/reference.html*. This opens the
> Developer Documentation window in Xcode,
> from which you can search for more detailed
> information on CIRippleTransition.

Table 6-5   Ripple Filter Fields

Field Name	Function
inputImage	A CIImage used for the starting image.
inputTargetImage	A CIImage used as the finish image.
inputShadingImage	A CIImage used for setting the shading for the ripple effect.
inputCenter	A CIVector representing the center of the effect, which is where the visual effect begins. The default value is 150,150.
inputExtent	A CIVector representing the input image extent. The default value is 0, 0, 300, 300.
inputTime	An NSNumber representing the input time of the transition. The default values are default: 0.00, minimum: 0.00, maximum: 1.00, slider minimum: 0.00, and slider maximum: 1.00.
inputWidth	An NSNumber representing the width of the input image. The default values are default: 100.00, minimum: 1.00, maximum: 0.00, slider minimum: 10.00, slider maximum: 300.00.
inputScale	An NSNumber representing the input scale. The default values are default: 50.00, minimum: -50.00, maximum: 0.00, slider minimum: -50.00, slider maximum: 50.00.

The ripple transition seems complex. However, when you create it, you can just call
-setDefaults on the filter. The only field you *must* specify when using this filter on a
layer is inputShadingImage. You will probably also want to specify the inputCenter field
so that you can specify the location of the transition's origin point.

In this example, we use the ripple transition filter for the key "bounds." This means that
whenever the bounds field of the layer is changed, the ripple effect will be used instead of
the default transition. In Figure 6-7, you can see what the effect looks like in its various
stages.

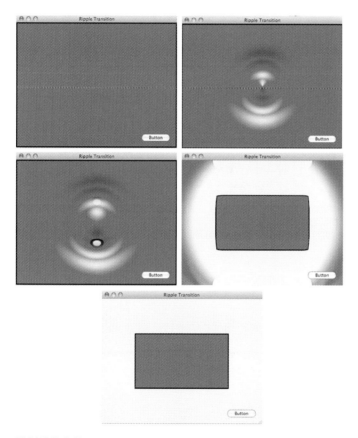

FIGURE 6-7   Ripple Transition Filter on a Core Animation Layer

To implement the ripple transition using encapsulation, simply create a derivative layer
named RippleLayer. The implementation of this layer code is in Listing 6-13.

LISTING 6-13   Ripple Layer Implementation

```objc
@interface RippleLayer : CALayer {


}

@end


@implementation RippleLayer

+ (id<CAAction>)defaultActionForKey:(NSString *)key;
{
if( [key isEqualToString@"bounds"] )
    {
        // Going to cheat a little bit here. Since this is a class
        // method, we can't get the dimensions from self. Instead,
        // we need to obtain this size some other way in a real-world
        // application.
        float w = 480.0;
        float h = 360.0;

        NSURL   *url = [NSURL fileURLWithPath:
                [[NSBundle mainBundle]
                pathForResource:@"Shading"
                        ofType:@"tiff"]];

        CIImage *shadingImage =
        [[CIImage alloc] initWithContentsOfURL: url];

        CIFilter *rippleFilter =
        [CIFilter filterWithName:@"CIRippleTransition"];
        [rippleFilter setDefaults];
        [rippleFilter setValue:shadingImage
                    forKey:@"inputShadingImage"];

        [rippleFilter setValue:[CIVector vectorWithX: 0.5*w Y: 0.5*h]
                    forKey:@"inputCenter"];


        CATransition *theTransition=[CATransition animation];
        [theTransition setFilter:rippleFilter];
        [theTransition setDuration:2.0f];
        return theTransition;
    }
```

LISTING 6-13   Continued

```
    // Cause the layer to use its default transition
    return nil;
}


@end
```

The new `RippleLayer` class is used in the application's delegate class. The complete `AppDelegate` code is in Listing 6-14.

LISTING 6-14   AppDelegate Implementation Using Encapsulation

```objc
#import "RippleLayer.h"

@interface AppDelegate : NSObject {
    IBOutlet NSWindow *window;
    RippleLayer *transitionLayer;

    BOOL toggle;
}

-(IBAction)doTransition:(id)sender;
@end


@implementation AppDelegate
-(void)awakeFromNib;
{
    [[window contentView] setWantsLayer:YES];

    CGColorRef green =
    CGColorCreateGenericRGB(0, 0.45, 0, 1);

    transitionLayer = [[[RippleLayer alloc] init] retain];
    [transitionLayer setFrame:
     NSRectToCGRect([[window contentView] frame])];

    [transitionLayer setBackgroundColor:green];
    [transitionLayer setDelegate:self];
    [transitionLayer setBorderWidth:3];

    // Keep the layer behind the button
    [[[window contentView] layer]
     insertSublayer:transitionLayer atIndex:0];
```

LISTING 6-14   Continued

```
    CFRelease(green);

}

-(IBAction)doTransition:(id)sender;
{

    CGRect contentRect =
    NSRectToCGRect([[window contentView] frame]);

    if(toggle)
    {
        [transitionLayer setBounds:contentRect];
    }
    else
    {
        CGRect newFrame =
        CGRectMake((contentRect.size.width / 2) - 100.0,
            (contentRect.size.height / 2) - 100.0,
            contentRect.size.width - 200.0,
            contentRect.size.height - 200.0);

        [transitionLayer setBounds:newFrame];
    }
    toggle = !toggle;

}

- (void)dealloc;
{
    [transitionLayer release], transitionLayer = nil;
    [super dealloc];
}


@end
```

Similarly, you can implement the ripple filter transition when using delegation using the code in Listing 6-15.

LISTING 6-15   AppDelegate Implementation Using Delegation

```
@interface AppDelegate : NSObject {
    IBOutlet NSWindow *window;
```

LISTING 6-15   Continued

```
    CALayer      *transitionLayer;
    CIImage      *shadingImage;
    CIVector     *extent;
    BOOL         toggle;
}

- (CIImage *)shadingImage;
-(IBAction)doTransition:(id)sender;

@end

@implementation AppDelegate
-(void)awakeFromNib;
{
    [[window contentView] setWantsLayer:YES];

    CGColorRef green =
    CGColorCreateGenericRGB(0, 0.45, 0, 1);

    transitionLayer = [CALayer layer];
    [transitionLayer setFrame:
     NSRectToCGRect([[window contentView] frame])];
    [transitionLayer setBackgroundColor:green];
    [transitionLayer setDelegate:self];
    [transitionLayer setBorderWidth:3];

    // Keep the layer behind our button.
    [[[window contentView] layer]
     insertSublayer:transitionLayer atIndex:0];

    CFRelease(green);
}

- (id<CAAction>)actionForLayer:(CALayer *)layer
                        forKey:(NSString *)key;
{
    if( layer == transitionLayer )
    {
        if( [key compare:@"bounds"] == NSOrderedSame )
        {
            float w = [[window contentView] frame].size.width;
            float h = [[window contentView] frame].size.height;

            CIFilter *rippleFilter =
            [CIFilter filterWithName:@"CIRippleTransition"];
```

LISTING 6-15   Continued

```objc
            [rippleFilter setDefaults];
            [rippleFilter setValue:[self shadingImage]
                          forKey:@"inputShadingImage"];

            [rippleFilter setValue:
             [CIVector vectorWithX: 0.5*w Y: 0.5*h]
                          forKey:@"inputCenter"];

            CATransition *theTransition=[CATransition animation];
            [theTransition setFilter:rippleFilter];
            [theTransition setDuration:2.0f];
            return theTransition;
        }
    }

    // Cause the layer to use its default transition
    return nil;
}

- (CIImage *)shadingImage
{
    if(!shadingImage)
    {
        NSURL  *url;
        url   = [NSURL fileURLWithPath:
                [[NSBundle mainBundle]
                 pathForResource:@"Shading"
                 ofType:@"tiff"]];

        shadingImage = [[CIImage alloc]
                initWithContentsOfURL: url];
    }

    return shadingImage;
}

-(IBAction)doTransition:(id)sender;
{
    CGRect contentRect =
    NSRectToCGRect([[window contentView] frame]);

    if(toggle)
    {
        [transitionLayer setBounds:contentRect];
```

LISTING 6-15   Continued

```
    }
    else
    {
        CGRect newFrame =
        CGRectMake(((contentRect.size.width / 2) - 100.0,
            (contentRect.size.height / 2) - 100.0,
            contentRect.size.width - 200.0,
            contentRect.size.height - 200.0);

        [transitionLayer setBounds:newFrame];
    }
    toggle = !toggle;
}

@end
```

The –doTransition method is identical regardless of which method you use to implement the transition filter. It uses a variable called toggle that keeps track of whether the layer covers the whole content area or its reduced size. The call to –setBounds on the layer causes the transition animation to occur. When the toggle is set, we transition to the content view frame, and we transition to the smaller frame when it isn't set. We then toggle the toggle variable.

To summarize, the main differences between encapsulation and delegation follow:

▶ Encapsulation requires you to create your own CALayer-derived layer class that will override + (id<CAAction>)defaultActionForKey:(NSString *)key;.

▶ Delegation requires that your application delegate implements -(id<CAAction>)actionForLayer:(CALayer *)layer after setting the layer's delegate to the AppDelegate instance, usually self.

> **NOTE**
>
> It's up to you whether you delegate or encapsulate. We tend to choose the encapsulation route as it makes things tidy. However, it is completely legitimate to use the delegation method should that prove to be cleaner or more convenient.

Summary

Whether providing a simple view effect, adding animations based on user interaction, changing filter parameters, or changing the default transition to be something more interesting, Core Image filters are a powerful and valuable component in the Core Animation toolbox.

CHAPTER 7

QuickTime Layers

IN THIS CHAPTER

▶ **Working with QTMovieLayer**

▶ **Working with QTCaptureLayer**

This chapter takes a close look at QTMovieLayer, a lightweight Core Animation layer that provides a simple mechanism for playing QuickTime movies using QTMovie objects from the QTKit framework.

We also look at the QTCaptureLayer, a lightweight Core Animation layer that provides a framework for capturing frames from an imaging device, such as the built-in iSight camera found in most Macs today. Setting up the capture session is the hard part, but after you have it set up, you can use the layer anywhere you want to capture live camera images.

The QuickTime layers provide all the functionality you need at a higher level than their view-based counter parts. This chapter shows you just how much you gain by using layers to take advantage of the QuickTime technologies.

Working with QTMovieLayer

The API for QTMovieLayer is simple. There are only three unique items to a QTMovieLayer:

> ▶ + layerWithMovie:

> ▶ - initWithMovie:

> ▶ - movie

The first two initialize the layer, and the third gets a reference back to the QTMovie object used to initialize the layer. Everything else is simply what you get from the parent CALayer class.

The QTMovie object from QTKit provides all you need for movie control, such as playback, scrubbing, fast forward, and so on. The difference is that QTMovie doesn't have the visual elements that QTMovieView does. Instead, you must tie your actions to outlets such as sliders and buttons. The action methods available to you in QTMovie are listed in Table 7-1.

Table 7-1   QTMovie's Action Methods

Method	Description
– autoplay	autoplay does the same thing as play except it is for use with streaming media. It will only start playing back the movie when enough data is available.
– play	Begins movie playback.
– stop	Stops movie playback.
– gotoBeginning	Sets the currentTime field in the QTMovie object to QTMovieZero, the movie beginning.
– gotoEnd	Sets the currentTime field in the QTMovie object to match the movie duration.
– gotoNextSelectionPoint	If a selection point has been set in the QTMovie object, sets the currentTime field to that selection point.
– gotoPreviousSelectionPoint	If a selection point has been set in the QTMovie object, sets the currentTime field to that selection point if that time is prior to the currentTime field's time.
– gotoPosterFrame	Sets the currentTime field in the QTMovie object to the poster frame time. If no poster frame is specified, currentTime is set to the beginning of the movie.
– setCurrentTime:	Sets the currentTime field in the QTMovie object to the QTTime you specify as a parameter.
– stepForward	Advances the movie ahead by one frame. The currentTime field is updated accordingly.
– stepBackward	Steps the movie back by one frame. The currentTime field is updated accordingly.

You can simply create an IBAction method in your controller and call any of these methods from those actions. See the upcoming section, "Adding Basic Playback Controls," to see how this is done.

Creating a Simple QTMovieLayer-Based Player

In the sample project for this chapter called Movie Player with Overlay (on the companion website), we created an application delegate class, called AppDelegate, that we associated with a controller object in Interface Builder. With this set up, the AppDelegate class gives us an entry point to create and display the QTMovieLayer. In this project, in addition to the QuartzCore framework, we added the QTKit framework. It is located at

/Developer/SDKs/MacOSX10.6.sdk/System/Library/Frameworks/QTKit.framework if you have the developer tools installed. (Change that path to use MacOSX10.5.sdk if you use Leopard rather than Snow Leopard.)

If all you want to do is play a movie, you simply implement playback on load in the `-awakeFromNib` method in the `AppDelegate` using the code in Listing 7-1.

LISTING 7-1   Implementing Simple Movie Playback

```
- (void)awakeFromNib;
{
    [[window contentView] setWantsLayer:YES];
    NSString *moviePath = [[NSBundle mainBundle]
                         pathForResource:@"stirfry" ofType:@"mov"];

    movie = [QTMovie movieWithFile:moviePath error:nil];

    if( movie )
    {
        QTMovieLayer *layer = [QTMovieLayer layerWithMovie:movie];
        [layer setFrame:NSRectToCGRect([[window contentView] bounds])];
        [[[window contentView] layer] addSublayer:layer];
        [movie play];
    }
}
```

The code begins by informing the `contentView` the window that it should be layer-backed with `–setWantsLayer`. Next the code instantiates a `QTMovie` object from a movie contained in the main bundle. If the movie is valid, we then initialize a `QTMovieLayer` with it. Next, the code sets the layer's frame to the content view's bounds and adds the layer as a sublayer of the content view. It then starts movie playback. That's it. That's all you need to display a movie in a `QTMovieLayer`. That being said, it won't be a very functional player if we don't give it some way to control playback.

Adding Basic Playback Controls

Now that we have the basic movie layer created, the next thing we need to do is add some controls to the view so we can play, pause, and go back or forward in the movie. In Interface Builder, add a button to start and stop playback along with two additional buttons: one to advance the frame and one to go back one frame.

> **NOTE**
>
> **Note on Sample Code**
>
> The sample code in the project called Movie Player with Overlay is complete and shows all the changes we discuss in this section. In other words, all the actions are already connected in Interface Builder for you, and the code reflects only the final state and not the intermediate code we mention.

Listing 7-2 demonstrates the implementation of these button actions.

LISTING 7-2   Control Buttons Implementation

```
- (IBAction)togglePlayback:(id)sender;{
    if( [movie rate] != 0.0 )
        [movie stop];
    else
        [movie play];
}


- (IBAction)stepBack:(id)sender;
{
    [movie stepBackward];
    [self updateSlider:nil];
}


- (IBAction)stepForward:(id)sender;
{
    [movie stepForward];
    [self updateSlider:nil];
}


- (IBAction)goToBeginning:(id)sender;
{
    [movie gotoBeginning];
    [self updateSlider:nil];
}


- (IBAction)goToEnding:(id)sender;
{
    [movie gotoEnd];
    [self updateSlider:nil];
}
```

These actions are connected to buttons we created in Interface Builder. Figure 7-1 shows a screenshot of the basic control buttons.

FIGURE 7-1   Playback Control Buttons

When you run the project, notice that the buttons we added to the window in Interface Builder are not visible. The problem is that the buttons are obscured by the movie layer (meaning, the buttons are behind the movie). To bring the buttons to the front, add the movie layer to the root layer, giving it an index of zero with a call to –insertSublayer:atIndex. Finally, change the –awakeFromNib call to –addSublayer to use the –insertSublayer:atIndex call instead, as follows:

```
[[[window contentView] layer] insertSublayer:layer atIndex:0];
```

Now if you run the project, the buttons are overlaid on top of the video, enabling you to click them and control the movie.

Tracking Progress and Changing Frames with a Slider

To complete our basic player functionality, we add a slider to the interface that provides a playback progress bar and displays the playback time across the top of the video. First, create an action in Xcode to handle changes to the slider, as shown in Listing 7-3.

LISTING 7-3   Implementing Slider Action

```
- (IBAction)sliderMoved:(id)sender;
{
    long long timeValue = movieDuration.timeValue * [slider doubleValue];
    [movie setCurrentTime:QTMakeTime(timeValue,
                                     movieDuration.timeScale)];
}
```

The slider will have a minimum of 0.0 and a maximum of 1.0. Set these values in Interface Builder by selecting the slider with a single mouse click and then providing the values in the slider minimum and maximum fields in the Slider Attributes Inspector. The slider value then provides a decimal fraction that when multiplied by total duration of the movie yields the current time in the movie. Use this time to set the currentTime of the QTMovie object when the slider position is changed. To do so, construct a QTTime structure by calling QTMakeTime with the time value you calculated and pass that to the movie's –setCurrentTime. This causes the QTMovieLayer to update the view to the current frame.

To obtain the current slider value (between 0.0 and 1.0 as we specified in Interface Builder) in code, you also need to create an NSSlider outlet in the AppDelegate by adding the following line to the header file:

```
IBOutlet NSSlider *slider;
```

In Interface Builder, add an NSSlider control to the window and make the connections from the AppDelegate to the slider control and from the slider control back to the AppDelegate's –sliderMoved action. Figures 7-2 and 7-3 demonstrate how to drag these connections in Interface Builder.

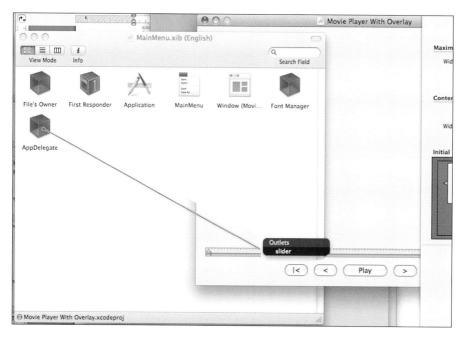

FIGURE 7-2   Dragging a Connection from AppDelegate to Slider

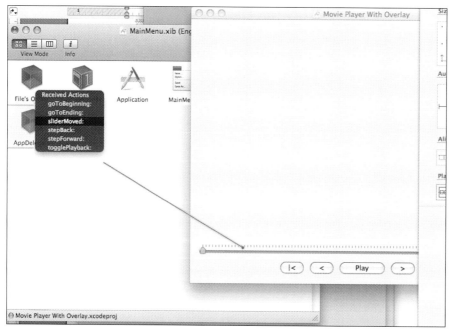

FIGURE 7-3   Dragging a Connection from Slider to AppDelegate

To update the slider's current position, a timer is implemented whenever playback has started. To add this, update the code for the –togglePlayback action, as shown in Listing 7-4.

LISTING 7-4   Implementing a Timer

```objc
- (IBAction)togglePlayback:(id)sender;
{
    if( [movie rate] != 0.0 )
    {
        [movie stop];
        [timer invalidate];
    }
    else
    {
        [movie play];
        timer = [NSTimer
                scheduledTimerWithTimeInterval:0.02
                                        target:self
                                      selector:@selector(updateSlider:)
                                      userInfo:NULL
                                       repeats:YES];

    }
}
```

The instance variable timer is instantiated whenever the movie starts playing. When the movie is stopped, we need to stop the timer by calling –invalidate on it.

The selector used on each tick of the timer is called –updateSlider. The implementation for this selector is shown in Listing 7-5.

LISTING 7-5   Implementing the Timer Selector

```objc
- (void)updateSlider:(NSTimer*)theTimer;
{
    QTTime current = [movie currentTime];
    double value = (double)current.timeValue /
    (double)movieDuration.timeValue;

    [slider setDoubleValue:value];
    [slider setNeedsDisplay];
}
```

This selector first obtains the current time and divides that by the movie's total time, which is stored in the movieDuration instance variable. This returns a value between 0.0

and 1.0, which is used directly by the slider. The slider value is set to this percentage, and –setNeedsDisplay is called to tell the slider to update its display.

Adding Overlays

Adding an overlay to a movie is often one of the first things a new QuickTime developer wants to do. This can be a bit of a challenge when using a QTMovieView, as views are heavyweight and don't provide a simple means for adding a subview that will display properly. If you use views, you either need to create a borderless subwindow that contains the overlay content, or you need to provide it by drawing in an OpenGL context. Both of those solutions add a significant amount of code and complexity to your application, so let's see how Core Animation can simplify this task.

To add an overlay using Core Animation, create a new CALayer-based layer—either actual or a derivative—and then call –addSublayer on QTMovieLayer. To demonstrate this, the -awakeFromNib call from Listing 7-1 has been modified in Listing 7-6 to add a CATextLayer to overlay the movie.

LISTING 7-6   Implementing an Overlay

```
- (void)awakeFromNib;
{
    [[window contentView] setWantsLayer:YES];
    NSString *moviePath = [[NSBundle mainBundle]
                        pathForResource:@"stirfry" ofType:@"mov"];

    movie = [QTMovie movieWithFile:moviePath error:nil];

    if( movie )
    {
        NSRect contentRect = [[window contentView] bounds];
        QTMovieLayer *layer = [QTMovieLayer layerWithMovie:movie];
        [layer setFrame:NSRectToCGRect(contentRect)];

        textLayer = [CATextLayer layer];
        [textLayer setString:@"Do Not Try This At Home!"];
        [textLayer setAlignmentMode:kCAAlignmentCenter];

        [textLayer setFrame:NSRectToCGRect(contentRect)];

        [layer addSublayer:textLayer];

        [[[window contentView] layer] addSublayer:layer];
        [movie play];
    }

}
```

Listing 7-6 adds code to instantiate a `CATextLayer` as a sublayer of the `QTMovieLayer`. The text is aligned at the center of the layer frame using `setAlignmentMode:kCAAlignmentCenter`. Now when the movie plays, you will see the text "Do Not Try This at Home!" displayed at the top of the frame.

Figure 7-4 shows what the basic overlay looks like. Notice that the text layer's frame is set to the same bounds as the window's content view. As such, the text displays at the top of the image.

FIGURE 7-4   Displaying "Do Not Try This at Home" Overlay

Overlaying a Time Code

One common requirement when building a movie player is the capability to see a time code for the movie as it is playing. Once again, the code to overlay a time stamp is fairly trivial when using Core Animation layers. To accomplish this, the first step is to create a `CATextLayer` as in the previous example, and then update the string field of the `CATextLayer` using –`setString` on a periodic basis.

In Listing 7-5, we implemented a timer for updating the slider position as the movie played. We can use this same timer to update the text overlay to use the current time of the movie as represented by the value we get back from a call to the `movie` object's `currentTime`.

Now create a function called -updateTimeStamp to update the time code display, as shown in Listing 7-7.

LISTING 7-7   Implementing Timestamp Update

```
- (void)updateTimeStamp;
{
    NSString *time = QTStringFromTime([movie currentTime]);
    [textLayer setString:time];
}
```

Next, you need to make a few changes to get the time code overlay to work. First, change the -awakeFromNib call to set the overlay text layer's start string to zero time,QTZeroTime, as shown in Listing 7-8.

LISTING 7-8   Setting the Initial Movie Time

```
- (void)awakeFromNib;
{
    [[window contentView] setWantsLayer:YES];
    NSString *moviePath = [[NSBundle mainBundle]
                           pathForResource:@"stirfry" ofType:@"mov"];

    movie = [QTMovie movieWithFile:moviePath error:nil];

    if( movie )
    {
        NSRect contentRect = [[window contentView] bounds];
        QTMovieLayer *layer = [QTMovieLayer layerWithMovie:movie];
        [layer setFrame:NSRectToCGRect(contentRect)];

        textLayer = [CATextLayer layer];
        [textLayer setString:QTStringFromTime(QTZeroTime)];
        [textLayer setAlignmentMode:kCAAlignmentCenter];

        [textLayer setFrame:NSRectToCGRect(contentRect)];

        [layer addSublayer:textLayer];

        [[[window contentView] layer] addSublayer:layer];
        [movie play];
    }
}
```

QTZeroTime is a QTTime structure that represents the beginning time of a movie. Next, change the –updateSlider selector that is called by the timer, as shown in Listing 7-9.

LISTING 7-9   Calling Time Stamp Update

```
- (void)updateSlider:(NSTimer*)theTimer;
{
    QTTime current = [movie currentTime];
        double value = (double)current.timeValue /
        (double)movieDuration.timeValue;

    [slider setDoubleValue:value];
    [slider setNeedsDisplay];

    [self updateTimeStamp];
}
```

With these changes in place, the time code overlay is updated in real time when the movie is running. In Xcode, load the Movie Player with the Overlay sample project, and click Build and Go to see the overlay in action. Figure 7-5 shows the time code overlay running. As you'll notice, the time is updated on a regular basis.

FIGURE 7-5   Displaying a Time Code Overlay

QTMovieLayer and contentsRect

In Chapter 2, "What Can and Should I Animate?," you saw all the different animatable parameters that are available to you. One of the more interesting parameters of a layer we covered there is the contentsRect as it specifies what portion of the layer contents you actually want to display. This is particularly interesting as it relates to the QTMovieLayer because you can duplicate the contents of the QTMovieLayer into another standard CALayer, and while doing so, you can specify which part or rectangle of the QTMovieLayer to display in that layer's contents.

So you might wonder how that is useful. Say you created a movie that contained a grid of individual videos. You could use this one reference video and duplicate its contents into numerous other CALayers and specify which portion of the layer should display in each CALayer. Or you could take a single movie and slice it up into a grid. Figure 7-6 shows a screenshot of the sample application from the companion website called CopyMovieContents that demonstrates this feature.

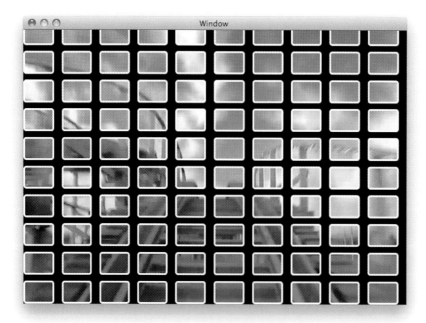

FIGURE 7-6   Copy Movie Contents into Individual CALayers

Each of the rectangles you see in the grid are individual CALayers all getting their contents from the same QTMovieLayer. For this application, we create a QTMovieLayer with the roller coaster movie located in */System/Library/Compositions/Rollercoaster.mov*.

We then add the layer to our view. Then we add each of our individual `CALayers` with their `contents` and `contentsRect` fields set.

The code to implement this is fairly simple. You set the contents of each `CALayer` to the contents of the movie layer, as shown in the following code:

```
[layer setContents:[movieLayer contents]];
```

Then you set the `contentsRect` to display only the portion of the movie layer that you want to show in that particular layer. You set the `contentsRect` field like this:

```
[layer setContentsRect:CGRectMake(0.25f, 0.25f, 0.25f, 0.25f)];
```

As you can recall from Chapter 2, this causes the contents of the `CALayer` to display one-quarter of the width and height starting one-quarter of the distance from the bottom-left corner of the movie layer.

Interestingly, this trick does not work with the `QTCaptureLayer` that we cover in the next section.

Working with QTCaptureLayer

`QTCaptureLayer` provides a means for displaying content from video devices connected to your computer. These devices include your iSight camera or a digital video camera connected via FireWire. To capture the video, you have to set up a `QTCaptureSession`, which does two things:

▶ It provides an interface to receive frames from the capture device.

▶ It enables you to save the images to a movie file and hand that session off to `QTCaptureLayer`.

The most complicated aspect of capturing video to display in the `QTCaptureLayer` is not in the layer at all. Rather, the `QTCaptureSession` object has the majority of the setup. This setup requires several steps that include obtaining a device, opening the device, adding the device to the capture session, and creating a video output object to add raw frames to the capture session.

It will be helpful if you open the sample project called Photo Capture and build the project. When you run it, you see a screen like the one in Figure 7-7.

FIGURE 7-7   Window of Photo Capture Sample Project

Listing 7-10 shows the code needed to create a QTCaptureSession object.

LISTING 7-10   Initializing the Capture Session

```
- (void)initCaptureSession;
{
    if(captureSession == nil)
    {
        NSError *error = nil;
        captureSession = [[QTCaptureSession alloc] init];

        // This finds a device, such as an iSight camera
        QTCaptureDevice *videoDevice =
        [QTCaptureDevice
        defaultInputDeviceWithMediaType:
        QTMediaTypeVideo];

        if (videoDevice == nil)
        {
            // Try a different device, such as miniDV camcorder
            videoDevice = [QTCaptureDevice
                    defaultInputDeviceWithMediaType:
                    QTMediaTypeMuxed];
        }

        // No need to continue if we can't find a device
        if (videoDevice == nil) return;
```

LISTING 7-10   Continued

```
        // Try to open the device
        [videoDevice open:&error];

        // No need to continue if device couldn't be opened
        if( error != nil ) return;

        // Create a device input object to add to the capture session
        QTCaptureDeviceInput *input =
        [[QTCaptureDeviceInput alloc]
        initWithDevice:videoDevice];
        [captureSession addInput:input error:&error];

        if( error != nil ) return;

        // Create video output to add raw frames to the session
        output = [[QTCaptureDecompressedVideoOutput alloc] init];
        [captureSession addOutput:output error:&error];

        if ( error != nil ) return;

        [self setSession:captureSession];
    }
}
```

This relatively small amount of code is quite amazing in what it provides. This abstractions Apple enables you to easily capture and display frames in real time. With QTCaptureSession created, the next thing to do is obtain a frame at any given time by setting a delegate for the QTCaptureDecompressedVideoOutput object. After the QTCaptureDecompressedVideoOutput object has been allocated, set its delegate to self using the following:

```
[output setDelegate:self];
```

This enables you to capture the output as an image file or to a QuickTime movie object. First, however, let's take a closer look at how QTCaptureLayer was initialized for the capture session.

Creating and Displaying the QTCaptureLayer

Although it is possible to create a QTCaptureLayer object directly with alloc and init, or with a convenience function such as +layerWithSession, we're going to subclass QTCaptureLayer so that we can hide QTCaptureSession's initialization in the init. We do this so that we can encapsulate all our capture functionality in the layer and then reuse the layer wherever we like in our applications that need capture functionality.

In the Photo Capture sample code, we have created this `QTCaptureLayer` derived class and named it simply `CaptureLayer`. Listing 7-11 shows the `init` code used to initialize the layer.

LISTING 7-11   QTCaptureLayer Derived Class Initialization

```
- (id)init;
{
    self = [super init];
    if( !self ) return nil;
    [self initCaptureSession];
    return self;
}
```

As you can see, we have called –`initCaptureSession` here from Listing 7-10. This way, when we initialize a new `CaptureLayer` object, `QTCaptureSession` is already fired up and ready to go. Next, add `CaptureLayer` to the window's root layer tree. You can see how this code is implemented in the `AppDelegate`'s –`awakeFromNib`, as shown in Listing 7-12.

LISTING 7-12   Implementing CaptureLayer in the AppDelegate

```
-(void)awakeFromNib;
{
    [[window contentView] setWantsLayer:YES];

    captureLayer = [[CaptureLayer alloc] init];

    // Use the frame from the generic NSView we have
    // named captureView
    [captureLayer setBounds:
    NSRectToCGRect([captureView frame])];
    [captureLayer setPosition:
     CGPointMake([captureView frame].size.width/2,
            [captureView frame].size.height/2)];

    [[captureView layer]
    insertSublayer:captureLayer atIndex:0];

    [captureLayer starCaptureSession];
}
```

When you run this code, you see that the view we created on the left of the window is now filled with whatever your iSight camera or miniDV camera is currently pointing at.

Capturing the Current Image

Naturally, you will likely want to capture the current image to take a picture, just as you would when using Apple's Photo Booth application. To implement this, the QTCaptureLayer-derived class called CaptureLayer is added to the application. This way, we can implement the -getCurrentImage function to return an NSImage* containing the current image when the action is triggered. Looking back to Listing 7-10, you can see that we set the delegate for the QTCaptureDecompressedVideoOutput object in the -initSession code. We now need to implement its delegate method,-captureOutput, as shown in Listing 7-13.

LISTING 7-13   Implementing the Capture Output Callback

```
- (void)captureOutput:(QTCaptureOutput *)captureOutput
  didOutputVideoFrame:(CVImageBufferRef)videoFrame
     withSampleBuffer:(QTSampleBuffer *)sampleBuffer
       fromConnection:(QTCaptureConnection *)connection
{
    // Store the current frame
    CVImageBufferRef imageBuffer;

    CVBufferRetain(videoFrame);

    // Synchronize access, as this delegate is not
    // called on the main thread.
    @synchronized (self)
    {
        imageBuffer = currentImageBuffer;
        currentImageBuffer = videoFrame;
    }

    CVBufferRelease(imageBuffer);
}
```

This delegate is continuously called at a regular interval by the QTCaptureSession API behind the scenes. The currentImageBuffer object is kept up to date in this delegate because it needs to be ready for when the user clicks the button to take a picture. When the user clicks the button to take the picture, the QTCaptureLayer-derived class is queried for the current image. To capture the picture into the layer, we have added the -getCurrentImage function, as shown in Listing 7-14.

LISTING 7-14   Implementing Current Image Capture

```
- (NSImage*)getCurrentImage;
{
    CVImageBufferRef imageBuffer;

    @synchronized (self)
    {
        imageBuffer = CVBufferRetain(currentImageBuffer);
    }

    if (imageBuffer) {
        // Create an NSImage
        NSCIImageRep *imageRep =
        [NSCIImageRep imageRepWithCIImage:
         [CIImage
          imageWithCVImageBuffer:imageBuffer]];

        NSImage *image = [[[NSImage alloc] initWithSize:
                   [imageRep size]] autorelease];
        [image addRepresentation:imageRep];
        CVBufferRelease(imageBuffer);
        return image;
    }
    return nil;
}
```

Access to the currentImageBuffer object is synchronized on a regular basis as it is written to by the captureOutput callback function in Listing 7-13. It runs on its own thread, making the synchronized block necessary. If the image buffer was successfully retained, we can convert it to an NSImage* and return it to the calling function.

Finally, we add an action to the AppDelegate that fires when the Capture Image button is pressed. The action grabs the current image from the QTCaptureLayer-derived class (CaptureLayer) and sets the NSImageView's image with it; Listing 7-15 shows how this is implemented.

LISTING 7-15   Setting the Image View with the Current Image

```
- (IBAction)grabImage:(id)sender;
{
    NSImage *image = [captureLayer getCurrentImage];
    [imageView setImage:image];
}
```

When you run the Photo Capture application, the view on the left displays the QTCaptureLayer in an NSView. When you click the Capture Image button, the view on the right updates by snagging the current image from the capture layer. When you set the image on the image view, it simply displays the image in its frame. If you want to save the image, you would obtain an NSData object by calling -representationUsingType on the NSImage. When you have this NSData object, you can then call -writeToFile: atomically: to write the file to disk.

Summary

The QuickTime Core Animation layers provide some powerful functionality both for displaying movies on disk and for real-time video display using a variety of supported capture devices. They make these complicated tasks almost trivial to implement in your own video applications.

CHAPTER 8

OpenGL Layer

IN THIS CHAPTER

▶ Rendering Video in a CAOpenGLLayer

▶ Rendering Multiple Video Channels

Using Core Animation's OpenGL layer, CAOpenGLLayer, you can gain more control over movie playback with everything from using Core Image filters on the video frame to compositing multiple video streams in the same context.

This chapter shows you how to render a video channel in a CAOpenGLLayer and duplicate the functionality from QuickTime layers, as shown in Chapter 7, "QuickTime Layers." Following that, we take a look at compositing multiple video channels in a grid layout on the CAOpenGLLayer, similar to what you might see in a video wall. This demonstrates just how much functionality and power you have at your disposal when using the CAOpenGLLayer.

Rendering Video in a CAOpenGLLayer

As discussed in Chapter 7, simple playback of video is typically handled by QTMovieView and QTMovieLayer. However, if you want to alter your current frame before rendering it, you are better off using OpenGL. As a first step, we look at how to simply display the frames unaltered in a CAOpenGLLayer. This mimics the functionality implemented in a QTMovieLayer in Chapter 7.

To take advantage of a CAOpenGLLayer, you need to subclass it—it cannot be used directly. The API for creating OpenGL content in a CAOpenGLLayer has been greatly simplified compared to what you had to do prior to Core Animation. In an NSOpenGLView, you had to set up everything yourself, but in the CAOpenGLLayer, you get the following for free.

▶ Preconfigured OpenGL Context

▶ Viewport automatically set to the CAOpenGLLayer's frame

▶ Preconfigured pixel format object

The setup code is so simplified that you need to be concerned with only two functions. The first function checks to see if the frame for the next time *should* be rendered, and the second function

> **NOTE**
>
> If you are new to OpenGL, you might not understand what having all this set up for you really means. The bottom line is that you gain a great deal of functionality without having to painstakingly write out the code yourself. Core Animation does all the heavy lifting for you, so you can focus on your OpenGL rendering code.

renders the content depending upon whether the first returned YES or NO. If you have a good understanding of these two functions, you have a very good understanding of how the CAOpenGLLayer works and, more important, how to use it. These functions are shown in Listing 8-1.

LISTING 8-1   CAOpenGLLayer Delegate Rendering Functions

```
- (BOOL)canDrawInCGLContext:(CGLContextObj)glContext
              pixelFormat:(CGLPixelFormatObj)pixelFormat
            forLayerTime:(CFTimeInterval)timeInterval
             displayTime:(const CVTimeStamp *)timestamp;


- (void)drawInCGLContext:(CGLContextObj)glContext
              pixelFormat:(CGLPixelFormatObj)pixelFormat
            forLayerTime:(CFTimeInterval)interval
             displayTime:(const CVTimeStamp *)timestamp;
```

The function -canDrawInCGLContext gets called only if you have set the layer's asynchronous property to YES. You can do so with the following call in your CAOpenGLLayer derived layer's init method:

```
[self setAsynchronous:YES];
```

You don't need to set this if you plan to update the content manually or according to some other scheme, such as a timer. In that case you simply need to call –setNeedsDisplay:YES on the layer whenever you want the content to be refreshed.

In our case, however, we want –canDrawInCGLContext to be called periodically because we are going to be constantly checking for a new frame to be ready while the movie is playing. To pull this off, set the asynchronous property to YES.

The function –drawInCGLContext gets called only if –canDrawInCGLContext returned YES. After it is called, it takes the responsibility for rendering your OpenGL content into a rendering context.

Layer Timing

Notice in both `-canDrawInCGLContext` and `-drawInCGLContext`, two fields relate to time:

- ▶ `forLayerTime`, which is a `CFTimeInterval`

- ▶ `displayTime`, which is a `CVTimeStamp`

We won't focus on `forLayerTime` because we won't be using it with `CAOpenGLLayer`; however, `displayTime` is important for this exercise.

Playing back movies correctly with a display's refresh rate and in-sync with the movie's sound can be tricky. However, Apple has achieved stable movie playback in the Mac OS using what they refer to as a *display link*. Here is how Apple defines a display link in the *Core Video Programming Guide*:[1]

> To simplify synchronization of video with a display's refresh rate, Core Video provides a special timer called a display link. The display link runs as a separate high priority thread, which is not affected by interactions within your application process.

> In the past, synchronizing your video frames with the display's refresh rate was often a problem, especially if you also had audio. You could make only simple guesses for when to output a frame (by using a timer, for example), which didn't take into account possible latency from user interactions, CPU loading, window compositing, and so on. The Core Video display link can make intelligent estimates for when a frame needs to be output, based on display type and latencies.

In essence this means that you must set up a callback that will get called periodically, at which point you can check to see if a new frame is available for display at the time specified in the callback's `inOutputTime` `CVTimeStamp` field. The display link callback signature is in Listing 8-2.

LISTING 8-2   Display Link Callback Signature

```
CVReturn MyDisplayLinkCallback (
        CVDisplayLinkRef displayLink,
        const CVTimeStamp *inNow,
        const CVTimeStamp *inOutputTime,
        CVOptionFlags flagsIn,
        CVOptionFlags *flagsOut,
        void *displayLinkContext);
```

---

[1]*Apple's* Core Video Programming Guide *(p. 10): http://developer.apple.com/mac/library/ documentation/GraphicsImaging/Conceptual/CoreVideo/CoreVideo.pdf.*

In a CAOpenGLLayer, however, setting up and using a display link callback is completely unnecessary as this is provided for you in both –canDrawInCGLContext and –drawInCGLContext. The time you use to check to see if a new frame is ready is provided in the parameter called displayTime.

So, to render a movie into the CAOpenGLLayer, in the –canDrawInCGLContext:

1. Check to see if the movie is playing back; if not, return NO.

2. If the movie is playing back, check to see if the context for the movie has been set up yet. If not, set it up with a call to –setupVisualContext.

3. Check to see if a new frame is ready.

4. If so, copy the current image into the image buffer.

5. If everything is successful, return YES.

6. If –canDrawInCGLContext returned YES, -drawInCGLContext gets called. Inside of that method, draw the OpenGL quads for the movie's current texture images.

The implementation of –canDrawInCGLContext is in Listing 8-3.

LISTING 8-3   Implementation of Delegate -canDrawInCGLContext

```
- (BOOL)canDrawInCGLContext:(CGLContextObj)glContext
            pixelFormat:(CGLPixelFormatObj)pixelFormat
            forLayerTime:(CFTimeInterval)timeInterval
            displayTime:(const CVTimeStamp *)timeStamp
{
    if( !qtVisualContext )
    {
        // If the visual context for the QTMovie has not been set up
        // we initialize it now
        [self setupVisualContext:glContext withPixelFormat:pixelFormat];
    }

    // Check to see if a new frame (image) is ready to be drawn at
    // the current time by passing NULL as the second param
    if(QTVisualContextIsNewImageAvailable(qtVisualContext,NULL))
    {
        // Release the previous frame
        CVOpenGLTextureRelease(currentFrame);

        // Copy the current frame into the image buffer
        QTVisualContextCopyImageForTime(qtVisualContext,
                                NULL,
                                NULL,
                                &currentFrame);
```

LISTING 8-3   Continued

```
        // Returns the texture coordinates for the
        // part of the image that should be displayed
        CVOpenGLTextureGetCleanTexCoords(currentFrame,
                                         lowerLeft,
                                         lowerRight,
                                         upperRight,
                                         upperLeft);
        return YES;
    }

    return NO;
}
```

Before you can draw anything on an OpenGL context, you must first set up the visual context for the QuickTime movie. The call to –setupVisualContext is shown in Listing 8-4.

LISTING 8-4   Implementation of QuickTime Visual Context

```
- (void)setupVisualContext:(CGLContextObj)glContext
          withPixelFormat:(CGLPixelFormatObj)pixelFormat;
{
    OSStatus error;

    NSDictionary          *attributes = nil;
    attributes = [NSDictionary dictionaryWithObjectsAndKeys:
                  [NSDictionary dictionaryWithObjectsAndKeys:
                   [NSNumber numberWithFloat:[self frame].size.width],
                   kQTVisualContextTargetDimensions_WidthKey,
                   [NSNumber numberWithFloat:[self frame].size.height],
                   kQTVisualContextTargetDimensions_HeightKey, nil],
                  kQTVisualContextTargetDimensionsKey,
                  [NSDictionary dictionaryWithObjectsAndKeys:
                   [NSNumber numberWithFloat:[self frame].size.width],
                   kCVPixelBufferWidthKey,
                   [NSNumber numberWithFloat:[self frame].size.height],
                   kCVPixelBufferHeightKey, nil],
                  kQTVisualContextPixelBufferAttributesKey,
                  nil];

    // Create the QuickTime visual context
    error = QTOpenGLTextureContextCreate(NULL,
                                         glContext,
```

LISTING 8-4   Continued

```
                               pixelFormat,
                               (CFDictionaryRef)attributes,
                               &qtVisualContext);

    // Associate it with the movie
    SetMovieVisualContext([movie quickTimeMovie],qtVisualContext);
}
```

Inside this call to –setupVisualContext, the movie is associated with the OpenGL context of the CAOpenGLLayer. That way, when –drawInCGLContext gets called, we will have everything set up to make the OpenGL calls, as shown in Listing 8-5.

LISTING 8-5   Implementation of drawInCGLContext

```
- (void)drawInCGLContext:(CGLContextObj)glContext
           pixelFormat:(CGLPixelFormatObj)pixelFormat
         forLayerTime:(CFTimeInterval)interval
          displayTime:(const CVTimeStamp *)timeStamp
{
    NSRect bounds = NSRectFromCGRect([self bounds]);

    GLfloat minX, minY, maxX, maxY;

    minX = NSMinX(bounds);
    minY = NSMinY(bounds);
    maxX = NSMaxX(bounds);
    maxY = NSMaxY(bounds);

    glMatrixMode(GL_MODELVIEW);
    glLoadIdentity();
    glMatrixMode(GL_PROJECTION);
    glLoadIdentity();
    glOrtho( minX, maxX, minY, maxY, -1.0, 1.0);

    glClearColor(0.0, 0.0, 0.0, 0.0);
    glClear(GL_COLOR_BUFFER_BIT);

    CGRect imageRect = [self frame];
    // Enable target for the current frame
    glEnable(CVOpenGLTextureGetTarget(currentFrame));
```

LISTING 8-5   Continued

```objc
// Bind to the current frame
// This tells OpenGL which texture we want
// to draw so when we make the glTexCord and
// glVertex calls, the current frame gets drawn
// to the context
glBindTexture(CVOpenGLTextureGetTarget(currentFrame),
              CVOpenGLTextureGetName(currentFrame));
glMatrixMode(GL_TEXTURE);
glLoadIdentity();
glColor4f(1.0, 1.0, 1.0, 1.0);
glBegin(GL_QUADS);

// Draw the quads
glTexCoord2f(upperLeft[0], upperLeft[1]);
glVertex2f  (imageRect.origin.x,
              imageRect.origin.y + imageRect.size.height);
glTexCoord2f(upperRight[0], upperRight[1]);
glVertex2f  (imageRect.origin.x + imageRect.size.width,
              imageRect.origin.y + imageRect.size.height);
glTexCoord2f(lowerRight[0], lowerRight[1]);
glVertex2f  (imageRect.origin.x + imageRect.size.width,
              imageRect.origin.y);
glTexCoord2f(lowerLeft[0], lowerLeft[1]);
glVertex2f  (imageRect.origin.x, imageRect.origin.y);

glEnd();

// This CAOpenGLLayer is responsible to flush
// the OpenGL context so we call super
[super drawInCGLContext:glContext
            pixelFormat:pixelFormat
            forLayerTime:interval
             displayTime:timeStamp];

// Task the context
QTVisualContextTask(qtVisualContext);

}
```

8

To understand all of this code, you likely need to understand OpenGL, which is beyond the scope of this book. However, take a look at these two lines from Listing 8-5:

```
glEnable(CVOpenGLTextureGetTarget(currentFrame));
glBindTexture(CVOpenGLTextureGetTarget(currentFrame),
              CVOpenGLTextureGetName(currentFrame));
```

These two lines tell OpenGL to enable and bind the drawing texture to the `currentFrame` (CVImageBufferRef) that we saved off in our call to -canDrawInCGLContext. In other words, this is how we tell OpenGL what to draw.

Why Use CAOpenGLLayer for Movie Playback?

You might be a little confused as to why we duplicated a functionality we easily implemented in Chapter 7 using QuickTime Layers. Why not just use a QTMovieLayer for movie playback?

If all you need is movie playback, you should indeed just use a QTMovieLayer instead. However, we are building up to the ultimate reason, which is to use OpenGL for simultaneously playing back multiple video streams.

If you were to try to playback multiple videos in multiple QTMovieLayers, you would find the performance degrades quickly. OpenGL enables us to get all the image data from each of the movie objects at once and composite them into a single context. This reduces the overhead and improves performance. This first section on the CAOpenGLLayer is provided as a building block that assists you in understanding how to composite multiple video streams, as covered in the next section.

Rendering Multiple Video Channels

The final goal for this chapter is to demonstrate how to render multiple QuickTime video streams in a single CAOpenGLLayer. As noted in the sidebar, the primary reason for using OpenGL here instead of QTMovieLayer boils down to performance. Performance degrades quickly when you load and playback multiple QTMovies using multiple QTMovieLayers. To improve performance, we instead get the current frame of each movie playing back and composite them all together in the same OpenGL context.

To achieve this is not much different from what we did in the previous section to render a single QuickTime movie using OpenGL. We create an image buffer for each QuickTime movie and check each of them periodically to see if the next frame is ready in the call to -canDrawInCGLContext. We also need to set up a way to display the movies in a grid by setting a drawing rectangle for each movie as they are initialized.

We could use copy and paste and simply duplicate the code we wrote in the previous section, but the code quickly becomes unwieldy and cumbersome to navigate. Instead we use an object-oriented approach and create the OpenGL-derived layer (called OpenGLVidGridLayer), a VideoChannel object that represents one video stream, and a VideoChannelController object that provides an interface for playback and rendering. Here is what each object does:

▶ OpenGLVidGridLayer
This object initializes the layer so that it runs asynchronously, sets the frame, sets the background color to black, sets the video paths array from what was passed in, initializes the VideoChannel and the VideoChannelController objects, calls –canDrawInCGLContext and –drawInCGLContext, and acts as a proxy to start playback of all the movies that were assigned to VideoChannel objects.

▶ VideoChannel
This object represents each video on the grid. It stores the rectangle that will be used to composite the video in the parent rectangle, checks to see if its assigned video is ready to draw the next frame, initializes the visual context using the width and height specified by the rectangle it was initialized with, draws the video assigned to it using OpenGL calls, and provides a proxy method for video playback.

▶ VideoChannelController
This object takes an array of VideoChannel objects, each initialized with a movie and rectangle, to be used to render in the grid. It provides a proxy function that instructs all VideoChannels to start or stop playback on their movies, provides a proxy function to see if all VideoChannels are ready to draw their next frame, provides a proxy function to tell all VideoChannels to set up their visual contexts, calls initial OpenGL drawing code that is common for all VideoChannels, and provides a proxy function to tell all VideoChannels to render their movies in their respective compositing rectangles.

This object-oriented approach is a double-edged sword. Although it enables us to organize things in a cleaner fashion, it makes it necessary to think about everything in terms of objects, so study theses descriptions so that you know where to look in the project code to figure out what is going on. The VideoChannelController object provides control for each of the VideoChannels and is probably the best place to start to see how things work. The OpenGLVidGridLayer only does initialization and provides the functionality to decide whether we should draw at the current time.

Figure 8-1 depicts the demo application, OpenGL VidGrid. The full display area in the window is the CAOpenGLLayer-derived class, called OpenGLVidGridLayer. Each of the individual movie clips displaying on the screen are represented in code by the VideoChannel class.

FIGURE 8-1   Visible Objects

Implementing the CAOpenGLLayer-Derived OpenGLVidGridLayer

The CAOpenGLLayer derived class, OpenGLVidGridLayer, provides the entry point for drawing all the video channels to the same OpenGL context. The initialization code accepts a list of QTMovie objects for which it calculates the display rectangle. It creates a VideoChannel object for each of the QTMovies and adds them to an array. The VideoChannelController object is then instantiated, and the array of VideoChannel objects is assigned to it. The implementation code is shown in Listing 8-6.

LISTING 8-6   Implementing OpenGLVidGridLayer Initialization Code

```
- (void)initVideoChannels;
{
    int i = 0;

    if( videoChannels != nil )
        [videoChannels release], videoChannels = nil;

    videoChannels = [[NSMutableArray alloc] init];

    // Create a grid kColCount across
    float vidWidth = [self frame].size.width / kColCount;
    vidWidth = vidWidth - kMargin;
```

LISTING 8-6   Continued

```objc
float vidHeight = [self frame].size.height;
if( [videoPaths count] > kColCount )
    vidHeight = [self frame].size.height /
        (((float)[videoPaths count])/kColCount);
vidHeight = vidHeight - kMargin;

int row = 0;
int col = 0;

for (i = 0; i < [videoPaths count]; ++i)
{
    NSString *path = [videoPaths objectAtIndex:i];
    QTMovie *m = [QTMovie movieWithFile:path error:nil];

    // Mute each video
    [m setMuted:YES];

    // Force the movie to loop
    [m setAttribute:[NSNumber numberWithBool:YES]
            forKey:QTMovieLoopsAttribute];

    float x = col*vidWidth;
    float y = row*vidHeight;

    if( i!= 0 && (i+1) % (int)kColCount == 0 )
    {
        row++;
    }
    CGRect currentRect = CGRectMake(x+kMargin,
                                    y+kMargin,
                                    vidWidth-kMargin,
                                    vidHeight-kMargin);

    // Instantiate a video channel for each QTMovie
    // object we've created
    VideoChannel *channel =
        [[[VideoChannel alloc] initWithMovie:m
                          usingDisplayRect:currentRect] autorelease];
    [videoChannels addObject:channel];

    col++;
    if( col > kColCount-1 )
        col = 0;
```

LISTING 8-6   Continued

```
    }

    if( videoController != nil )
    {
        [videoController release];
    }
    videoController = [[VideoChannelController alloc] init];

    [videoController setVideoChannels:videoChannels];

}
```

Previously in this chapter, we looked at how to render a single video clip in an OpenGL context. We have taken that code and placed it into classes that encapsulate that functionality. The VideoChannelController class holds the VideoChannel objects so that they can be controlled. It passes the OpenGL context to each VideoChannel object and tells them to draw their content (the movies) to that context.

In the AppDelegate for this project, we instantiate a CAOpenGLLayer-derived layer called OpenGLVidGridLayer and pass it an array of NSStrings containing movie paths, as shown in Listing 8-7.

LISTING 8-7   Initializing the OpenGLVidGridLayer in the AppDelegate

```
-(void)awakeFromNib;
{
    NSString *path1 = @"/System/Library/Compositions/Eiffel Tower.mov";
    NSString *path2 = @"/System/Library/Compositions/Fish.mov";
    NSString *path3 = [[NSBundle mainBundle] pathForResource:@"stirfry"
                                                      ofType:@"mp4"];
    NSString *path4 = @"/System/Library/Compositions/Rollercoaster.mov";
    NSString *path5 = @"/System/Library/Compositions/Sunset.mov";
    NSString *path6 = @"/System/Library/Compositions/Yosemite.mov";

    NSArray *paths = [NSArray arrayWithObjects:path1,
                        path2,
                        path3,
                        path4,
                        path5,
                        path6, nil];

    gridLayer = [[OpenGLVidGridLayer alloc]
                    initWithVideoPaths:paths
```

LISTING 8-7   Continued

```
                  usingContentFrame:
                  NSRectToCGRect([[window contentView] bounds])];

    [[window contentView] setWantsLayer:YES];
    [[[window contentView] layer] addSublayer:gridLayer];
    [gridLayer playMovies];
}
```

When `OpenGLVidGridLayer` is allocated, we pass it the array of movie file paths and the content frame in which each movie will render.

When the root layer of the window's content view is made layer-backed using [[window contentView] setWantsLayer:YES], add the `OpenGLVidGridLayer` to the root layer as a sublayer, and then call –playMovies, which simply calls [videoController togglePlaybackAll]. This function iterates through each of the `VideoChannel` objects inside the `VideoChannelController` and instructs them to start playing back each movie in their designated container.

Listing 8-8 shows how we have overridden the calls to –canDrawInCGLContext and –drawInCGLContext in the OpenGLVideGridLayer.

LISTING 8-8   Implementation of Drawing Functions

```
- (BOOL)canDrawInCGLContext:(CGLContextObj)glContext
                pixelFormat:(CGLPixelFormatObj)pixelFormat
                forLayerTime:(CFTimeInterval)timeInterval
                displayTime:(const CVTimeStamp *)timeStamp
{

    if( ![videoController isPlaying] )
        return NO;

    [videoController setVisualContext:glContext
                    withPixelFormat:pixelFormat];

    BOOL ready = [videoController
                channelsReadyToDraw:(CVTimeStamp*)timeStamp];

    return ready;

}
```

LISTING 8-8   Continued

```
- (void)drawInCGLContext:(CGLContextObj)glContext
             pixelFormat:(CGLPixelFormatObj)pixelFormat
            forLayerTime:(CFTimeInterval)interval
             displayTime:(const CVTimeStamp *)timeStamp
{

    NSRect        bounds = NSRectFromCGRect([self bounds]);

    [videoController drawAllInRect:bounds];

    // This forces OpenGL to flush the context
    [super drawInCGLContext:glContext
               pixelFormat:pixelFormat
              forLayerTime:interval
               displayTime:timeStamp];

    [videoController taskAll];


}
```

These functions are fairly simple because we have offloaded the majority of the work to the VideoChannelController object. The VideoChannelController then instructs all the VideoChannel objects to do their work, and the call to –canDrawInCGLContext checks to see if the movies are running. If not, we don't need to render, and NO is returned. In that case, -drawInCGLContext won't be called either. When the movies are running, however, the visual context for rendering the QuickTime videos are set up before checking to see if the current image buffer for each of the VideoChannels is ready to draw into using a call to –channelsReadyToDraw in the VideoChannelController object. You can see how it is implemented Listing 8-9.

LISTING 8-9   Implementing channelsReadyToDraw Function

```
- (BOOL)channelsReadyToDraw:(CVTimeStamp*)timeStamp;
{
    BOOL stillOk = NO;
    int i = 0;
    for (i=0; i<[videoChannels count]; ++i)
    {
        VideoChannel *currentChannel =
                    [videoChannels objectAtIndex:i];

        if( [currentChannel readyToDrawNextFrame:timeStamp] )
        {
```

LISTING 8-9   Continued

```
            stillOk = YES;
        }
        if( !stillOk )
            return NO;
    }
    return stillOk;
}
```

The code iterates through the list of VideoChannel objects and checks each to see if they are ready to draw. If any of them fail readiness, NO is returned for the current call to -canDrawInCGLContext. Listing 8-10 shows an implementation of the call to the VideoChannel's -readyToDrawNextFrame function.

LISTING 8-10   Implementing readyToDrawNextFrame Function

```
- (BOOL)readyToDrawNextFrame:(CVTimeStamp*)timeStamp;
{
  if(QTVisualContextIsNewImageAvailable(qtVisualContext,NULL))
  {
    CVOpenGLTextureRelease(currentFrameImageBuffer);

    QTVisualContextCopyImageForTime(
                    qtVisualContext,
                    NULL,
                    NULL,
                    &currentFrameImageBuffer);

    CVOpenGLTextureGetCleanTexCoords(
                    currentFrameImageBuffer,
                    lowerLeft,
                    lowerRight,
                    upperRight,
                    upperLeft);
    return YES;
  }
  return NO;
}
```

If you look closely, you see that this code is similar to the code used in Listing 8-3 to render a single video channel. This function checks to see if a new image is available for the visual context using the specified timeStamp. If it is available, the previous image buffer is released, the current image is copied to the image buffer, the texture coordinates are reset, and YES is returned; otherwise NO is returned.

This result bubbles back up the call stack to the CAOpenGLLayer-derived class, OpenGLVidGridLayer's -canDrawInCGLContext. If all the channels are ready to draw, YES is returned and -drawInCGLContext is called.

When -drawInCGLContext is called, we pass the main rectangle of the window

> **NOTE**
>
> Look back at the call to -drawInCGLContext in Listing 8-8. It is also greatly simplified as we have offloaded most of the work to the VideoChannelController and VideoChannel objects.

to the video controller with a call to [videoController drawAllInRect:bounds], where bounds is the rectangle, as shown in Listing 8-11.

LISTING 8-11   Implementing drawAllInRect

```
- (void)drawAllInRect:(NSRect)rect;
{
    GLfloat     minX, minY, maxX, maxY;

    minX = NSMinX(rect);
    minY = NSMinY(rect);
    maxX = NSMaxX(rect);
    maxY = NSMaxY(rect);

    glMatrixMode(GL_MODELVIEW);
    glLoadIdentity();
    glMatrixMode(GL_PROJECTION);
    glLoadIdentity();
    glOrtho(minX, maxX, minY, maxY, -1.0, 1.0);

    glClearColor(0.0, 0.0, 0.0, 0.0);
    glClear(GL_COLOR_BUFFER_BIT);

    int i = 0;
    for (i=0; i<[videoChannels count]; ++i)
    {
        VideoChannel *currentChannel = [videoChannels objectAtIndex:i];
        [currentChannel drawChannel];
    }

}
```

If you compare Listing 8-11 with Listing 8-5, you can see some clear similarities. The OpenGL calls we make here are setup calls to draw the quads properly. When those setup calls are made, we iterate through the list of VideoChannel objects and tell each of them to draw their current frame instead of doing all the drawing code as we did in Listing 8-5.

Keep in mind that the rectangles for each of the VideoChannels to draw in were set when the VideoChannels were initially created (see –initVideoChannels in Listing 8-6, previously in this chapter).

When we iterate through the VideoChannel objects, we call –drawChannel, as shown in Listing 8-12.

LISTING 8-12   Implementing the VideoChannel drawChannel

```
- (void)drawChannel;
{
  [self drawImage];
}


- (void)drawImage;
{
    [self drawImage:mainDisplayRect withOpacity:opacity];
}


- (void)drawImage:(CGRect)imageRect withOpacity:(GLfloat)op;
{
    glEnable(
        CVOpenGLTextureGetTarget(
                currentFrameImageBuffer));

    glBindTexture(
        CVOpenGLTextureGetTarget(
                currentFrameImageBuffer),
            CVOpenGLTextureGetName(
                    currentFrameImageBuffer));

    glMatrixMode(GL_TEXTURE);
    glLoadIdentity();
    glColor4f(1.0, 1.0, 1.0, op);
    glBegin(GL_QUADS);

    glTexCoord2f(upperLeft[0], upperLeft[1]);
    glVertex2f  (imageRect.origin.x,
                imageRect.origin.y + imageRect.size.height);

    glTexCoord2f(upperRight[0], upperRight[1]);
    glVertex2f  (imageRect.origin.x + imageRect.size.width,
                imageRect.origin.y + imageRect.size.height);
```

8

LISTING 8-12   Continued

```
    glTexCoord2f(lowerRight[0], lowerRight[1]);
    glVertex2f  (imageRect.origin.x + imageRect.size.width,
                imageRect.origin.y);

    glTexCoord2f(lowerLeft[0], lowerLeft[1]);
    glVertex2f  (imageRect.origin.x, imageRect.origin.y);

    glEnd();

}
```

The -drawChannel method calls the default implementation of another function,
-drawImage, which simply calls another function with the same name that takes two
parameters:

▸ displayRect, which is passed mainDisplayRect for the main window rectangle

▸ opacity, which receives the value 1.0 for full opacity

This might seem like more levels of indirection than necessary, but it gives you the flexibility to alter this call and give it a different opacity if you want the video to render with
some level of transparency rather than fully opaque.

We have shown the core code you need to render multiple video channels in this section,
but you need to run the example project, OpenGLVidGrid, to see how it all works.

Summary

Core Animation provides such a powerful abstraction for many of Apple's technologies.
Harnessing the power of OpenGL while not having to understand all the underlying
concepts is helpful to programmers who need to use it but who don't want to or have the
time to become experts. As we have seen in this chapter, rendering to an OpenGL context
is within the realm of what most Cocoa programmers can attain. It also helps to introduce you to OpenGL concepts so that you can go to that next level if you want.
Regardless of where you are in your programming efforts, the CAOpenGLLayer gives you
what you need to harness the power of OpenGL in your applications.

CHAPTER 9

Quartz Composer Layer

IN THIS CHAPTER

▶ **Creating a Multi-Video Stream with Quartz Composer**

▶ **The Quartz Composition Layer and OpenGL**

Quartz compositions provide a method for developing complex visualizations. Quartz Composer is a visual development tool that enables you to create visualizations such as screensavers and motion graphic animations by simply dragging and dropping *patches* and connecting the different inputs and outputs from one patch to another. Although you can create your own custom patches, there are plenty of patches to choose from in Quartz Composer's toolbox. Simply drag the patches you are interested in to the patch editor and start connecting the inputs and outputs.

> **NOTE**
>
> Okay, it's not that simple, but you get the general idea. If you want to learn more about how to use Quartz Composer, be on the lookout for *Real-Time Motion Graphics with Quartz Composer*, by Graham Robinson and Surya Buchwald, coming soon from Addison-Wesley.

Inputs are often things such as images or the video input of your iSight camera. Outputs are often things such as composited images that have had some effect applied to them, such as a filter, mask, or transformation.

If you are not familiar with Quartz Composer, you might want to do a search for *.qtz* files on your computer, and open them in Quartz Composer to see the kinds of visualizations that are possible.

In this chapter, you create a simple Quartz Composition using Quartz Composer. You then load the composition into a QCCompositionLayer and add some Cocoa controls for controlling the various input values of the composition.

Creating a Multi-Video Stream with Quartz Composer

In keeping with the theme of the previous two chapters, we continue to use video as the rendering medium. This composition will consist of two Movie Loader source patches and two Billboard patches that display the movies loaded by our Movie Loader patches. Movie Loader patches simply do what the name implies—they load movies from disk to be used as an input source for a composition. It is a type of source patch. Billboard patches are renderer patches that display the video for us. You connect the output image of the Movie Loader patch to the input image of the Billboard patch and the movie will render.

Quartz Composer is found in */Developer/Applications*. Go ahead and start it.

To create the composition, follow these steps:

1. Select **File** > **New Blank** in Quartz Composer to create a new blank composition.

2. Drag two Movie Loader Source patches from the Patch Browser to the editor in the Root Macro Patch.

3. Drag two Billboard Renderer patches from the Patch Browser to the editor in the Root Macro Patch.

4. Drag a Clear Renderer patch from the Patch Browser to the editor in the Root Macro Patch.

5. Click the Image output of one of the Movie Loader patches, and drag it to the Image input of one of the Billboard patches.

6. Click the Image output of the other Movie Loader patch, and drag it to the Image input of the remaining Billboard patch.

7. Click the Clear patch number badge and set it to Layer 1. This ensures that our clear color is the backmost layer.

8. Select one of the Movie Loader patches and provide a path to a QuickTime movie in the Movie Location input parameter in the patch inspector (see Figure 9-1). Repeat this for the other Movie Loader patch.

9. As shown in Figure 9-2, adjust the X Position and Width parameters for each of the Billboard patches so that the videos display side by side.

    For Billboard Layer 2, specify Width: 0.85, X Position: -0.4856.

    For Billboard Layer 3, specify Width: 0.85, X Position: 0.4856.

    These settings cause the videos to display side by side.

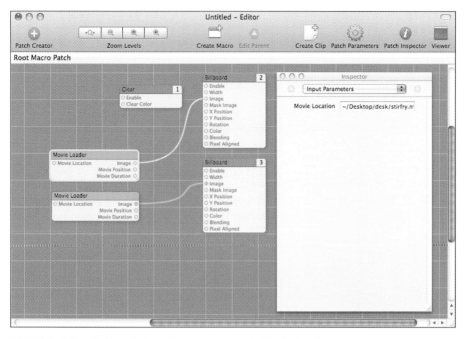

FIGURE 9-1   Set Movie Location Parameter in Movie Loader

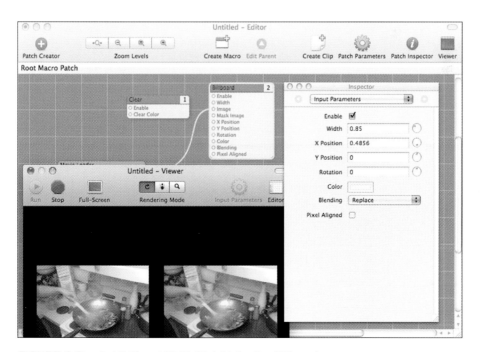

FIGURE 9-2   Set X/Y and Width/Height for the Billboards

10. Save the composition to a *.qtz* file.

11. If the composition is not already running, click the Run button in the composition viewer to watch the two videos play back.

Creating Controllable Parameters

The power of using Quartz Compositions is found in its capability to provide inputs and outputs that are controllable outside of the composition. Our QCCompositionLayer provides a way to set any parameter that we have published in the composition.

When we created our composition, we explicitly specified the path to the movie files we want to use in the Movie Loader patches. What if instead we decide we want to allow the user to specify the paths to video files to use and pass those paths along to the composition? This is done by publishing the Movie Location parameters of the Movie Loader patches.

To publish the Movie Location input parameters, do the following:

1. In Quartz Composer, Control-click the Movie Location input on the first (top) Movie Loader patch and select **Published Input** > **Movie Location**.

2. Name the input **movie1_location** and press Enter.

3. Control-click the Movie location input on the other Movie Loader patch and select **Published Input** > **Movie Location**.

4. Name the input **movie2_location** and press Enter.

5. Save the composition.

Now, the locations of the movie files can be set from within our application code. Next, we create an Xcode project that uses a QCCompositionLayer to display the composition.

Creating the Xcode Project

To create our hosting application, do the following:

1. In Xcode, press Shift-⌘-N and select Cocoa Application in the Project Templates dialog.

2. Name the project Dual Video QC Composition and click Save.

3. Expand the Frameworks group, Control-click the Linked Frameworks subgroup, and select **Add** > **Existing Frameworks**.

4. In the resulting dialog, navigate to */System/Library/Frameworks* and select both *QuartzCore.framework* and *Quartz.framework*. You need to click Add twice, when prompted.

5. Control-click the Classes group and select **Add** > **New File**.

6. In the New File template dialog, select **Objective-C class** under the Cocoa group and click Next.

7. Name the file *AppDelegate.m* and make sure Also Create "AppDelegate.h" is checked. Click Finish.

8. Click *AppDelegate.h* to open the file in the code editor and add the following code:

```
@interface AppDelegate : NSObject {
    IBOutlet NSWindow *window;
}
```

9. Click *AppDelegate.m* to open the file in the code editor and add the following code:

```
@implementation AppDelegate
- (void)awakeFromNib;
{
    [[window contentView] setWantsLayer:YES];
}
@end
```

10. Under the Resources group in your project, double-click *MainMenu.xib* to open the nib in Interface Builder.

11. From the Library palette, drag an NSObject object into *MainMenu.xib* and rename it to AppDelegate.

12. Make sure your AppDelegate object is selected. In the object inspector, click the Identity tab and change the Class field to AppDelegate.

13. In *MainMenu.xib*, Control-click on File's Owner and drag the connection to the AppDelegate object. Select **delegate** in the ensuing context menu.

14. In the *MainMenu.xib*, Control-click on AppDelegate and drag the connection to the Window object. Select **window** in the ensuing context menu.

15. Save the XIB file and return to Xcode.

The project is now set up. In the preceding steps we created an application delegate that we can use to provide functionality between our views and our data. In the next section, we demonstrate how to implement adding a Quartz Composition layer, QCCompositionLayer, to our window.

Adding a QCCompositionLayer to the Window

Now that we have an outlet defined for the window in the AppDelegate class, we can add the QCCompositionLayer to the root layer of the window's content view. Listing 9-1 demonstrates how this is done in our –awakeFromNib method.

LISTING 9-1   Implementing the QCCompostionLayer

```
- (void)awakeFromNib;
{
    [[window contentView] setWantsLayer:YES];

    NSString *path = [[NSBundle mainBundle]
                pathForResource:@"DualStirfry"
                ofType:@"qtz"];

    qcLayer = [[QCCompositionLayer alloc] initWithFile:path];

    // Set the composition frame to be the same
    // size as the window content.
    [qcLayer setFrame:NSRectToCGRect([[window contentView] frame])];

    // Insert the layer at index zero so that any controls we add
    // to the window won't be obscured by the layer.
    [[[window contentView] layer] insertSublayer:qcLayer atIndex:0];
}
```

The instance variable qcLayer is declared in the AppDelegate header file. We initialize it here in the -awakeFromNib because we are guaranteed that our window and view are initialized and can, therefore, be used.

Notice that the path we use to load the Quartz Composition file we created earlier is obtained from the main bundle. At this point you should add your Quartz Composition file that you created earlier to the project by Control-clicking the Resources group in the project tree and selecting Add Existing Files. Navigate to the location of your Quartz Composition file and click Add when you've located it. Now the file will be included in the application bundle when it is built and you can access it using the code specified in Listing 9-1.

Passing Parameters to the Quartz Composition

The parameters or inputs that we published while creating the Quartz Composition called movie1_location and movie2_location can now be accessed through key-value coding. We have set default values for these fields in the actual composition, but now we can set them to something else based on user input. We just need to add a couple of buttons and an open file dialog to set the path for each input parameter based upon user selection.

To obtain the path for the selected file, you need to create two buttons in Interface Builder and two IBActions in Xcode. First create the actions in Xcode. Listing 9-2 demonstrates how to use an NSOpenPanel to obtain the path to a movie file and then set the parameter called movie1_location.

LISTING 9-2   Obtain Movie Path Using NSOpenPanel

```
- (IBAction)setMovie1Location:(id)sender;
{
    NSOpenPanel *openPanel;

    openPanel = [NSOpenPanel openPanel];
    [openPanel setCanChooseDirectories:NO];
    [openPanel setAllowsMultipleSelection:NO];
    [openPanel setResolvesAliases:YES];
    [openPanel setCanChooseFiles:YES];

    if ([openPanel runModalForTypes:nil] == NSOKButton)
    {
        [qcLayer setValue:[openPanel filename]
            forInputKey:@"movie1_location"];
    }
}
```

You can duplicate this code in a second IBAction method called –setMovie2Location and simply change the input key to movie2_location.

The Quartz Composition layer provides the method –setValue:forInputKey through the QCCompositionRenderer protocol specifically for setting the value of a published input inside of your composition. What is interesting, though, is that we could also set the movie location field using Key-Value Coding with a call to –setValue:forKeyPath. You can simply change the –setValue to use the following instead:

```
[qcLayer setValue:[openPanel filename]
   forKeyPath:@"patch.movie1_location.value"];
```

Prior to the availability of QCCompositionLayer, you had to use a QCView object to display Quartz Compositions in a Cocoa application. If you wanted to control patches using bindings, you also had to instantiate a QCPatchController. The keypath, patch.movie1_location.value is the keypath you need if you use a QCPatchController because "patch" refers to the root level patch in the composition. This mechanism is preserved in a QCCompositionLayer, so you can access the value directly using bindings. This is especially useful for when you want to bind a value for one of your Cocoa controls using Interface Builder.

Getting Image Data from the Composition

In the same way that we published the inputs for our movie locations, we can publish outputs as well, but first let's change our composition to add a filter to the image output. Then we can capture that image output back in our Cocoa application.

To add a filter to the compositions:

1. Open the Quartz Composition file in Quartz Composer, and drag a Dot Screen patch from the filters in the Patch Creator list to the editing area.

2. Drag the Image output of the second Movie Loader to the Image input of the Dot Screen patch.

3. Drag the Image output of the Dot Screen patch to the Image input of the second Billboard patch.

Your composition should now look like what you see in Figure 9-3.

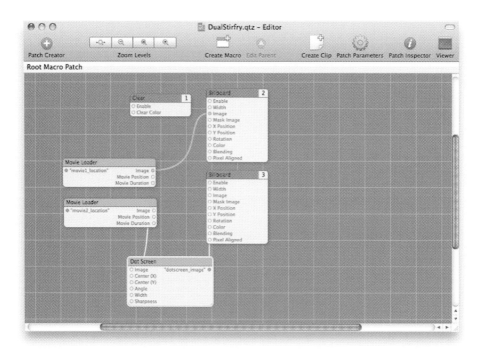

FIGURE 9-3   Composition with Dot Screen Patch

Now we need to publish the Image output for the Dot Screen patch so that we can obtain the current image with the filter applied at any time during the video playback. To publish the Image output of the Dot Screen patch, follow these steps:

1. Control-click the Dot Screen patch.

2. Select **Published Outputs > Image**.

3. Name it dotscreen_image and press Enter.

4. Save the composition.

Obtaining the Current Image in Code

Now that we have published the Image output in our composition, we can obtain the image data for the current image as an NSImage object. In fact, we can obtain the image data in several different formats by specifying the type in our call to –valueForOutputKey:ofType. In the example code we are simply going to set the contents field of our root layer to the current image. In that case, we want to obtain a CGImageRef instead of an NSImage. This is trivial because all we need to do is specify CGImage as the type to return to our –valueForOutputKey call. Listing 9-3 demonstrates how we can obtain the current image as a CGImageRef and set the contents of the root layer.

LISTING 9-3   Obtaining Image Data as CGImageRef

```
- (IBAction)getDotScreenImage:(id)sender;
{
    CGImageRef image = (CGImageRef)
    [qcLayer valueForOutputKey:@"dotscreen_image"
                    ofType:@"CGImage"];

    [[[window contentView] layer] setContents:(id)image];
}
```

We request the dotscreen_image output from the composition with a type of CGImage, and we get back a CGImageRef object that we use to set the contents of the root window content view layer.

The call to –valueForOutputKey:ofType can return an NSImage, NSBitmapImageRep, CGImage, CIImage, CVPixelBuffer, CVOpenGLBuffer, or CVOpenGLTexture. Simply substitute for the name CGImage and change the type returned according to the image type you want to receive instead.

Notice that the –getDotScreenImage call is an IBAction. In interface builder, you need to add a button to the window and connect it to this action in the AppDelegate object. Figure 9-4 shows what the example project looks like when run.

Figure 9-5 shows what the example project looks like when the Get Image button has been pressed. It sets the contents field of the root layer to the current image from Movie 2, which has had the dot screen filter applied to it.

You determine which inputs and outputs are available to your code in Quartz Composer. You can develop complex visualizations and then easily control them programmatically. Just keep in mind that you can access only inputs and outputs that are available in the Root Patch. If you create a *macro patch* (a patch that encapsulates other patches), you need to expose inputs and outputs at the Root Patch level, or you cannot access them in your calls to –setValue:forInputKey and –valueForOutputKey:ofType.

FIGURE 9-4   Running the QCCompositionLayer Example Project

FIGURE 9-5   Setting the Contents of the Root Layer to the Current Filtered Image

The Quartz Composition Layer and OpenGL

All the power of OpenGL is at your fingertips in a `QCCompositionLayer` as it inherits directly from `CAOpenGLLayer`, which we discuss in detail in Chapter 8, "OpenGL Layer." What we learned in that chapter is that we first determine whether we should draw using `-canDrawInCGLContext` and then draw in the context using `-drawInCGLContext`. We can override both of these methods if we create our own `QCCompositionLayer`-derived class and add additional functionality.

This gives you the power to do any additional rendering you might want to do before displaying the current frame in the composition. Remember that Quartz Compositions are playing, which is to say that they are rendering to the screen on a regular basis. The frequency is not something that you control because it is related to your hardware and the video refresh rate. What you do know, however, is that if `-drawInCGLContext` has been called, the next frame is ready to be rendered, and `-drawInCGLContext` has provided you a `CGLContextObj` object into which you can render your own drawing. Listing 9-4 demonstrates what the default implementation of a `QCQuartzCompositionLayer` derived class looks like.

LISTING 9-4   Default QCCompositionLayer Derived Class Implementation

```
@interface QuartzLayer : QCCompositionLayer {

}
@end

@implementation QuartzLayer

- (BOOL)canDrawInCGLContext:(CGLContextObj)glContext
            pixelFormat:(CGLPixelFormatObj)pixelFormat
          forLayerTime:(CFTimeInterval)timeInterval
          displayTime:(const CVTimeStamp *)timeStamp;
{

    return [super canDrawInCGLContext:glContext
                      pixelFormat:pixelFormat
                    forLayerTime:timeInterval
                    displayTime:timeStamp];

}

- (void)drawInCGLContext:(CGLContextObj)glContext
            pixelFormat:(CGLPixelFormatObj)pixelFormat
          forLayerTime:(CFTimeInterval)timeInterval
          displayTime:(const CVTimeStamp *)timeStamp;
{
```

LISTING 9-4   Continued

```
    // Call super to ensure the OpenGL context gets flushed.
  [super drawInCGLContext:glContext
          pixelFormat:pixelFormat
          forLayerTime:timeInterval
          displayTime:timeStamp];
}
@end
```

The call to -canDrawInCGLContext can be overridden depending on whatever criteria you specify. When rendering video like we did in the Chapter 8, we used this call to determine if the next video frame were ready to draw. If it were, we returned YES; otherwise we returned NO. Then, if we returned YES, -drawInCGLContext actually handled the drawing of our quads in the OpenGL context. Take a look at Chapter 8 if you want understand how to take advantage of this feature.

Summary

Quartz compositions provide a simple way to create complex visualizations. The limit is only in what you can think up. This sounds like a cliché, however, it is actually the truth. There are times when your application requires animation or other visual elements and you might be tempted to code them by hand. You might want to reconsider that approach depending on how complex the visualization is.

Why write code when you can simply add the elements and effects to a Quartz composition and control those effects and elements by publishing inputs and outputs? When you start thinking this way, ideas can begin to open up in your mind. The Core Animation Quartz Composition Layer, QCCompositionLayer, provides an intuitive way to incorporate your compositions into your Cocoa applications.

CHAPTER 10

Other Useful Layers

IN THIS CHAPTER

▶ **CAShapeLayer**

▶ **CAGradientLayer**

▶ **CAReplicatorLayer**

Core Animation provides a plethora of layers to help you accomplish many and various tasks. This chapter covers several notable layers, including

▶ CAShapeLayer, a layer that provides a simple way to composite a shape in the layer tree using a Core Graphics path.

▶ CAGradientLayer, a layer that enables you to simply draw a gradient in your layer tree by specifying the colors, a start point, end point, and gradient type.

▶ CAReplicatorLayer, which replicates any sublayers that have been added to it. These replicated layers can be transformed (as discussed in Chapter 5, "Layer Transforms") to produce dazzling effects.

The layers discussed in this chapter are not ones normally used on a daily basis but are more of a specialty nature. When a special effect is needed or an unusual shape needs to be worked with, these are the layers that can accomplish that goal.

CAShapeLayer

So far through our discussion of CALayer objects, they have always been rectangles. This generally makes sense because views and windows are also rectangles. However, there are situations where we want a layer to be another shape; perhaps a circle or a triangle. In the first release of Core Animation (on iPhone 2.x and Mac OS X 10.5 Leopard), we had to create a transparent layer and draw the desired shape onto the rectangle. Further, if we needed to click on that layer, we then needed to do a complicated hit test to determine if the click was within the desired shape or outside of it.

Fortunately, with the update to Core Animation that was included in iPhone OS 3.0 and Mac OS X 10.6 Snow Leopard, there is another option: the CAShapeLayer, which is specifically designed to solve this issue. With CAShapeLayer, you can specify the path for any shape by creating a Core Graphics path and assign it to the CAShapeLayer's path property. You can then specify a fill color for the shape using -setFillColor on the layer.

Listing 10-1 demonstrates how to create a CAShapeLayer and add it to the layer tree. In this example, a new CAShapeLayer is created, and it is instructed to take on the shape of a simple triangle.

LISTING 10-1   Initializing a CAShapeLayer and Adding It to the Layer Tree

```
- (void)viewDidLoad
{
  [super viewDidLoad];

  UIImage *balloon = [UIImage imageNamed:@"balloon.jpg"];

  [[[self view] layer] setContents:(id)[balloon CGImage]];

  CGMutablePathRef path = CGPathCreateMutable();
  CGPathMoveToPoint(path, NULL, 0, 100);
  CGPathAddLineToPoint(path, NULL, 200, 0);
  CGPathAddLineToPoint(path, NULL, 200, 200);
  CGPathAddLineToPoint(path, NULL, 0, 100);

  shapeLayer = [[CAShapeLayer alloc] init];
  [shapeLayer setBounds:CGRectMake(0, 0, 200, 200)];
  [shapeLayer setFillColor:[[UIColor purpleColor] CGColor]];
  [shapeLayer setPosition:CGPointMake(200, 200)];
  [shapeLayer setPath:path];

  [[[self view] layer] addSublayer:shapeLayer];
}
```

The first thing you notice in Listing 10-1 is that it starts out with the -viewDidLoad method, which tells us that this code is for an iPhone project. We grab an image from the main bundle by calling [UIImage imageNamed:] and then set the view's layer contents to display the image. Next, create a Core Graphics path with a call to CGPathCreateMutable. We add lines to the path to draw a rectangle. Next we create our shape layer giving it a size of 200 × 200 pixels. We set the fill color to purple and then set its path to the path we just created. Now, when we add the layer to the layer tree with a call to -addSublayer, you can see something like the image in Figure 10-1.

FIGURE 10-1   CAShapeLayer Displaying a Triangle

Although this example is shown to be running on iPhone OS, the CAShapeLayer is also available as of Mac OS X 10.5 Snow Leopard and can be used in any application targeted at that version of the desktop OS.

Manipulating the Path Stroke

CAShapeLayer enables you to manipulate the appearance of the stroke around the perimeter of the shape you have drawn. For example, you can set the stroke width with the lineWidth property, or you could set the stroke color by calling –setStrokeColor passing it a CGColorRef. Listing 10-2 demonstrates several of the fields that you can change to manipulate the stroke of the shape.

LISTING 10-2   Path Stroke Manipulations

```
- (void)viewDidLoad
{
  [super viewDidLoad];

  UIImage *balloon = [UIImage imageNamed:@"balloon.jpg"];

  [[[self view] layer] setContents:(id)[balloon CGImage]];
```

LISTING 10-2   Continued

```objc
CGMutablePathRef path = CGPathCreateMutable();
CGPathMoveToPoint(path, NULL, 0, 100);
CGPathAddLineToPoint(path, NULL, 200, 0);
CGPathAddLineToPoint(path, NULL, 200, 200);
CGPathAddLineToPoint(path, NULL, 0, 100);

shapeLayer = [[CAShapeLayer alloc] init];
[shapeLayer setBounds:CGRectMake(0, 0, 200, 200)];
[shapeLayer setFillColor:[[UIColor purpleColor] CGColor]];
[shapeLayer setPosition:CGPointMake(200, 200)];
[shapeLayer setPath:path];

[shapeLayer setStrokeColor:[[UIColor redColor] CGColor]];
[shapeLayer setLineWidth:10.0f];
[shapeLayer setLineJoin:kCALineJoinRound];
[shapeLayer setLineDashPattern:
 [NSArray arrayWithObjects:[NSNumber numberWithInt:50],
  [NSNumber numberWithInt:2],
  nil]];

[[[self view] layer] addSublayer:shapeLayer];
}
```

The first thing we do is set the stroke color to red and set its width to 10 pixels. To round the corners of the path, kCALineJoinRound is used to join the lines and round corners. The radius of the corners is based on the thickness of the lines being joined and the angle of the intersection of the lines and, therefore, cannot be adjusted directly. The last thing we give the line is a dashed pattern. In Listing 10-2, the layer is stroked with 50 units of red-colored line to create the dash, followed by 2 units of unpainted space, which gives you the gap between the dashes.

What Is a "Unit"?

The term *unit* is used here instead of *pixels* because of *resolution independence*. Apple introduced to developers the concept of resolution independence at WWDC 2006 as part of its migration strategy for Mac OS X Leopard and beyond. The benefit of resolution independence guarantees that regardless of which device the application is used on—be it an iPhone, iPod touch, a MacBook Pro screen, or a 30-inch Apple Cinema HD Display—will look the same from one screen to the next, regardless of what the user-space-unit is. As you can imagine, if we were to use pixel-perfect settings instead of units, the layer would look much, much different from one screen (and one resolution) to the next.

This pattern could get very complex if we wanted it to. When you specify the pattern you want to use, odd number values are painted and even numbered values are unpainted. For example, if you specify the values 5, 10, 15, 20, the stroke will show 5 units painted, followed by 10 units unpainted, followed by 15 units painted, followed by 20 units unpainted. This pattern can be specified with any interval you like. Just remember: *Odd equals painted and even equals un-painted.* The units defined within the NSArray are expected to be NSNumber objects and placing anything else in that array can have unexpected results.

Figure 10-2 shows the shape layer with the stroke, as specified in Listing 10-2. Note that one of the corners appears to be missing because the gap in the line pattern falls directly on that corner.

FIGURE 10-2   The Shape Layer with a Red-Dashed Stroke

Using CAShapeLayer as a Layer Mask

All CALayer-derived Core Animation layers have a property called mask. This property enables you to mask everything in the layer *except* the portion where the layer mask has content. For example, if you set the image layer's mask to a shape layer instead of adding it to the layer tree, it allows only part of the image to show through where the shape layer has been drawn. Listing 10-3 demonstrates the difference if we wanted to use a shape layer as a mask instead of as a sublayer.

LISTING 10-3   Using CAShapeLayer as a Layer Mask

```
- (void)viewDidLoad
{
  [super viewDidLoad];

  UIImage *balloon = [UIImage imageNamed:@"balloon.jpg"];

  [[[self view] layer] setContents:(id)[balloon CGImage]];

  CGMutablePathRef path = CGPathCreateMutable();
  CGPathMoveToPoint(path, NULL, 0, 100);
```

LISTING 10-3   Continued

```
CGPathAddLineToPoint(path, NULL, 200, 0);
CGPathAddLineToPoint(path, NULL, 200, 200);
CGPathAddLineToPoint(path, NULL, 0, 100);

shapeLayer = [[CAShapeLayer alloc] init];
[shapeLayer setBounds:CGRectMake(0, 0, 200, 200)];
[shapeLayer setFillColor:[[UIColor purpleColor] CGColor]];
[shapeLayer setPosition:CGPointMake(200, 200)];
[shapeLayer setPath:path];

[[[self view] layer] setMask:shapeLayer];
}
```

The initialization code for the layer is identical to the code in Listing 10-1. The difference in Listing 10-3 is that we have changed the method call from –addSublayer to –setMask, passing it the CAShapeLayer. Figure 10-3 shows what the view looks like after applying this change.

FIGURE 10-3   Using a Layer Mask to Create a Triangle Filled with the Image

The stroke manipulations can also be applied when using the shape layer as a mask. In fact, if you change the code from Listing 10-2 to set the layer mask instead of adding the layer as we did in Listing 10-3, the view will now look like what you see in Figure 10-4. See Listing 10-4 for the specific code changes.

LISTING 10-4   Using a CAShapeLayer with Stoke Manipulations as a Mask

```
- (void)viewDidLoad
{
  [super viewDidLoad];

  UIImage *balloon = [UIImage imageNamed:@"balloon.jpg"];

  [[[self view] layer] setContents:(id)[balloon CGImage]];

  CGMutablePathRef path = CGPathCreateMutable();
  CGPathMoveToPoint(path, NULL, 0, 100);
  CGPathAddLineToPoint(path, NULL, 200, 0);
  CGPathAddLineToPoint(path, NULL, 200, 200);
  CGPathAddLineToPoint(path, NULL, 0, 100);

  shapeLayer = [[CAShapeLayer alloc] init];
  [shapeLayer setBounds:CGRectMake(0, 0, 200, 200)];
  [shapeLayer setFillColor:[[UIColor purpleColor] CGColor]];
  [shapeLayer setPosition:CGPointMake(200, 200)];
  [shapeLayer setPath:path];

  [shapeLayer setStrokeColor:[[UIColor redColor] CGColor]];
  [shapeLayer setLineWidth:10.0f];
  [shapeLayer setLineJoin:kCALineJoinRound];
  [shapeLayer setLineDashPattern:
   [NSArray arrayWithObjects:[NSNumber numberWithInt:50],
    [NSNumber numberWithInt:2],
    nil]];

  [[[self view] layer] setMask:shapeLayer];
}
```

As can be seen in Figure 10-4, the stroke manipulation is reflected in the masking of the image and changes the clean edges into a jagged pattern that follows the shape of the CAShapeLayer.

FIGURE 10-4   Using a Stroked Layer as a Layer Mask

CAGradientLayer

One of the more common effects you have likely seen on Mac OS X and the iPhone is composited images that look like they have a reflective surface underneath them. This effect can be somewhat difficult to produce, but with the CAGradientLayer, it becomes fairly trivial.

> **NOTE**
>
> At the time of this writing, CAGradientLayer supports only linear gradients. This section provides a quick and simple way to add gradients to your application without relying on Core Graphics for the heavy lifting.

The basic concept behind creating a reflective surface (as seen in iChat or in image displays in iWeb) is to use a copy of the main image flipped and placed beneath the main image. Then you apply a gradient to the flipped image to make it look like it is fading into the foreground, as shown in Figure 10-5.

The sample code in Listing 10-5 creates three layers—one for the main image and one for the image reflection—and then applies a gradient layer to use as the mask for the reflection layer on the bottom.

FIGURE 10-5   Image Reflection with Gradient Layer

LISTING 10-5   Applying Reflection Using a Gradient Layer

```
- (void)viewDidLoad
{
  [super viewDidLoad];

  [[[self view] layer] setBackgroundColor:
   [[UIColor blackColor] CGColor]];

  UIImage *balloon = [UIImage imageNamed:@"balloon.jpg"];

  // Create the top layer; this is the main image
  CALayer *topLayer = [[CALayer alloc] init];
  [topLayer setBounds:CGRectMake(0.0f, 0.0f, 320.0, 240.0)];
  [topLayer setPosition:CGPointMake(160.0f, 120.0f)];
  [topLayer setContents:(id)[balloon CGImage]];

  // Add the layer to the view
  [[[self view] layer] addSublayer:topLayer];
```

10

LISTING 10-5   Continued

```
// Create the reflection layer; this image is displayed beneath
// the top layer
CALayer *reflectionLayer = [[CALayer alloc] init];
[reflectionLayer setBounds:CGRectMake(0.0f, 0.0f, 320.0, 240.0)];
[reflectionLayer setPosition:CGPointMake(158.0f, 362.0f)];
// Use a copy of the image contents from the top layer
// for the reflection layer
[reflectionLayer setContents:[topLayer contents]];

// Rotate the image 180 degrees over the x axis to flip the image
[reflectionLayer setValue:DegreesToNumber(180.0f)
                 forKeyPath:@"transform.rotation.x"];

// Create a gradient layer to use as a mask for the
// reflection layer
CAGradientLayer *gradientLayer = [[CAGradientLayer alloc] init];
[gradientLayer setBounds:[reflectionLayer bounds]];
[gradientLayer setPosition:
 CGPointMake([reflectionLayer bounds].size.width/2,
             [reflectionLayer bounds].size.height/2)];

[gradientLayer setColors:[NSArray arrayWithObjects:
                          (id)[[UIColor clearColor] CGColor],
                          (id)[[UIColor blackColor] CGColor],
                          nil]];

// Override the default start and end points to give the gradient
// the right look
[gradientLayer setStartPoint:CGPointMake(0.5,0.35)];
[gradientLayer setEndPoint:CGPointMake(0.5,1.0)];

// Set the reflection layer's mask to the gradient layer
[reflectionLayer setMask:gradientLayer];

// Add the reflection layer to the view
[[[self view] layer] addSublayer:reflectionLayer];
}
```

This application uses three layers to achieve the desired effect. The top layer takes up the upper half of the screen and displays the original image. The bottom, or reflection, layer takes up the bottom half of the screen and shows a copy of the top layer's contents flipped on the *x*-axis. The image is flipped using key-value coding with the following call:

```
[reflectionLayer setValue:DegreesToNumber(180.0f)
                 forKeyPath:@"transform.rotation.x"];
```

This sets the layer's transform to 180 degrees from its original to give you the flipped image effect.

Finally, a gradient layer is applied to the reflection layer. Because we want to use the gradient layer as a mask, the gradient layer uses the same bounds and position as the reflection layer and is added to the layer tree of the reflection layer. You can adjust the way the gradient layer displays by altering its `startPoint` and `endPoint` properties as we have done in Listing 10-5.

CAReplicatorLayer

`CAReplicatorLayer` is an unusual and powerful subclass of `CALayer`. Its main job is to replicate any sublayers that have been added to it. These sublayers can be replicated a number of times based on the value of the `-instanceCount` property. In addition to replicating its sublayers, `CAReplicatorLayer` will shift their colors and transform the layers based on values stored in the following instance properties:

▶ `instanceTransform`

▶ `instanceColor`

▶ `instanceRedOffset`

▶ `instanceGreenOffset`

▶ `instanceBlueOffset`

▶ `instanceAlphaOffset`

One use for `CAReplicatorLayer` is to mimic the image reflections similar to what you see in CoverFlow. You can create a `UIView` that automatically creates a reflection of its subviews (and sublayers). The example we build is shown in Figure 10-6.

FIGURE 10-6   A Reflection Layer Generated with the CAReplicatorLayer

Building the UIView

You can begin this project by selecting the basic Window iPhone template in Xcode. Add a `UIView` subclass to this template, called `ReplicatorView`. The entire purpose for subclassing UIView is so we can override the +layerClass method and dictate what kind of layer this UIView will be backed with, as shown in Listing 10-6.

LISTING 10-6   Overriding the +layerClass Method

```
+ (Class)layerClass
{
  return [CAReplicatorLayer class];
}
```

This class method is called whenever an instance of the ReplicatorView is initialized. Instead of having a CALayer backing the view, we will automatically have CAReplicatorLayer as the backing layer.

Because we are subclassing the UIView, add the setup code shown in Listing 10-7 to the -initWithFrame: method of the ReplicatorView class. This setup code tells CAReplicatorLayer what to do with the sublayers (and subviews) it is about to receive.

LISTING 10-7   Overriding the +layerClass Method

```
- (id)initWithFrame:(CGRect)frame
{
  if (!(self = [super initWithFrame:frame])) return nil;

  CGFloat reflectionBase = 230.0f;

  CATransform3D transform = CATransform3DMakeScale(1.0, -1.0, 1.0);
  transform = CATransform3DTranslate(transform, 0.0, frame.size.height
- 2.0 * reflectionBase, 0.0);
  CAReplicatorLayer *replicatorLayer = (CAReplicatorLayer*)[self layer];
  [replicatorLayer setInstanceTransform:transform];
  [replicatorLayer setInstanceRedOffset:-0.5];
  [replicatorLayer setInstanceGreenOffset:-0.5];
  [replicatorLayer setInstanceBlueOffset:-0.5];
  [replicatorLayer setInstanceAlphaOffset:-0.45];
  [replicatorLayer setInstanceCount:2];

  return self;
}
```

After calling super, a transform is used to both flip the layer it is associated with and to shift that layer down 230 pixels. The reason for shifting the layer down 230 pixels is because we know the ReplicatorView will be 220 pixels high, so we want to position the layer 10 pixels below the top of its parent view.

After applying the transform, shift the colors (red, green, blue, and the alpha value) of the duplicated layers closer to black. The reason for this color shift is because the background of the window to which the view is added is black. This gives the layer a nice glossy reflection.

> **NOTE**
>
> In a production application this transform would probably need to be calculated at a later point in the application's execution.

All of these "instance" properties are used to instruct `CAReplicatorLayer` what to do with the layers it is generating. The initial layer remains untouched, but each subsequent layer from the first (based on the `instanceCount` property) will have transform and offset values applied. In addition, if the layer is duplicated more than once, each subsequent layer will receive the transform of the previous copy and an increase of its own. In this project, if we had more than one copy, we would see them fading closer and closer to black, and they would alternate vertically while being moved further and further down the screen.

Utilizing the ReplicatorView

Finally, we need to initialize an instance of the `ReplicatorView`, add it to the window, and then give it a subview to replicate. This is all accomplished in the `AppDelegate`, as shown in Listing 10-8.

LISTING 10-8 Adding the ReplicatorView to the Window

```
- (void)applicationDidFinishLaunching:(UIApplication *)application
{
  CGRect frame = [[UIScreen mainScreen] applicationFrame];
  UIView *replicatorView = nil;
  replicatorView = [[ReplicatorView alloc] initWithFrame:frame];

  [window addSubview:replicatorView];

  UIImage *lacey = [UIImage imageNamed:@"Lacey1.png"];
  UIImageView *imageView = [[UIImageView alloc] initWithImage:lacey];
  [imageView setFrame:CGRectMake(10, 10, 300, 220)];
  [imageView setContentMode:UIViewContentModeScaleAspectFit];

  [replicatorView addSubview:imageView];

  [window setBackgroundColor:[UIColor blackColor]];
  [window makeKeyAndVisible];

  [imageView release], imageView = nil;
  [replicatorView release], replicatorView = nil;
}
```

10

In this final piece, we initialize a new `ReplicatorView` with a `frame` the same size as the application itself and add it to the window. The image to be displayed is loaded into a `UIImageView`, and the `-contentMode` of that `UIImageView` is set so that it scales the image to fit the frame. Finally, the `UIImageView` is added to the instance of the `ReplicatorView`.

If you wanted to add more than one component to the `ReplicatorView`, you would need to adjust the `instanceCount` appropriately so that each sublayer added has one replicated layer.

Summary

Each of `CALayer`'s subclasses are very useful on their own. However, they can be applied together and along with other `CALayer` subclasses to provide some startling effects. For example, a combination of `CAReplicatorLayer` and `CAShapeLayer` can produce a perfectly aligned pie chart with identically sized wedges.

In the next chapter, we discuss how to add user interaction to Core Animation layers. The combination of `CAShapeLayers` with User Interaction can create dazzling user interfaces that go beyond the standard widgets that both the Desktop and iPhone offer.

PART IV

Advanced Core Animation

IN THIS PART

CHAPTER 11 User Interaction   177

CHAPTER 12 Performance   193

CHAPTER 13 Core Animation on the iPhone   207

CHAPTER 11

User Interaction

IN THIS CHAPTER

▶ **The Click of a Mouse**

▶ **Hit Testing CALayer Objects**

▶ **Hit Test**

▶ **Example Application: Color Changer**

▶ **LZButtonLayer**

▶ **Interface Builder**

▶ **Building the Layers**

▶ **Watching the Mouse**

▶ **Keyboard Events**

▶ **Layer-Backed Views**

W hat is the point of a graphical interface if a user cannot interact with it? However, a quick exploration of the Core Animation API reveals that it has no direct way to receive user interaction!

This chapter focuses on how to add interaction points to an application, specifically to Core Animation. We look at both mouse interaction and keyboard input.

The Click of a Mouse

The most common interaction users expect from your application is the ability to click the mouse on various interface elements to perform some function, such as clicking a Save button. In a normal Cocoa application, these type of events are handled with NSResponder. However, because Core Animation was designed to be as light as possible, CALayer does not inherit from NSResponder, and the layer cannot accept mouse events. Instead, you need to route the event through NSView.

When working with layer-backed views, your app can capture mouse events in an NSView and process them there. However, things get a little more interesting when you work in a configuration in which there is only one NSView for an entire stack of CALayer objects. Because the NSView is the only object that receives events, it must figure out what layer was clicked on and what action to take.

Hit Testing CALayer Objects

When an application has only one (or at least very few) NSView object, all user interaction becomes the responsibility of that lone NSView. It receives all mouse and keyboard input and needs to determine how to process that input. Before diving into the meat of figuring out how to receive events, we first need to create a custom `NSView` that receives mouse events and hands them off to a delegate object, as shown in Listing 11-1.

LISTING 11-1   LZContentView Header for Receiving Mouse Events

```
#import <Cocoa/Cocoa.h>

@interface LZContentView : NSView
{
  IBOutlet id delegate;
}

@end
```

The header subclasses `NSView` adds one instance variable (or ivar) to the object; the `delegate`. Because this `delegate` is assigned in Interface Builder, it is flagged as an `IBOutlet`. Whenever we want to bind an object in Interface Builder that is not defined as an `id`, we need to declare it as an `IBOutlet` to let Interface Builder know it should be exposed.

We want to capture only the `-mouseDown:` and `-mouseUp:` events in the `NSView` subclass, as shown in Listing 11-2. When captured, those events are sent to the `delegate`, which handles all other interactions.

LISTING 11-2   LZContentView Implementation File for Receiving Mouse Events

```
#import "LZContentView.h"

@implementation LZContentView

- (void)awakeFromNib
{
}

- (void)mouseDown:(NSEvent*)theEvent
{
  [delegate mouseDown:theEvent];
}

- (void)mouseUp:(NSEvent*)theEvent
{
  [delegate mouseUp:theEvent];
}

@end
```

Hit Test

When a user clicks on an application, two NSEvent objects are generated for that click. One event is generated when the mouse button is pushed down and a second when the button is released. To follow this example, applications should also differentiate between mouseDown and mouseUp events and react accordingly.

When acting on a mouse event, the first thing we need to do is to determine which layer is being clicked on. Because the NSView has an unknown number of layers in its hierarchy, we cannot assume which layer is being clicked just by its location. Fortunately, CALayer has a -hitTest: method designed to solve this issue. When CGPoint is passed to the root CALayer, it returns the deepest CALayer that the point falls within. This enables you to quickly determine which CALayer has been clicked so that your app can act accordingly.

> **NOTE**
>
> This is an important point to note. Most events in OS X that we think of as reacting to a mouse click are actually reacting to NSEvent's mouseUp method. For example, click on a window's Close button and drag the mouse cursor off the button before releasing the mouse button. You notice that the window did not close. This is intended as a last chance for the user to cancel an action they did not intend.

Example Application: Color Changer

To demonstrate how the hit test works, we build a simple application that has three buttons: Red, Green, and Blue, along with a color bar that displays the choice, as shown in Figure 11-1.

The buttons and the color bar are built using CALayer objects. In the first version of this application, we determine which button is clicked on and respond.

FIGURE 11-1   Color Chooser Example

LZButtonLayer

The first step to building this application is building the buttons. The buttons are composed of two CALayer objects:

▶ The main layer (the LZButtonLayer itself), which handles the border and corner radius (as shown in Listing 11-3)

▶ A CATextLayer object, which display the text (as shown in Listing 11-4)

The header, shown in Listing 11-3, retains a reference to the `CATextLayer` sublayer, which enables you to adjust its text as needed. We also have a reference to the associated color object. The header also includes a pair of accessors, `-string` and `-setString`, which set the strings on the `CATextLayer` sublayer. Finally, the `-setSelected` method informs the layer when it is actively being clicked.

> **WARNING**
>
> Because `CATextLayer` objects cannot be centered vertically, you cannot build the buttons on a single layer. Therefore, each button needs to be in its own layer so that we can place each one where we want it.

LISTING 11-3   LZButtonLayer Header File

```
#import <Cocoa/Cocoa.h>

@interface LZButtonLayer : CALayer
{
    __weak CATextLayer *textLayer;
    CGColorRef myColor;
}

@property (assign) CGColorRef myColor;

- (NSString*)string;
- (void)setString:(NSString*)string;
- (void)setSelected:(BOOL)selected;

@end
```

Whenever `[CALayer layer]` is called, the init method is also called as the default initializer, as shown in Listing 11-4. The button layer overrides the default initializer and configures the button itself. When the `[super init]` finishes its task, the background layer of the button is configured by setting its `cornerRadius`, `bounds`, `borderWidth`, and `borderColor`.

Next, the `textLayer` is initialized. Even though the `textLayer` is an auto-released object (because we did not call alloc or copy when we created it), we continue referencing it. Because we define this as a weak reference, we are not retaining it but instead letting the layer hierarchy handle its retention. With the `CATextLayer` initialized, the

> **NOTE**
>
> **Weak References**
>
> Weak references were added in Mac OS X Leopard (v 10.5) and effectively zero out the reference if the referenced object is released. This is primarily used when the garbage collector is turned on, but it is a helpful flag to use when doing non-GC development (such as for the iPhone) as well.

next step is to set the layer's default properties and assign its position attribute to the center of the button's background layer.

LISTING 11-4   LZButtonLayer -init

```
#import "LZButtonLayer.h"


@implementation LZButtonLayer


@synthesize myColor;


- (id)init
{
  if (![super init]) return nil;

  [self setCornerRadius:10.0];
  [self setBounds:CGRectMake(0, 0, 100, 24)];
  [self setBorderWidth:1.0];
  [self setBorderColor:kWhiteColor];

  textLayer = [CATextLayer layer];
  [textLayer setForegroundColor:kWhiteColor];
  [textLayer setFontSize:20.0f];
  [textLayer setAlignmentMode:kCAAlignmentCenter];
  [textLayer setString:@"blah"];
  CGRect textRect;
  textRect.size = [textLayer preferredFrameSize];
  [textLayer setBounds:textRect];
  [textLayer setPosition:CGPointMake(50, 12)];

  [self addSublayer:textLayer];

  return self;
}
```

The -string and -setString: methods (shown in Listing 11-5) retrieve and pass the string value into the underlying CATextLayer. This provides opaque access to the underlying CATextLayer as a convenience.

LISTING 11-5   LZButton -setString: and -string: Implementations

```
- (NSString*)string;
{
  return [textLayer string];
}
```

LISTING 11-5   Continued

```
- (void)setString:(NSString*)string;
{
  [textLayer setString:string];
  CGRect textRect;
  textRect.size = [textLayer preferredFrameSize];
  [textLayer setBounds:textRect];
}
```

The –setSelected: method (as shown in Listing 11-6) provides visible feedback to the user so that they can see the click has an effect on the application. To show this effect, we add and remove a Core Image filter (CIBloom) to the button layer depending upon the BOOL value being passed in.

LISTING 11-6   LZButton -setSelected: Implementation

```
- (void)setSelected:(BOOL)selected
{
  if (!selected) {
    [self setFilters:nil];
    return;
  }
  CIFilter *effect = [CIFilter filterWithName:@"CIBloom"];
  [effect setDefaults];
  [effect setValue: [NSNumber numberWithFloat: 10.0f]  forKey: @"inputRadius"];
  [effect setName: @"bloom"];
  [self setFilters: [NSArray arrayWithObject:effect]];
}
```

> **NOTE**
>
> Remember that Core Image filters are currently only available on the desktop. Therefore, the filter changes in the -setSelected: method will not work on a Cocoa Touch device.

Interface Builder

With the LZButton layer designed, the next thing we build is the AppDelegate. The AppDelegate contains all the layers; add them to the window's contentView and receive the delegate calls.

The only thing we do in Interface Builder is change the window's contentView to an instance of LZContentView. After the class type has been changed, bind the ContentView's delegate to the `AppDelegate`. This enables the `AppDelegate` to receive `mouseUp` and `mouseDown` events from `contentView`.

Building the Layers

After launching, the application builds the interface layers before presenting the window to the user. The best way to do this is to implement the `-awakeFromNib` method in the `AppDelegate` class, as shown in Listing 11-7. This method is called before the application renders anything onscreen and is processed as the application starts up. We want to set up everything before display to avoid an ugly redraw as the application appears on screen.

LISTING 11-7   AppDelegate –awakeFromNib implementation

```
- (void)awakeFromNib
{
  NSView *contentView = [window contentView];
  [contentView setWantsLayer:YES];
  CALayer *contentLayer = [contentView layer];
  [contentLayer setBackgroundColor:kBlackColor];

  redButton = [LZButtonLayer layer];
  [redButton setString:@"Red"];
  [redButton setPosition:CGPointMake(60, 22)];
  [redButton setMyColor:kRedColor];

  [contentLayer addSublayer:redButton];

  greenButton = [LZButtonLayer layer];
  [greenButton setString:@"Green"];
  [greenButton setPosition:CGPointMake(200, 22)];
  [greenButton setMyColor:kGreenColor];

  [contentLayer addSublayer:greenButton];

  blueButton = [LZButtonLayer layer];
  [blueButton setString:@"Blue"];
  [blueButton setPosition:CGPointMake(340, 22)];
  [blueButton setMyColor:kBlueColor];

  [contentLayer addSublayer:blueButton];

  colorBar = [CALayer layer];
  [colorBar setBounds:CGRectMake(0, 0, 380, 20)];
  [colorBar setPosition:CGPointMake(200, 100)];
```

LISTING 11-7   Continued

```
[colorBar setBackgroundColor:kBlackColor];
[colorBar setBorderColor:kWhiteColor];
[colorBar setBorderWidth:1.0];
[colorBar setCornerRadius:4.0f];


[contentLayer addSublayer:colorBar];
}
```

In Listing 11-7, the –awakeFromNib grabs a reference to the window's contentView and makes it layer-backed. We then grab a reference to the contentView's layer and use it as the root layer for the rest of the interface.

When we have the rootLayer, the next step is to initialize three copies of the LZButtonLayer that we previously built, assign each one to a color, and set their position within the root layer. When each button is fully initialized, add it as a sublayer to the root layer.

Finally, create a generic CALayer, named colorBar, and add it as a sublayer to the root layer. Because colorBar is a CALayer, it needs to be fully defined here.

This now gives us the interface shown earlier in Figure 11-1. Next, add the interaction code to the AppDelegate that tells us which layer is being interacted with. To start the interaction, we abstract the hit test because it will be used in multiple places. This enables you to reuse the code and avoid having multiple copies of it through the application.

LISTING 11-8   AppDelegate –buttonLayerHit Implementation

```
- (LZButtonLayer*)buttonLayerHit
{
  NSPoint mouseLocation = [NSEvent mouseLocation];
  NSPoint translated = [window convertScreenToBase:mouseLocation];
  CGPoint point = NSPointToCGPoint(translated);

  CALayer *rootLayer = [[window contentView] layer];
  id hitLayer = [rootLayer hitTest:point];
  if (![hitLayer isKindOfClass:[LZButtonLayer class]]) {
    hitLayer = [hitLayer superlayer];
    if (![hitLayer isKindOfClass:[LZButtonLayer class]]) {
      return nil;
    }
  }
  return hitLayer;
}
```

When accessing `mouseLocation`, it gives us the location clicked as screen coordinates (*x* and *y* values). These coordinates are not the same as those used by the application, so you need to convert them to window coordinates by using one of the methods built into the `NSWindow` and `NSView` classes. Also, because `CALayer` objects deal in `CGPoints` instead of `NSPoints`, we also need to change the window coordinate's returned `NSRect` into a `CGRect`.

Now that we have the correct mouse coordinates, we need to find out which is the deepest layer under the mouse. A call to `-hitTest:` on the `rootLayer` returns the correct `CALayer` information.

The *deepest layer* is defined as the layer that has no sublayers that would contain the point being passed in. For instance, if you click on the text within `LZButtonLayer`, `CATextLayer` is returned from the `-hitTest:` call because it has no sublayers that contain the `CGPoint` being passed in. If, however, the edge of the button is clicked, then `LZButtonLayer` is returned instead. Finally, the root layer is returned if the background root layer is clicked (see Figure 11-2).

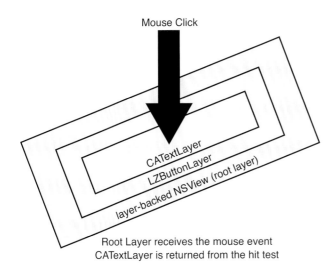

FIGURE 11-2   The Hit Test

However, we care only if the user clicked on `LZButtonLayer`. It is possible that the user thought they were clicking on `LZButtonLayer`, but were in fact clicking its sublayer. Therefore, an additional check was added. If the clicked layer were not a `LZButtonLayer`, we check that layer's superlayer to see if it is a `LZButtonLayer`. If the clicked layer is, then its superlayer is returned instead. If neither the clicked layer nor its superlayer is a `LZButtonLayer`, we return `nil`.

With the hit test method defined, it's now time to handle `mouseUp` and `mouseDown` events using the code shown in Listing 11-9.

LISTING 11-9   AppDelegate -mouseDown: Implementation

```
- (void)mouseDown:(NSEvent*)theEvent;
{
  [[self buttonLayerHit] setSelected:YES];
}
```

When the mouseDown event is received, we want to tell the selected button that it is selected and have it change its appearance. Because the –buttonLayerHit method returns only LZButtonLayer or nil, we can safely nest its call within the –setSelected: call, as shown in Listing 11-10.

LISTING 11-10   AppDelegate -mouseUp: Implementation

```
- (void)mouseUp:(NSEvent*)theEvent;
{
  LZButtonLayer *hitLayer = [self buttonLayerHit];
  [hitLayer setSelected:NO];
  [colorBar setBackgroundColor:[hitLayer myColor]];
}
```

Watching the Mouse

Playing with this initial version shows a few issues right away. If the mouse button is pressed over the LZButtonLayer and released while off of it, the button stays selected. Worse, if one button is pressed and released on another, the second button's color is selected while the first button stays selected!

To fix these issues, we need to refine the mouseUp and mouseDown methods, as shown in Listing 11-11.

LISTING 11-11   Updated AppDelegate -mouseDown: Implementation

```
- (void)mouseDown:(NSEvent*)theEvent;
{
  LZButtonLayer *layer = [self buttonLayerHit];
  if (!layer) return;
  selectedButton = layer;
  [selectedButton setSelected:YES];
  NSRect buttonRect = NSRectFromCGRect([selectedButton frame]);
  buttonDownTrackingArea = [[NSTrackingArea alloc] initWithRect:buttonRect
options:(NSTrackingMouseEnteredAndExited | NSTrackingActiveInActiveApp |
NSTrackingEnabledDuringMouseDrag | NSTrackingAssumeInside) owner:self
userInfo:nil];
  [[window contentView] addTrackingArea:buttonDownTrackingArea];
}
```

The key issue here is that we need to determine when the mouse has left the button. However, tracking the mouse all the time throughout the entire window is processor-intensive, so you don't want to do that; we want to limit mouse tracking as much as possible. To accomplish this, add an NSTrackingArea to the contentView when the mouseDown event is received, and we limit this NSTrackingArea to the rectangle containing the button that was pressed.

The AppDelegate is set within the NSTrackingArea as the owner of the area, which tells the area to notify AppDelegate whenever the mouse enters or exits the rectangle, but only when we are the active application. We also tell NSTrackingArea to assume it is starting within the rectangle so that the first event we receive is when the mouse exits.

In addition to adding an NSTrackingArea, we also keep a pointer to the button that was pressed. This pointer is used in other methods to turn the selection of the button on and off and to properly handle the mouseUp event.

This addition to the –mouseDown: method causes two other methods to be called: -mouseExited: and –mouseEntered:; both are defined in Listing 11-12.

LISTING 11-12   AppDelegate -mouseExited: Implementation

```
- (void)mouseExited:(NSEvent*)theEvent
{
  [selectedButton setSelected:NO];
}

- (void)mouseEntered:(NSEvent*)theEvent
{
  [selectedButton setSelected:YES];
}
```

After adding these methods, the button that was pressed selects and unselects as the mouse enters and exits its rectangle. This gives the user visual feedback while the mouse button is down so that they know the button click can still be canceled.

LISTING 11-13   AppDelegate -mouseUp: Implementation

```
- (void)mouseUp:(NSEvent*)theEvent;
{
  if (!selectedButton) return;
  [[window contentView] removeTrackingArea:buttonDownTrackingArea];
  [selectedButton setSelected:NO];
  LZButtonLayer *hitLayer = [self buttonLayerHit];
  if (hitLayer != selectedButton) {
    selectedButton = nil;
    return;
  }
```

LISTING 11-13   Continued

```
CGColorRef newBackgroundColor;
if (CGColorEqualToColor([colorBar backgroundColor], [selectedButton myColor])) {
  newBackgroundColor = kBlackColor;
} else {
  newBackgroundColor = [selectedButton myColor];
}
CABasicAnimation *animation = [CABasicAnimation
animationWithKeyPath:@"backgroundColor"];
[animation setFromValue:(id)[colorBar backgroundColor]];
[animation setToValue:(id)newBackgroundColor];
[animation setRemovedOnCompletion:NO];
//[animation setDelegate:self];
[animation setAutoreverses:NO];
[colorBar addAnimation:animation forKey:@"colorChange"];
[colorBar setBackgroundColor:newBackgroundColor];
}
```

The changes required in the mouseUp, as shown in Listing 11-13, are the most aggressive. First, if there was no button selected previously, we abort right away. This prevents an accidental click if the mouse is moved over a button after the mouse button has been pressed.

Next, remove the tracking area to stop receiving mouseEntered and mouseExited events. Now that the mouse button is up, there is no need to further update the LZButtonLayer.

The next step is to find out if the mouse is currently over the same LZButtonLayer that we started with. We do this by requesting the current LZButtonLayer that is under the mouse. If that is not the same LZButtonLayer that we started with, we abort by setting the selectedButton to nil and returning out of the method. This prevents the wrong button from being clicked when the user presses down the mouse on one button but releases the mouse over a different button.

After all the logic checks have passed, set the backgroundColor of the colorBar. While doing this, first check to see if the backgroundColor is already set to the button's color. If it is, the background is set to black instead. Otherwise we set it to the button's color.

Now when the application is run, not only does the colorBar change to the appropriate color, but also we can cancel a click of the button by moving the mouse off the button and then releasing.

Keyboard Events

Keyboard and mouse events are handled in a similar way. As with mouse events, only NSResponder objects can receive keyboard events. However, unlike mouse events, keyboard events do not have a point and are passed only to the current first responder. In the color application example, the window is the first responder. Because we want to receive and process key events, we first want to make our `LZContentView` accept first responder status. We do this by overriding the `-acceptsFirstResponder` method, as shown in Listing 11-14.

LISTING 11-14   LZContentView -acceptsFirstResponder Implementation

```
- (BOOL)acceptsFirstResponder
{
  return YES;
}
```

Like the `mouseUp` and `mouseDown` events in Listing 11-14, we want to handle key events within the delegate instead of directly in the view. Therefore, the `-keyUp:` method passes the event to the delegate, as shown in Listing 11-15.

LISTING 11-15   LZContentView -keyUp: Implementation

```
- (void)keyUp:(NSEvent *)theEvent
{
  [delegate keyUp:theEvent];
}
```

Back in the `AppDelegate`, we need to give the `contentView` first responder status on start up so that it can receive key events. To do this, call `[window setFirstResponder: contentView]` within the `-awakeFromNib` method.

Now that the events are routed to where we want them, it is time to do something with them. When the `-keyUp:` event is triggered, we want to set the background color based on the key that was pressed. See Listing 11-16.

LISTING 11-16   Updated AppDelegate -keyUp: Implementation

```
- (void)keyUp:(NSEvent *)theEvent
{
  CGColorRef newColor;
  if ([[theEvent charactersIgnoringModifiers] isEqualToString:@"r"]) {
    newColor = kRedColor;
  } else if ([[theEvent charactersIgnoringModifiers] isEqualToString:@"g"]) {
    newColor = kGreenColor;
  } else if ([[theEvent charactersIgnoringModifiers] isEqualToString:@"b"]) {
    newColor = kBlueColor;
  } else {
    [super keyUp:theEvent];
    return;
  }
```

LISTING 11-16   Continued

```
if (CGColorEqualToColor([colorBar backgroundColor], newColor)) {
  newColor = kBlackColor;
}
[colorBar setBackgroundColor:newColor];
}
```

We are testing for the three key events in this method: r, g, and b. If the incoming event does not match any of those three, we abort by passing the event up the chain and returning out of the method. If it does match, we test against the current background color of the colorBar and either set it or unset it as appropriate.

Layer-Backed Views

So far, we have discussed situations in which the entire user interface is built using Core Animation with a single "root" NSView supporting it all. The other equally common situation is working with layer-backed views as opposed to stand-alone layers.

Unlike the single NSView design, layer-backed views are subclasses of NSResponder. Therefore, it is possible to accept mouse and keyboard input at a much lower level. However, you need to consider a few things when adding user interaction to a layer-backed view design:

▶ **Keyboard input**
As previously mentioned, because keyboard input does not have an input "point," the application needs to keep track of which NSResponder receives the key events. This is done via the responder chain. When developing custom layer-backed NSView objects, we need to be aware of the responder chain and handle it appropriately. If we receive an event and we don't handle it, we need to pass it up the responder chain so that a potential parent can handle it. If we do not pass the event up, we can accidentally block things such as keyboard shortcuts to the menus, and so on.

▶ **Mouse coordinates**
Mouse events are easier to handle than keyboard events. When a custom NSView receives the mouse event, it is guaranteed to belong to either that NSView or one of its children. However, care does need to be taken to properly translate the coordinates of that event. As previously discussed in Listing 11-8, [NSEvent mouseLocation] returns the coordinates of the mouse in screen coordinates. Those need to be first translated to the coordinates of the window and then translated again to the view that received the event. Because each NSResponder has its own internal grid, we need to make sure we work with the correct coordinates before responding to the click.

Summary

This chapter introduced you to the concepts behind capturing user input in a Core Animation environment. Using the concepts discussed in this chapter, you can build compelling interactive interfaces.

Although it is easier to develop user interfaces that take advantage of layer-backed views, you can build the entire interface in stand-alone layers, or build custom layers that get passed in the mouse and/or keyboard events and allow them to be handled in smaller chunks than what was demonstrated here.

11

CHAPTER 12

Performance

IN THIS CHAPTER

▶ **Hardware Acceleration**

▶ **Rules of Thumb**

▶ **Tiled Layers**

▶ **Multithreaded Animation**

Core Animation was designed with performance in mind. It first appeared as Layer Kit and was designed to run on a small device (the iPhone and iPod touch), which had a limited amount of RAM, a small CPU, and unlike most desktop computers, a tiny GPU. Corc Animation was built for speed and efficiency, but that doesn't mean you can't tweak your code even more.

As with any other complex system, performance is a consideration when dealing with Core Animation. Fortunately, Core Animation does a lot of the heavy performance lifting for you. However, when working with a complex animation, you can refine the code even further to give your Core Animation-based apps an added performance boost.

This chapter shows you how to get the most from Core Animation. The chapter starts off with some guidelines; things to keep in mind as you're programming with Core Animation and trying to eek the most out of your code. Then you learn how to leverage the GPU, how to multi-thread your animations, and utilize CATiledLayer to present large images to the user without bogging down your application.

Hardware Acceleration

One of the major benefits of using Core Animation is that it takes advantage of the Mac's built-in hardware to its advantage. Previously, when developers would need to animate some part of the user interface, it generally took place on the *central processing unit (CPU)*, consumed CPU cycles, and was relatively slow. Making a user interface animate without stuttering took a great deal of time and usually involved working with the *graphics processing unit (GPU)* through OpenGL or some other technology. With Core Animation, you get the hardware acceleration for free! All you need to do is define the animation, kick it off, and let it run. You don't have to worry about loading it onto the GPU because Core Animation handles that automatically.

This is something to keep in mind while designing your user interfaces. What might be considered a complicated animation is more than likely trivial for the GPU to perform. Sliding rectangles around on the screen, transforming them in a 3D space, and so on is what the GPU was *designed* to do. Only when we start to push the limits of the GPU do we start to see performance degradation.

---

iPhone Hardware Rendering

Hardware acceleration occurs on both the desktop and in Cocoa Touch for the iPhone and iPod touch. Although the GPU is smaller on a Cocoa Touch device, we still get its benefit and get to hand off that animation to the GPU. However, unlike the desktop, there is a limited amount of resources on Cocoa Touch devices. As such, it is generally not a good idea to do processor-intensive work while the animation runs.

Your application should wait until any animations have finished running before performing any other tasks that might consume vital resources. Having said that, it is possible to perform other activities on background threads, or even on the main thread, while an animation runs. However, there is a balancing act between having the animation run smoothly and getting several tasks completed at the same time.

If you need to perform other tasks during an animation, be sure to flag them as potential performance bottlenecks, so they can be reviewed later, just in case it becomes obvious that the animations perform poorly.

Rules of Thumb

The following sections present those guidelines mentioned in the introduction as something that you need to keep in mind as you create your animations.

Avoid Offscreen Rendering

Whether you work with a desktop application or a Cocoa Touch device, you want to limit your drawing to only those areas visible to the user. Fortunately the `-drawRect:` method passes in only the rectangle that is dirty, so you can control exactly how much is drawn in each cycle of the run loop.

Limit the Use of Filters and Shadows

Filters and shadows take quite a bit of time to calculate and render within Core Animation. Therefore, it is recommended that you keep these to a minimum and that you avoid animating either one if possible. Here are some helpful tips:

▶ Especially in the case of filters, it is possible to render a static, temporary image, with the filter applied. This static image can then be used in place of the layer (with filters applied) during an animation to speed up rendering. When the animation is complete, the filtered-layer can then be swapped back in. Although this might not apply in all situations, it can yield significant performance advantages. This can be accomplished by asking the topmost layer to `-drawInContext:` that creates the static image that can be swapped in.

▶ Shadows are expensive. Because they are a partially transparent layer, they require large calculations to determine each pixel (because each pixel needs to be calculated on each layer until an opaque layer is hit). If shadows end up overlapping this increases the cost dramatically. Consider limiting shadows to only the outer layers and allow the inner layers to generate without any effects. See "Minimize Alpha Blending" later in this chapter.

Use Transition Effects Wisely

Transition effects offer great ways to give visual clues to the users that their view of the data or application is changing and how it is changing. From views sliding in and out of the window to layers curling away, the intention is obvious to the users. However, transitions such as filters and shadows (mentioned in the previous section), can be expensive with regard to performance.

Therefore, when designing your applications you should consider how many transitions you are applying to the visible application at one time or how quickly they are being applied.

Avoid Nested Transforms

As part of the power of Core Animation, it is possible to transform multiple layers that reside within each other. For example, you can have layers within layers all of which are transformed on their z-axis. However, it should be noted that these transforms are applied in real time and are not cached. Therefore when you move or animate a layer that has multiple levels of transforms, each transform needs to be recalculated for each frame of the animation.

To increase performance, avoid using multiple levels of transforms while your animations run.

Minimize Alpha Blending

Similar to the nested transforms discussed earlier, alpha blending is also calculated in real time. When a layer has partial transparency, that transparency is recalculated for every frame of an animation. Beware of this when animating layers that have transparency, and try to minimize the calculations as much as possible. Sliding layers behind other layers that are transparent can incur a large performance penalty.

Fortunately, there is an easy way to determine which layers have alpha blending and remove it. This is especially useful on the iPhone with its limited resources. To check for alpha blending, launch your application on the iPhone with Instruments running on the desktop. In Instruments, add the Core Animation instrument in addition to any others you want to use.

FIGURE 12-1   The Color Blended Layers Switch in Instruments

When your application runs on the iPhone and you have Instruments attached to it, to turn on the Color Blended Layers, switch in the Core Animation Instrument, as shown in Figure 12-1.

As soon as you enable this switch, you see an immediate effect on the iPhone. The entire iPhone screen turns either red or green. In fact, this switch can be turned on without any applications running, and you can see its effect on the home screen, as shown in Figure 12-2.

When enabled, the Color Blended Layers option colors the layers, so you can quickly identify the trouble spots in your app. Areas marked in green do not have any alpha blending, whereas areas marked in red do. The goal with this is to eliminate as much of the red as possible. For example, in the TransparentCocoaTouch application, you can see that all the UILabel objects have a transparent background, as shown in Figure 12-3.

FIGURE 12-2   Color Blended Layers Mode on the iPhone Springboard

FIGURE 12-3   iPhone Application with Color Blended Layers Mode Turned On

When you examine the code for these areas, you can see where the issue lies. Specifically, look at the -initWithFrame:reuseIdentifier: of the CustomTableViewCell object; this is where the trouble lies (see Listing 12-1).

LISTING 12-1   [CustomTableViewCell -initWithFrame:reuseIdentifier:]

```
- (id)initWithFrame:(CGRect)frame reuseIdentifier:(NSString*)ident
{
  if (!(self = [super initWithFrame:frame reuseIdentifier:ident])) return nil;

  UIView *contentView = [self contentView];

  imageView = [[UIImageView alloc] initWithFrame:CGRectMake(5, 5, 64, 64)];
  [imageView setContentMode:UIViewContentModeScaleAspectFit];
  [contentView addSubview:imageView];
  [imageView release];

  titleLabel = [[UILabel alloc] initWithFrame:CGRectZero];
  [titleLabel setFont:[UIFont boldSystemFontOfSize:14.0f]];
  [titleLabel setBackgroundColor:[UIColor clearColor]];
  [contentView addSubview:titleLabel];
  [titleLabel release];
```

LISTING 12-1   Continued

```
descriptionLabel = [[UILabel alloc] initWithFrame:CGRectZero];
[descriptionLabel setNumberOfLines:0];
[descriptionLabel setFont:[UIFont systemFontOfSize:6.0f]];
[descriptionLabel setBackgroundColor:[UIColor clearColor]];
[contentView addSubview:descriptionLabel];
[descriptionLabel release];

[[NSNotificationCenter defaultCenter] addObserver:self
                       selector:@selector(imageUpdated:)
                          name:kImageDownloadComplete
                        object:nil];


return self;
}
```

As you can see, the UILabel objects, titleLabel and descriptionLabel, both have their -backgroundColor set to [UIColor clearColor], causing an alpha blending to occur. To correct this, change that UIColor to be the same color as the background for the entire UITableViewCell. This eliminates the alpha blending and improves performance, as shown in Listing 12-2.

LISTING 12-2   Corrected [CustomTableViewCell -initWithFrame:reuseIdentifier:]

```
- (id)initWithFrame:(CGRect)frame reuseIdentifier:(NSString*)ident
{
  if (!(self = [super initWithFrame:frame reuseIdentifier:ident])) return nil;

  UIView *contentView = [self contentView];

  imageView = [[UIImageView alloc] initWithFrame:CGRectMake(5, 5, 64, 64)];
  [imageView setContentMode:UIViewContentModeScaleAspectFit];
  [contentView addSubview:imageView];
  [imageView release];

  titleLabel = [[UILabel alloc] initWithFrame:CGRectZero];
  [titleLabel setFont:[UIFont boldSystemFontOfSize:14.0f]];
  [titleLabel setBackgroundColor:[UIColor whiteColor]];
  [contentView addSubview:titleLabel];
  [titleLabel release];
```

LISTING 12-2   Continued

```
descriptionLabel = [[UILabel alloc] initWithFrame:CGRectZero];
[descriptionLabel setNumberOfLines:0];
[descriptionLabel setFont:[UIFont systemFontOfSize:6.0f]];
[descriptionLabel setBackgroundColor:[UIColor whiteColor]];
[contentView addSubview:descriptionLabel];
[descriptionLabel release];

[[NSNotificationCenter defaultCenter] addObserver:self
                              selector:@selector(imageUpdated:)
                                  name:kImageDownloadComplete
                                object:nil];

    return self;
}
```

Tiled Layers

Core Animation has a great feature that enables you to display and quickly view highly detailed images within your application. CATiledLayer is designed to display large images without having to load the entire image into memory and cause performance issues.

To demonstrate the usefulness of CATiledLayer, open the TiledLayers sample application that accompanies this chapter. In this application, a very large image (6064 × 4128) is loaded and the ability to zoom in and out of it is enabled. Normally, large images are loaded fully into memory before they are displayed, and that can cause a huge performance issue. However, by loading the image into a CATiledLayer, Core Animation handles all of the memory issues for us. Core Animation loads in only parts of the image as needed rather than pulling in the entire file. All you need to do to configure the CATiledLayer is to give it the levels of detail used to determine zoom levels, along with the tile size.

> **NOTE**
>
> CATiledLayer solves a number of problems that occur in both desktop development and iPhone development. Specifically it enables you to handle large images, multiresolution data, and handles on-demand loading automatically.

In the TiledLayers application, a single CATiledLayer is initialized in the main window and is assigned an NSSegmentedControl (via Interface Builder) to manage the levels of zoom. The resulting window is shown in Figure 12-4.

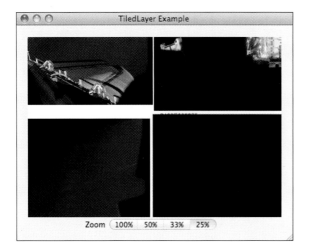

FIGURE 12-4   Tiled Layer Application

When the interface has been designed, construct the CATiledLayer in the -awakeFromNib method of the Application Delegate, as shown in Listing 12-3.

LISTING 12-3   -awakeFromNib

```
- (void)awakeFromNib
{
  NSString *imagePath = [[NSBundle mainBundle] pathForResource:@"BigSpaceImage"
                         ofType:@"png"];
  NSData *data = [NSData dataWithContentsOfFile:imagePath];
  image = [[CIImage imageWithData:data] retain];

  tiledLayer = [CATiledLayer layer];
  [tiledLayer setBounds:CGRectMake(0, 0, 6064, 4128)];
  float midX = NSMidX(NSRectFromCGRect([[view layer] frame]));
  float midY = NSMidY(NSRectFromCGRect([[view layer] frame]));
  [tiledLayer setPosition:CGPointMake(midX, midY)];
  [tiledLayer setLevelsOfDetail:4]; //number of levels
  [tiledLayer setTileSize:CGSizeMake(256, 256)];
  [tiledLayer setDelegate:self];

  [[view layer] addSublayer:tiledLayer];
}
```

When the app has the path to the image, the path is loaded into a CIImage call and stored for later use. CATiledLayer is initialized and applied to the bounds of the image that will be displayed. Next, the image is positioned within the root layer by setting its position and configuring the levels of available zoom. The last step is to assign the

AppDelegate as delegate for the layer so that we can receive events when drawing needs to occur.

NSSegmentedControl is bound to the -zoom: method, which sends an event every time the segmented control changes state. The index of the selected segment is used to determine the image's current scale before displaying the image within the CATiledLayer. This is accomplished by setting its sublayerTransform with a CATransform3DMakeScale call, passing in the *x* and *y* values based on the segmented control (see Listing 12-4).

12

LISTING 12-4   -zoom:

```
- (IBAction)zoom:(id)sender
{
    CGFloat zoom = 1.0 / ([sender selectedSegment] + 1);
    [[view layer] setSublayerTransform:CATransform3DMakeScale(zoom, zoom, 1.0)];
}
```

The final method you need to implement is a delegate of the CATiledLayer. This method enables us to override the layer's -drawInContext: method without having to subclass CALayer. In the default implementation of -drawInContext:, it looks for a delegate and checks to see if the delegate implements -drawLayer:inContext:. If both of those conditions are true, the -drawLayer:inContext: is called, as shown in Listing 12-5.

LISTING 12-5   -drawLayer:inContext:

```
- (void)drawLayer:(CALayer*)layer inContext:(CGContextRef)context
{
  [[CIContext contextWithCGContext:context options:nil] drawImage:image
atPoint:CGPointMake(0, 0) fromRect:CGRectMake(0, 0, 6064, 4128)];
}
```

This method uses the image initialized in -awakeFromNib and draws it into the context using the image size as the rectangle for drawing. It should be noted that you don't need to handle any form of zoom calculations, scaling, or transforms in this method. The CATiledLayer handles that automatically.

How Does This Work?

CATiledLayer loads images into tiles, hence the name. Each tile corresponds to a level of detail based on a tile size that you set. When you request a level of detail, CATiledLayer takes the original image, scales it to the desired size, and breaks it into individual tiles before drawing the tiles on-screen. Because these tiles are cached by CATiledLayer, you can scroll around the image and change levels of detail very quickly.

CATiledLayer caches only so many tiles at once, and when it hits that limit it starts dropping tiles out of the cache as needed. If we request that tile again in the future, it is generated again for our use. This means that tiles appear in an asynchronous manner as they are generated for us, and users see a delay as the tiles are generated and drawn in the layer. A great demonstration of this effect is the Google Maps application on iPhone, as shown in Figure 12-5. If you zoom out or zoom into a different level of tiles, the images that are not yet available display as a simple gray grid. As the tiles are loaded, they replace this grid with the actual information.

FIGURE 12-5   Google Maps Application on the iPhone

Multithreaded Animation

Core Animation is internally thread safe because it was designed with multicore systems in mind.

What this means in practical terms is that you can manipulate Core Animation layers on multiple threads without risk of corrupting its data internally and, equally important, that it does the right thing. However, the one area of Core Animation that is not necessarily thread safe is when it comes to accessing properties of a CALayer.

> **NOTE**
>
> **What Is a Lock?**
>
> A lock is when one object grabs the "access flag" to another object. Only a single object can have that access flag at a time when locks are engaged. Any subsequent object must wait until the flag is available before it can proceed to access the affected object.

If your application is accessing a property on its main thread and that same property gets accessed on a background thread at the same time, the results are undefined. It is possible that the change will not go through or that it could cause a crash deep within the Core Animation API or any other result. When you try to fetch a property and change it and then restore the property to its previous state, those actions should be wrapped in a lock to make them atomic, as shown in Listing 12-6.

> **NOTE**
>
> **What Does Atomic Mean?**
>
> Atomic is defined as consisting of a set of operations that can be combined so that they appear to the rest of the system to be a single operation with only two possible outcomes: success or failure.

LISTING 12-6   Locking Layer Changes

```
[layer lock]
float opacity = layer.opacity;
layer.opacity = opacity + .1;
[layer unlock];
```

In this example, a [CATransaction lock] is requested to prevent any other thread from obtaining the same lock, effectively blocking the other threads. This serializes access to the layer and its properties and guarantees that the accessed property won't change before you are done with it.

Care should be taken when working with layers on multiple threads for a couple reasons:

▶ Holding a lock too long can cause the user interface to stop drawing. Because access to that layer is blocked, you cannot access it on another thread, and other parts of the system also cannot access it until the lock is released. Remember, any time you lock a layer, you need to unlock it as quickly as possible.

▶ The second issue, which is inherit to all threading locks and not just Core Animation, is the contempt of *circular locks*. If you lock a layer with a thread and that layer needs access to another property locked by another thread waiting for access to the lock, that can cause the entire application to become unresponsive to user interaction, resulting in the eventual crash of that application.

> **NOTE**
>
> **What Is a Circular Lock?**
>
> A circular lock (or deadlock) is a situation wherein two or more competing threads are waiting for the other to finish, and thus neither ever does. This is illustrated in Figure 12-6.

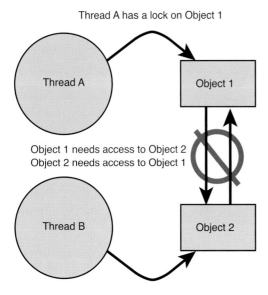

Thread A has a lock on Object 1

Object 1 needs access to Object 2
Object 2 needs access to Object 1

Thread B has a lock on Object 2

FIGURE 12-6   A Theoretical Circular Lock

Mutlithreading with Filters

Unlike Core Animation, Core Image filters are not thread safe. This means that you should only manipulate Core Image filters on a single thread. It is possible, however, to adjust a filter on more than one thread by using key-value coding (KVC) and key paths to manipulate the properties. For example, if you have a layer with a filter named *acme* and it has a property named *job*, you can adjust it with code similar to the following:

```
[layer setValue:myValue forKeyPath:@"layer.filters.acme.job"];
```

The layer would guarantee that the change is atomic and, therefore, thread safe.

Threads and Run Loops

When working with Core Animation on multiple threads, you need to be aware that any thread that calls -setNeedsDisplay on a layer is going to get the -display message as well. If you flag a layer as needing the display from a thread other than the main thread, you need to set up a run loop to ensure that the thread still runs when the -display call occurs. If you don't, the -display call never occurs because the thread it is looking for will have terminated, causing unexpected results.

Although it is possible to call -setNeedsDisplay from a thread other than the main thread, it is a lot of work for very little effect or benefit. It is highly recommended that these calls be localized to the main thread by utilizing -performSelectorOnMainThread:.

Summary

In this chapter, we walked through a lot of tips and tricks with regard to performance. As is always recommended when dealing with performance issues, finish the code first. Do not spend time optimizing the code for a "possible" bottleneck until that bottleneck is confirmed.

It is also highly recommended to test potential bottlenecks and have recordable results. Sometimes, a simple fps (frames per second) recording is sufficient to test the bottleneck. With recordable results, we can confirm that any performance changes were positive instead of being a no-op or, worse, having a negative impact.

12

CHAPTER 13

Core Animation on the iPhone

IN THIS CHAPTER

▶ The (Cold Hard) Facts About Core Animation on the iPhone

▶ Building a Core Animation Application for Cocoa Touch

▶ Core Animation and Cocoa Touch Example

▶ Doing Animations at the UIView Level

Until now, we discussed Core Animation as it exists on the desktop. However, Core Animation is also available as part of Cocoa Touch, which runs on the iPhone and iPod touch. When it comes to Cocoa Touch, Core Animation is a foundational part of the user interface for those devices. As the story goes, Core Animation was originally written for Cocoa Touch and then exported to Mac OS X Leopard and expanded for use in desktop applications. Considering how intertwined Core Animation is with the entire user interface, it certainly makes sense.

In this chapter, we walk through a few example projects that utilize Core Animation on Cocoa Touch. Each project demonstrates a different way to use Core Animation effectively.

As with the desktop version of Core Animation, there is no single right away to use the API. Core Animation is designed to be extremely flexible and useful in a variety of situations. With Core Animation developed originally for Cocoa Touch, it is even more flexible than its desktop counterpart.

The (Cold Hard) Facts About Core Animation on the iPhone

As noted in the introduction, Core Animation was originally developed for Cocoa Touch for the iPhone, and was originally known as Layer Kit. However, several features of Core Animation are not available, or at least not exposed, in the public APIs. Quite a few of the items listed in this section were not available in Cocoa Touch until the iPhone 3.0 SDK.

The Good

Core Animation is already "turned on" for every UIView in the user interface on Cocoa Touch. Although you still need to import the QuartzCore framework to get access to its header files, you do not need to implicitly turn on layers on any UIView element.

The Bad

Core Animation on Cocoa Touch is significantly limited compared to its desktop version. A number of the features that we expect on the desktop simply are not available (at this time) within Cocoa Touch. Many of the features listed here are currently unavailable in Cocoa Touch, but they might become available at a later date:

- ▶ **Borders** (*not available before 3.0*)
  Prior to the release of version 3.0 of the iPhone OS, borders were not public and, therefore, we could not access them. However, they are now fully available for our use. You can see a demonstration of them in Chapter 11, "User Interaction."

- ▶ **Corners** (*not available before 3.0*)
  As with borders, adjusting the corner radius is not available prior to 3.0.

- ▶ **Masks** (*not available before 3.0*)
  As with Borders and Corners, masks are not available before 3.0.

- ▶ **Shadows**
  Currently, there is no shadow support in Cocoa Touch. Whether this is a permanent situation is unknown; Apple hasn't used Shadows in its own applications. This might be due to the lack of Core Image filters in Cocoa Touch.

- ▶ **Layout Managers**
  At first glance, this one seems surprising. However, unlike its desktop cousin, the user interface of Cocoa Touch has exactly two sizes, 480 × 320 and 320 × 480. Therefore, a Layout Manager would be rather heavy for just those two situations.

- ▶ **Core Image**
  Core Image is currently not available for Cocoa Touch. Although the CALayer objects have the capability to accept filters, because of the lack of Core Image there are no filters that can be applied to layers. Therefore the filters property on CALayer objects is undefined.

> **NOTE**
>
> New features are being added and existing features are being exposed to the public with each release of Cocoa Touch and the iPhone SDK. If you are a registered iPhone developer (see *http://developer.apple.com/iphone*), you should receive an email whenever there is an update to the SDK.

▶ CATextLayer

At first, this one is as surprising as the missing layout managers. But as we discuss in greater detail, the UIView objects are fairly lightweight in themselves, and it is just as easy to use a UILabel in the place of a CATextLayer.

Some of these items that are lacking can be quite frustrating, whereas others would clearly be overkill on the device.

Building a Core Animation Application for Cocoa Touch

To demonstrate Core Animation on the iPhone, we write an application similar to the example we developed previously for the desktop in Chapter 5, "Layer Transforms." In that example, we used a UILabel and animated it in a star pattern. The end result of the project for this example is shown in Figure 13-1.

Setting Up the Xcode Project

Start this project by creating a new Cocoa Touch project within Xcode and select the Window-Based Application project template, as shown in Figure 13-2.

1. Launch Xcode and create a new project (Shift-⌘-N), and save it to ~/Documents/CAProjects. Name the project Star.

FIGURE 13-1   Star Label Animation Application

2. In Xcode, double-click the *MainMenu.xib* file to open it in Interface Builder.

3. From the Library panel, drag a Rounded Rect Button to the Window. In the Button Attributes panel, enter Draw in the Title field to give the button a label.

4. Next, go back to the Library panel and drag a Label to the Window. Using the alignment guides, align the Label at the top-center part of the Window.

5. In the Label Attributes panel, enter Star in the Title field. When you do so, you notice that the position of the word Star changes. To make this look a little better, click the center alignment button in the Layout section to center-align the word Star in the Window.

FIGURE 13-2　New Project Selection in Xcode

Building the UIWindow

This project template gives you the very bare bones of a structure and creates a nib for you to work with. After you create the project, the first thing you want to do is make a few changes to the nib. With the nib file open, you can see there is one Window, which is the delegate for the UIApplication (aptly named AppDelegate, or a variation thereof), and the File's Owner, which for the main nib is the UIApplication itself. As with all nib files, we have the conveyance First Responder object, as shown in Figure 13-3.

The first changes we want to make are to add a button and a label to the window. The button is a Rounded Rect Button from the library. Give it a title value of Draw. This button will be placed directly on the Window and centered at the bottom. The button can easily be centered by selecting the **Size** palette in Interface Builder and clicking on the center horizontal button.

The second addition is a UILabel object that needs to be centered near the top and given a title of Star. With this object, though, we want to use a little more precision for its alignment, so go to the Size Inspector and change its dimensions to 139 × 89, and its width to 42 with a height of 22, as shown in Figure 13-4.

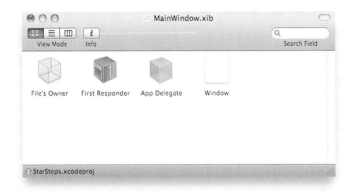

FIGURE 13-3   Main Nib

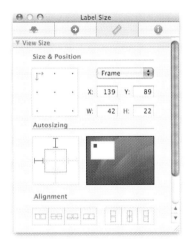

FIGURE 13-4   Change the Size Dimensions

The last change you want to make is to set the background color of the UIWindow itself to black and the text color of the label to white. The final result will look like Figure 13-5.

Adding the QuartzCore Framework and Binding the Objects

Back in Xcode, we need to add the QuartzCore framework to the project. To do this open the targets section in the source list; right-click on the target and select **Add > Existing Frameworks** in the context menu. In the sheet that opens to the Frameworks folder, scroll down and select **QuartzCore.framework;** then click the Add button. After the framework has been added to the project, you can compile against its headers without warnings. As with the desktop implementation, you either need to add #import <QuartzCore/CoreAnimation.h> to the top of each class or add it to the *Prefix.pch* file to insure it is included in all class files for the project.

FIGURE 13-5   Our Completed UIWindow

With the framework imported, the next step is to bind the objects that you added to the nib. Therefore, you want to add a UILabel and a UIButton property to the header of the application's delegate, aptly named StarStepsAppDelegate. You also want to add a method to serve as the action for the button when it is clicked. The resulting header file is shown in Listing 13-1.

LISTING 13-1   The Application Delegate Header

```
#import <QuartzCore/CoreAnimation.h>

@interface StarStepsAppDelegate : NSObject <UIApplicationDelegate>
{
  UIButton *drawButton;
  UIWindow *window;
  UILabel *textLabel;
}

@property (nonatomic, retain) IBOutlet UIWindow *window;
@property (nonatomic, retain) IBOutlet UIButton *drawButton;
@property (nonatomic, retain) IBOutlet UILabel *textLabel;


- (IBAction)drawStar:(id)sender;

@end
```

After the header is configured, the next step is to go back to Interface Builder and complete the bindings. You can do this by Control-dragging from the application delegate to the window, button, and label; binding each of these to their appropriate IBOutlets. Control-drag from the Star App Delegate to

▶ The background of the window, and select window from the Outlets pop-up.

▶ The UILabel, and select textLabel from the Outlets pop-up.

▶ The UIButton, and select drawButton from the Outlets pop-up.

When complete, Control-drag from the button back to the application's delegate and select the -drawStar: Events method. This causes the -drawStar: method to be invoked when the button is touched.

With the header complete it is time to begin the implementation details. Because the configuration settings for this application were handled in Interface Builder, the only thing that needs to be done to the -applicationDidFinishLaunching: (in the project's StarStepsAppDelegate) method is to bring the window to the front and make it the Key Responder, as shown in Listing 13-2.

LISTING 13-2   The -applicationDidFinishLaunching: Method

```
- (void)applicationDidFinishLaunching:(UIApplication *)application
{
  [window makeKeyAndVisible];
  [textLabel setCenter:CGPointMake(160.0f, 100.0f)];
}
```

Next, we need to implement the -drawStar: method shown in Listing 13-3, again in the StarStepsAppDelegate class. This method first disables the draw button (to avoid it being clicked multiple times during the animation) and then configures a CGPath for UILabel to follow. Finally, it applies that path to the UILabel using a CAKeyframeAnimation.

LISTING 13-3   The -drawStar: Implementation

```
- (IBAction)drawStar:(id)sender;
{
  NSLog(@"%@:%s fired", [self class], _cmd);
  [drawButton setEnabled:NO];
  CGMutablePathRef starPath = CGPathCreateMutable();
  CGPathMoveToPoint(starPath,NULL,160.0f, 100.0f);
  CGPathAddLineToPoint(starPath, NULL, 100.0f, 280.0f);
  CGPathAddLineToPoint(starPath, NULL, 260.0, 170.0);
  CGPathAddLineToPoint(starPath, NULL, 60.0, 170.0);
  CGPathAddLineToPoint(starPath, NULL, 220.0, 280.0);
  CGPathCloseSubpath(starPath);
```

LISTING 13-3   Continued

```
CAKeyframeAnimation *animation = nil;
  animation = [CAKeyframeAnimation animationWithKeyPath:@"position"];
  [animation setDuration:10.0f];
  [animation setDelegate:self];
[animation setPath:starPath];
CFRelease(starPath), starPath = nil;
[[textLabel layer] addAnimation:animation forKey:@"position"];
}
```

When implemented, this method makes the UILabel move in a star pattern, following the CGPath we defined. When the path has finished CAKeyframeAnimation notifies the application delegate (because it is also the animation's delegate) via the method in Listing 13-4.

LISTING 13-4   CAAnimation Delegate Method

```
- (void)animationDidStop:(CAAnimation *)theAnimation finished:(BOOL)flag
{
  [drawButton setEnabled:YES];
}
```

Adding the animationDidStop: method completes our work on the Star application. Running the application produces a black window with the button and label. Pressing the button causes the label to trace a star-shaped pattern on the screen. When the animation receives the callback, the button is reenabled so that the animation can be fired again.

Core Animation and Cocoa Touch Example

Another example of working with Core Animation on Cocoa Touch is integrating with the touch system. Unlike a key press or mouse event on a desktop computer, the touch system is designed for taps, drags, and multitouch events. This example focuses on touches and drags.

All UIView objects are capable of receiving touch events, but they are turned off by default. To enable touch events, call the -setUserInteractionEnabled: method on the UIView and pass the Boolean value of YES. After you do that, you begin receiving touch events that occur within the bounds of the view. There are four possible events that we can receive:

- ▶ touchesBegan
- ▶ touchesEnded
- ▶ touchesMoved
- ▶ touchesCancelled

Each of these events is rather self-explanatory, but there are a few points worth mentioning.

Because Cocoa Touch is designed as a multitouch system, it is possible to receive more than one UITouch event in any of the touches*XXX* methods. However, this occurs only if we specifically enable multitouch in our UIView. Multitouch is enabled via the -setMultipleTouchEnabled: method on the UIView and by passing the Boolean value of YES. Even with multitouch enabled, however, only touches that actually occur within the view's bounds will be passed to that view. Therefore, if the view is small enough, it is quite possible that an intended multitouch event will result in a single UITouch event being passed to the UIView.

Touch events occur in a specific order and never deviate from it. All touch event workflows start with a touchesBegan event and always end with either a touchesEnded or a touchesCancelled event. A single event flow (beginning with touchesBegan) never has both a touchesCancelled and a touchesEnded. It is possible to receive zero or more touchesMoved events between touchesBegan and the end of the flow. There is no limit to the number of touchesMoved events that a particular flow can receive; they are not timed events. As such, if a user touches the screen, moves her finger, pauses, and then moves it again, no events will be sent to the receiver during the pause period.

Finally, touch events—no matter how many actual touch points are involved—will be sent all at once. In other words, if we start with a single finger touching the screen, we get one touchesBegan. If a second finger is added, another touchesBegan event is sent for the second finger, but a UITouch event is included in that call for the first finger. If one or both fingers are moved, a single touchesMoved event is sent for both fingers. Each of the touches*XXX* methods pass in NSSet to the receiving class. This NSSet contains one or more UITouch objects that describe the current state of that touch event. An NSSet is used as the order of these events has no value, and you should not assume that a UITouch event set will be passed in any specific order.

Setting Up the Xcode Project

In this example, we present users with a single box on the screen represented by a UIView object. When the users tap on the box, it rotates through a set number of colors. If they touch and drag the box, it follows their finger around on the screen. This demonstrates how to determine the difference between a tap and a drag, and how to animate the reaction to a user touching the screen. We also make it so the box transforms slightly in response to the action when the user taps on the box.

For this project, we begin with a window-based template, as shown in Figure 13-6. This template provides us with just a window without any type of navigational aid. Within this project we create two additional classes: TouchMeViewController and

NOTE

We recommend running the finished project in the iPhone Simulator to see how it works and reacts before following along with how to build the application.

TouchableView. The application's delegate instantiates a TouchMeViewController and adds it as a subview to the window that is constructed in the MainWindow xib file. The TouchMeViewController itself instantiates a TouchableView and adds it to its main view. Because it receives the touch events, TouchableView is the focus of this example.

FIGURE 13-6   Start with a Window-Based Project

Building the TouchMeViewController

The TouchMeViewController is a subclass of the UIViewController and does not require any protocol implementations. Therefore, the implementation file only has the -init and -loadView methods, as shown in Listing 13-5.

LISTING 13-5   TouchMeViewController.m Implementation

```
- (id)init
{
  if (![super init]) return nil;
  return self;
}
```

LISTING 13-5   Continued

```
- (void)loadView
{
  CGRect frame = [[UIScreen mainScreen] applicationFrame];
  UIView *view = [[UIView alloc] initWithFrame:frame];
  [view setBackgroundColor:[UIColor blackColor]];

  CGRect box = CGRectMake(10, 10, 100, 100);
  touchView = [[TouchableView alloc] initWithFrame:box];
  [view addSubview:touchView];
  [touchView release];

  [self setView:view];
  [view release];
}
```

In the TouchMeViewController we build only a single UIView and add the TouchableView to it. No other implementation is required. That view is added to the UIWindow for the application. To do this, we need to update the application delegate's header, as shown in Listing 13-6.

LISTING 13-6   Application Delegate's Header

```
@class TouchMeViewController;

@interface AppDelegate : NSObject <UIApplicationDelegate>
{
  UIWindow *window;
  TouchMeViewController *viewController;
}

@end
```

We have added a reference to the TouchMeViewController in the application delegate's header so that we can release it at the appropriate time. With the header updated, we next need to update the -applicationDidFinishLaunching: method to instantiate the TouchMeViewController. When the TouchMeViewController is instantiated, add its associated view to the window, as shown in Listing 13-7.

LISTING 13-7   Application Delegate's Implementation

```
- (void)applicationDidFinishLaunching:(UIApplication *)application
{
  window = [[UIWindow alloc] initWithFrame:[[UIScreen mainScreen] bounds]];
```

LISTING 13-7   Continued

```
  viewController = [[TouchMeViewController alloc] init];

  [window addSubview:[viewController view]];
  [window makeKeyAndVisible];
}

- (void)dealloc
{
  [viewController release];
  [window release];
  [super dealloc];
}
```

The only reason we hang onto the `TouchMeViewController` reference is to allow its later release with the `dealloc` method. All the control in this example is handled directly in the `UIView` subclass implemented in the next section.

Implementing the TouchableView

Although the `touchesXXX` methods are stateful, they do not pass us stateful information. Therefore we need to keep track of the current state of the touches. We need to keep track of both where the touch began at and where the last move update was. This enables us to move the square if the move is sufficient to justify it, and also enables us to test for a tap as opposed to an actual move. To keep all this stateful information, we need to implement the header, as shown in Listing 13-8.

LISTING 13-8   TouchableView Header

```
@interface TouchableView : UIView
{
  CGPoint touchBeganPoint;
  CGPoint lastUpdatedPoint;
  NSArray *colorArray;
  NSInteger colorIndex;
}

@end
```

In addition to the beginning touch point and the last updated point, we also keep track the currently displayed color and the full array of colors that the view can rotate through. There are a number of things we need to set up in the view's subclass, the first of which is to override the superclass's `-initWithFrame:` method, as shown in Listing 13-9.

LISTING 13-9   TouchableView -initWithFrame: Implementation

```
- (id)initWithFrame:(CGRect)frame
{
  if (!(self = [super initWithFrame:frame])) return nil;

  colorArray = [[NSArray alloc] initWithObjects:[UIColor greenColor],
               [UIColor blueColor], [UIColor redColor], nil];
  colorIndex = 0;
  [self setBackgroundColor:[colorArray objectAtIndex:colorIndex]];

  touchBeganPoint = CGPointZero;
  [self setUserInteractionEnabled:YES];
  return self;
}
```

After calling the super's initWithFrame, build the color array for the view to rotate through and set the initial colorIndex to zero. Next, set the view's backgroundColor based on that index, and then set the userInteractionEnabled to YES so that the application can receive single touch events.

With touch events enabled, we need to implement all the touch methods to receive those events. The first one is -touchesBegan: withEvent:, as shown in Listing 13-10.

LISTING 13-10   -touchesBegain:withEvent: Implementation

```
- (void)touchesBegan:(NSSet *)touches withEvent:(UIEvent *)event
{
  UITouch *beginTouch = [touches anyObject];
  touchBeganPoint = [beginTouch locationInView:[self window]];
  lastUpdatedPoint = [beginTouch locationInView:[self window]];
}
```

This method records the location of the beginning touch with touchBeganPoint and sets the lastUpdatedPoint to the same location. We grab any of the touches from the set because we are configured only for single touch events, so it is irrelevant as to which touch we get.

Now that the touch workflow is set, we need to wait for the next event before we can perform any action. One of three possible methods will be called, the easiest of which to implement is the -touchesCancelled:withEvent:, as shown in Listing 13-11.

LISTING 13-11   -touchesCancelled:withEvent: Implementation

```
- (void)touchesCancelled:(NSSet *)touches withEvent:(UIEvent *)event
{
  touchBeganPoint = CGPointZero;
  lastUpdatedPoint = CGPointZero;
}
```

A cancel event occurs only when something interrupts the application. For example, this might happen when there is an incoming SMS message, phone call, or some other external event on the iPhone. As such, don't treat a cancel as a failure but as an opportunity to reset the state.

If the event is not canceled, you can send either of the following two methods next: -touchesEnded:withEvent: or -touchesMoved:withEvent:. For this application, we implement -touchesEnded:withEvent:, as shown in Listing 13-12.

LISTING 13-12   -touchesEnded:withEvent: Implementation

```
- (void)touchesEnded:(NSSet *)touches withEvent:(UIEvent *)event
{
  CGPoint touchPoint = [[touches anyObject] locationInView:[self window]];
  float deltaX = touchPoint.x - touchBeganPoint.x;
  float deltaY = touchPoint.y - touchBeganPoint.y;
  touchBeganPoint = CGPointZero;
  lastUpdatedPoint = CGPointZero;

  touchBeganPoint = CGPointZero;
  lastUpdatedPoint = CGPointZero;
  if (deltaX > MAX_TAP_DELTA && deltaY > MAX_TAP_DELTA) {
    return;
  }

  ++colorIndex;
  if (colorIndex >= [colorArray count]) colorIndex = 0;

  CGColorRef color = [[colorArray objectAtIndex:colorIndex] CGColor];

  [UIView beginAnimations:nil context:NULL];
  [UIView setAnimationDelegate:self];
  [UIView setAnimationDuration:0.15f];

  [UIView setAnimationDidStopSelector:@selector(throbReset:context:)];
  [self setTransform:CGAffineTransformMakeScale(1.4, 1.4)];
```

LISTING 13-12   Continued

```
[[self layer] setBackgroundColor:color];

[UIView commitAnimations];
}
```

Using this method, we first determine the delta of the current UITouch based on the touchBeganPoint. If the *x* or *y* delta is greater than the tap threshold, the touch is treated as the end of a move and resets the state. If the touch is within the tap threshold, however, we need to change the background color of the view and cause it to throb for visual feedback.

After rotating the color index and grabbing a reference for the next color, we begin an animation block. This tells the iPhone OS that all the property changes within this block should be performed together as a single animation transaction. We then set ourselves as the delegate for the animation. Because we want the transform to reverse, we need to add another transform to the delegate call. This enables us to reset the scale back to normal after the initial zoom as completed.

After setting the delegate, we give it an @selector to call back on when the animation is complete. Finally, we apply the grow transform, set the background color, and commit the animations. This now causes the view to expand by 40 percent and change its background color in a smooth animation. After this animation block is complete, we need to apply another transform with the -throbReset: context: method to undo the grow transform, as shown in Listing 13-13.

LISTING 13-13   -throbAnimationDidStop:finished:context: Implementation

```
- (void)throbReset:(NSString*)animationID
          context:(void*)context
{
  [UIView beginAnimations:nil context:NULL];
  [UIView setAnimationDuration:0.15];
  [self setTransform:CGAffineTransformMakeScale(1.1, 1.1)];
  [UIView commitAnimations];
}
```

Another animation block is created within this method. Its duration is set to be the same as the previous animation, and it applies another transform to the view to reduce its size back down before committing the animation.

Finally, we need to implement the -touchesMoved:withEvents: method, which is responsible for animating the view's move and for updating the state information so any subsequent moves are handled correctly. See Listing 13-14.

LISTING 13-14   -touchesMoved:withEvents: Implementation

```
- (void)touchesMoved:(NSSet *)touches withEvent:(UIEvent *)event
{
    [UIView beginAnimations:nil context:NULL];
    CGPoint touchPoint = [[touches anyObject] locationInView:[self window]];
    float deltaX = touchPoint.x - lastUpdatedPoint.x;
    float deltaY = touchPoint.y - lastUpdatedPoint.y;

    float newCenterX = [[self layer] position].x + deltaX;
    float newCenterY = [[self layer] position].y + deltaY;

    CGPoint center = CGPointMake(newCenterX, newCenterY);
    [[self layer] setPosition:center];
    lastUpdatedPoint = touchPoint;
    [UIView commitAnimations];
}
```

This method begins an animation block that properly moves the animation. The delta of the move is calculated based on the lastUpdatedPoint; that delta is then applied to the view's center. Because the frame is a derived value for UIView objects, you need to change the center instead of the frame if you want to animate the action. If you tried to animate the frame, the change would occur, but it wouldn't animate because the call from the -setFrame: to the -setCenter: isn't part of the animation block.

After the center of the view's layer is updated, you can update the state information for the next move (or end/cancel) and call and commit the animations.

With the -touchesMoved:withEvent: method fully implemented, you have completed work on the sample application. When you run the app, you can see that a tap on the screen invokes a color change to the view if that tap is within the view's bounds, and a drag of the view causes it to move in parallel to the touch. The resulting application is shown in Figure 13-7.

We implemented a few different animations in this section, some of which are

FIGURE 13-7   The Completed TouchMe Application

discussed in greater detail in the next section. What we have seen in this demonstration is that we can smoothly move elements around the screen by utilizing Core Animation and creating some impressive effects with only a few lines of code.

The techniques in this section, along with high quality graphics, can be used to create dazzling custom user interface elements that behave in any manner you choose.

Doing Animations at the UIView Level

In addition to manipulating the Core Animation layers directly, we can also apply a less aggressive design to our animations. There are numerous situations in which we want to provide some animation in a user interface, but it is overkill to build up a `CABasicAnimation` just to provide a simple animation.

Fortunately, there is another way to do just that. The desktop has a way to perform simple implicit animations by calling `-animator` on any object that can handle it. On Cocoa Touch it is a bit different and is handled by class methods on the `UIView` class.

In this example, we build a Cocoa Touch application that presents the user with an image and a button. When the button is pressed, the image bounces three times on the screen. While the image is bouncing, the button hides. You can download the example project and run it in the simulator. The final application is shown in Figure 13-8.

FIGURE 13-8   The Completed Application

Building the Application

For this example, we start with the view-based template from Xcode. From the template, open the main view controller and add two items. This example uses an image from the Xcode Tools examples, along with a `UIButton` that was added to the view. The result is shown in Figure 13-9.

Building the View Controller

The next step in the application is to add the logic to the view controller. In the sample application included with this chapter, the view controller we are editing is named *MainViewController.m*. Depending on the version of Xcode you run, the generated name from the template might be different.

FIGURE 13-9   The Completed View in Interface Builder

In the header for the controller, we add IBOutlet references for the UIImageView and for the UIButton. We use properties to make it clear that both of these are assignments and do not need to be released. The header is shown in Listing 13-15.

LISTING 13-15   MainViewController.m Header

```
@interface MainViewController : UIViewController
{
  UIImageView *animImageView;
  UIButton *button;
}

@property (assign) IBOutlet UIImageView *animImageView;
@property (assign) IBOutlet UIButton *button;

- (IBAction)action:(id)sender;

@end
```

In addition to the IBOutlet references, we have added a -action: method call to IBAction, which is called when the user presses the button on the view.

The implementation file is also quite sparse. Because we do not retain anything, we do not need a -dealloc method. Likewise, because the controller is named the same as the xib file, the controller does not need an -init method. Therefore, the controller needs methods to handle only the user pressing the button and a method to be called when the animation completes. Start by implementing the -action: method, as shown in Listing 13-16.

LISTING 13-16   MainViewController.m -action: Implementation

```
- (IBAction)action:(id)sender;
{
  [UIView beginAnimations:@"Hide Button" context:nil];
  [[self button] setAlpha:0.0];
  [UIView commitAnimations];

  [UIView beginAnimations:@"Slide Around" context:nil];

  [UIView setAnimationDuration:1.0];
  [UIView setAnimationDelegate:self];
  [UIView setAnimationDidStopSelector:@selector(viewAnimationDone:)];
  [UIView setAnimationRepeatCount:3];
  [UIView setAnimationRepeatAutoreverses:YES];

  CGPoint center = [[self animImageView] center];
  center.y += 100;

  [[self animImageView] setCenter:center];

  [UIView commitAnimations];
}
```

This method implements two separate animations. The first fades the button out of view, and the second moves the UIImageView up and down within its parent.

To perform an animation at the UIView level, we need to first call +beginAnimations: context: on the UIView class. This tells the view that all the calls following it are to be animated if possible. This continues until +commitAnimations is called on the UIView.

In the first animation, we have one call within the begin and commit calls, and that sets the alpha value of the UIView to 0.0, leaving the duration of the animation set to default.

The second animation is quite a bit more complicated. Because we want the bounce to be slower than the default animation, we first set the duration by calling +setAnimationDuration: and passing it a value of 1.0. Next, set the view controller as the delegate for the animation so that it can be notified when the animation is complete. We also set the `animationDidStopSelector` so that the animation has a method to call upon completion.

Next, because we want the animation to repeat, set the `animationRepeatCount` to 3 and set the `animationRepeatAutoreverses` to YES. This gives the illusion of the image bouncing three times.

The last setting to perform is actually moving the image. First grab the current center point of the `UIImageView` and then increase the y by 100 pixels. Then set that adjusted `CGPoint` back as the new center for the `UIImageView` and commit the animation.

When the animation is complete, the same animation is performed on the button, except in reverse, by setting its alpha value to 1.0. The implementation of this method is shown in Listing 13-17.

LISTING 13-17   MainViewController.m -action: Implementation

```
- (void)viewAnimationDone:(NSString*)name
{
  [UIView beginAnimations:@"Show Button" context:nil];
  [[self button] setAlpha:1.0];
  [UIView commitAnimations];
}
```

The end result is a fairly convincing bounce of the image view. This same technique can be used to slide an element onto the view, cause things to fade in and out, or create virtually any other animation that acts on the animatable properties of a view.

Summary

Using Core Animation in Cocoa Touch is similar to the Desktop, and most of the techniques that we learned throughout this book can be used interchangeably. The primary issue we need to be concerned with in Cocoa Touch is performance. The current devices that run Cocoa Touch are significantly less powerful than any modern desktop computer, and it is much easier to overload them with animations, resulting in poor performance.

Index

A

–acceptsFirstResponder method, 189

–actionForLayer: method, 31

–action: method, 225-226

–addAnimation: method, 9

adding

blur animation to mouseDown events, 89

close box, 61-62

filters to Core animation layers, 84

Gaussian Blur Filter to layers, 84

–addSublayer method, 162

allocating layers, 35-36

alpha blending, 196-199

anchor points, 74-75

animation

adding animation to layers, 9

adding list of animations to layer, 41-42

animator proxy object, 28

applied filters, 85-89

attribute animation, 18

basic animation to keyframe animation, 50

CABasicAnimation object, 40-41

Cartesian coordinate system, 3-4

color animation, 16-17

content animation, 19-20

design principles, 22

disabling, 31

filter animation, 19

grouping, 41-44

on iPhone. See iPhone, Core Animation on

layer animation

   animating layer positions, 36-37

   animating versus setting layer properties, 37-38

   implicit layer animation, 38-39

   visual stickiness, 39-40

layers, resizing, 31-32

masking animation, 20-21

monitoring progress of, 52

motion animation, 17-18

multithreaded animation, 202

   with filters, 204

   locking layer changes, 203

   threads and run loops, 204

overlays, 118-119

pacing, 9-10

projects

   application delegate class, 12, 33

   creating Xcode projects, 33-34

   setting up Xcode projects for OS X, 12-13

removing from layers, 9

simple animations, 27-28

Star Label Animation. See Star Label Animation application

time codes, 119-121

at UIView level

   building application, 223

   MainViewController, 223-226

views, resizing, 30

visibility field animation, 18

what not to animate, 23-24

when to use Core Animation, 23

windows, resizing, 28-29

–animationDidStop: method, 214

animator proxy object, 28

AppDelegate, 12, 33

   –awakeFromNib method, 183-184

   –buttonLayerHit method, 184

   for filter slider, 96-98

   for ripple transition

      AppDelegate implementation with delegation, 106-109

      AppDelegate implementation with encapsulation, 105-106

–applicationDidFinishLaunching: method, 70, 76-77, 173, 213, 217

applied filters, animating, 85-89

atomic operations, 203

attributes, animating, 18

–autoplay method, 112

Autoreverses property (CABasicAnimation class), 40

–awakeFromNib method, 34, 113, 118-120, 126, 142-143, 153-154, 183-184, 200

B

background color, animating from red to green, 16-17

background threads, 5

–backgroundColorAnimation method, 17

basic animation, 50

beginTime property, 41-42

binding objects in Star Label Animation application, 211-214

–animationDidStop: method, 214

–applicationDidFinishLaunching: method, 213

–drawStar: method, 213

StarStepsAppDelegate interface, 212

blur animation, adding to mouseDown events, 89

BlurView objects, initializing, 88

–buttonLayerHit method, 184-185

C

CAAnimation object, 9

CABasicAnimation class

  animating layer positions, 36-37

  animating versus setting layer properties, 37-38

  animation grouping, 41-44

  implicit layer animation and default timing function, 38-39

  properties, 40-41

  visual stickiness, 39-40

CAEAGLLayer class, 7

CAGradientLayer class, 8, 168-171

CALayer class, 5-6

  hit testing CALayer objects, 177-179

–canDrawInCGLContext method, 132-135, 159-160

CAOpenGLLayer class, 5

  overview, 5-7, 131

  and Quartz Composition layer, 159-160

  rendering multiple video channels, 138-139

    OpenGLVidGridLayer, 139-148

    VideoChannel, 139

    VideoChannelController, 139

  rendering video in, 131-132

    advantages, 138

    –canDrawInCGLContext method, 132-135, 159-160

    display link callback signature, 133

    display links, 133

    –drawInCGLContext: method, 132, 136-137

    implementation of QuickTime visual context, 135-136

    layer timing, 133-138

capture sessions, initializing, 124-125

–captureOutput: method, 127

capturing current image, 127-129

CAReplicatorLayer class, 8

  adding ReplicatorView to window, 173-174

  creating ReplicatorView, 171-173

  properties, 171

Cartesian coordinate system, 3-4

CAScrollLayer class, 7

CAShapeLayer class, 8

  adding to layer tree, 161-163

  as layer mask, 165-167

  initializing, 161-163

  path stroke manipulations, 163-165

CATextLayer class, 7

CATiledLayer class, 7, 199-202

CATransaction class, 31-32

CATransform3DMakeRotation method, 73-74

CATransform3DMakeScale method, 72

centering layers, 35

central processing unit (CPU), 193

CGImageRed, obtaining image data as, 157

–channelsReadyToDraw: function, 144

circular locks, 203-204

classes

AppDelegate, 12, 33

–awakeFromNib method, 183-184

–buttonLayerHit method, 184

for filter slider, 96-98

for ripple transition, 105-109

CABasicAnimation

animating layer positions, 36-37

animating versus setting layer properties, 37-38

animation grouping, 41-44

implicit layer animation and default timing function, 38-39

properties, 40-41

visual stickiness, 39-40

CAEAGLLayer, 7

CAGradientLayer, 8, 168-171

CALayer, 5-6

hit testing CALayer objects, 177-179

CAOpenGLLayer

overview, 5-7, 131

rendering multiple video channels, 138-148

rendering video in, 131-138

layer timing, 133-138

CAReplicatorLayer, 8

adding ReplicatorView to window, 173-174

creating ReplicatorView, 171-173

properties, 171

CAScrollLayer, 7

CAShapeLayer, 8

adding to layer tree, 161-163

initializing, 161-163

as layer mask, 165-167

path stroke manipulations, 163-165

CATextLayer, 7

CATiledLayer, 7, 199-202

CATransaction, 31-32

LZButton, 181-182

LZButtonLayer, 179-182

LZContentView, 178

MainViewController, 223-226

–action: implementation method, 225-226

header, 224

OpenGLVidGridLayer, 139-148

–channelsReadyToDraw: function, 144

–drawAllInRect: function, 146

–drawChannel: function, 147-148

implementation of drawing functions, 143-144

initialization code, 140-142

initializing in AppDelegate, 142-143

–readyToDrawNextFrame: function, 145

QCCompositionLayer, 7, 153-154

QCQuartzCompositionLayer, 159-160

QTCaptureLayer, 7, 123

creating and displaying, 125-127

current image, capturing, 127-129

initializing capture session, 124-125

QTMovieLayer

action methods, 112

contentsRect, 122-123

overlays, 118-119

overview, 7, 111-112

QTMovieLayer–based player, 112-118

time codes, 119-121

ReplicatorView

adding to window, 173-174

creating, 171-173

TouchableView, 218-223

header, 218

–initWithFrame: method, 219

–throbAnimationDidStop:finished:context: method, 221

–touchBegan:withEvent: method, 219

–touchesCancelled:withEvent: method, 220

–touchesEnded:withEvent: method, 220-221

–touchesMoved:withEvent: method, 222

TouchMeViewController, 216-218

Application Delegate's header, 217

Application Delegate's method, 217

TouchMeViewController.m method, 216

VideoChannel, 139

VideoChannelController, 139

Cocoa Touch, Core Animation on

animations at UIView level

building application, 223

MainViewController, 223-226

benefits, 208

limitations, 208-209

overview, 207

Star Label Animation application

QuartzCore framework and object binding, 211-214

setting up Xcode project, 209

UIWindow, 210-211

Xcode project setup, 209

touch system application

overview, 214-215

TouchableView, 218-223

TouchMeViewController, 216-218

Xcode project setup, 215-216

transforms in, 69

color animation

animating background color from red to green, 16-17

Color Changer sample application

–awakeFromNib method, 183-184

–buttonLayerHit method, 184-185

–hitTest: method, 185

Interface Builder, 182

LZButtonLayer, 179-182

–mouseDown: method, 185-187

–mouseEntered: method, 187

–mouseExited: method, 187

–mouseUp: method, 186-188

combining transforms, 76-79

compositions (Quartz Composer)

adding filters to, 156

creating, 150-152

getting image data from, 155-156

input parameters, 152

passing parameters to, 154-155

constants, kCAFillModeForwards, 40

containers, NSAnimatablePropertyContainer, 28

content, animating, 19-20

contents property, 19

contentsRect property, 19, 122-123

control buttons, adding to Movie Player with
   Overlay project, 113-115

controllers
   MainViewController, 223-226
      –action: implementation, 225-226
      header, 224
   TouchMeViewController, 216-218
      Application Delegate's header, 217
      Application Delegate's
         implementation, 217
      TouchMeViewController.m
         implementation, 216
   VideoChannelController, 139

controlling filter values with data bindings,
   92-98

coordinate system, 3-4

Core Animation layers, adding filters to, 84

Core Graphics path, specifying, 46

Core Image filters, 83

CPU (central processing unit), 193

current image, capturing, 127-129

custom transitions, 101-108
   delegating, 101-102
   encapsulating, 101-102
   Ripple transition, 102-106
      AppDelegate implementation with
         delegation, 106-109
      AppDelegate implementation with
         encapsulation, 105-106
      RippleLayer interface, 104-105

D

Dashboard effect, 10

data bindings, controlling filter values, 92-98

deepest layer, 185

default timing function, 38-39

default transitions, 98-100

–defaultActionForKey: method, 102

delegating custom transitions, 101-102,
   106-109

design elements, 23

design principles, 22

disabling animation, 31

display links
   callback signature, 133
   definition of, 133

–doItIn: method, 11

–doTransition method, 109

–drawAllInRect: function, 146

–drawChannel: function, 147-148

–drawInCGLContext method, 159-160

–drawInCGLContext: method, 132, 136-137

–drawInContext: method, 195

–drawLayer: method, 201

–drawStar: method, 213

dreadlocks, 203-204

Duration property (CABasicAnimation class), 40

E

Edit Mode (iPhone/iPod Touch), 56

encapsulating custom transitions, 101-102,
   105-106

events

keyboard events, 188-190

mouse events

Color Changer sample application, 179-188

hit testing CALayer objects, 177-179

overview, 177

F

Fade transitions, 99

filters

adding to Core animation layers, 84

adding to Quartz Compositions, 156

animating, 19

applied filters, 85-89

controlling values with data binding, 92-98

key paths, 95

multithreading with, 204

performance issues, 195

"sticky" effect, 91-92

transitions

custom transitions, 101-108

default transitions, 98-100

user input, receiving, 89-90

–filters method, 94-95

frameOrigin property, 30

frameSize property, 30

From Bottom transitions, 99

From Left transitions, 99

From Right transitions, 99

From Top transitions, 99

functions. *See* methods

G

Gaussian Blur Filter, 84

–getCurrentImage method, 127-128

–getDotScreenImage: method, 157

–gotoBeginning method, 112

–gotoEnd method, 112

–gotoNextSelectionPoint method, 112

–gotoPosterFrame method, 112

–gotoPreviousSelectionPoint method, 112

–grabImage: method, 128

gradient layer. *See* CAGradientLayer class

graphic artists, 22

graphics processing unit (GPU), 194

green background color, animating, 16-17

group animation, 41-44

H

hardware acceleration, 193-194

HIG (Human Interface Guidelines), 22

hit testing CALayer objects, 177-179

–hitTest: method, 179, 185

Human Interface Guidelines (HIG), 22

I

–(IBAction)action:(id)sender method, 77-79

Icon Dance application, 58, 65

icon shaking, implementing with keyframe animation, 57-61

    close box, adding, 61-62

    rotation axis and layer geometry, 61

    starting/stopping, 64-65

images

    capturing current image, 127-129

    as layer content, 63

    reflection, applying with CAGradientLayer class, 168-171

implicit layer animation, 38-39

–init method, 181

–initCaptureSession method, 124-125

initializing CAShapeLayer, 161-163

–initVideoChannels method, 140-142

–initWithFrame: method, 172, 219

–initWithFrame:reuseIdentifier: method, 197-199

interaction

    keyboard events, 188-190

    layer–backed views, 190

    mouse events

        Color Changer sample application, 179-188

        hit testing CALayer objects, 177-179

        overview, 177

Interface Builder for Color Changer sample application, 182

interfaces

    RippleLayer, 104-105

    StarStepsAppDelegate, 212

interpolation, 46

iPhone, Core Animation on, 11

    animations at UIView level

        building application, 223

        MainViewController, 223-226

    benefits, 208

    Edit Mode, 56

    Icon Dance application, 65

    keyframe steps animation, 56

    limitations, 208-209

    nondeletable applications, 57

    overview, 207

    Star Label Animation application

        QuartzCore framework and object binding, 211-214

        setting up Xcode project, 209

        UIWindow, 210-211

        Xcode project setup, 209

    touch system application

        overview, 214-215

        TouchableView, 218-223

        TouchMeViewController, 216-218

        Xcode project setup, 215-216

iPod Touch

    Edit Mode, 56

    nondeletable applications, 57

ivars, 86

J-K

kCAFillModeForwards constant, 40

kCAMediaTimingFunctionEaseInEaseOut method, 39

kCATransitionFade constant, 99

kCATransitionFromBottom constant, 99

kCATransitionFromLeft constant, 99

kCATransitionFromRight constant, 99

kCATransitionFromTop constant, 99

kCATransitionMoveIn constant, 99

kCATransitionPush constant, 99

kCATransitionReveal constant, 99

key paths (filter), 95

key times, 51

key–value coding (KVC), 86

keyboard events, 188-190

keyframe animation, 45-50

    from basic animation, 50

    implementing icon shake, 57-65

    interpolation, 46

    monitoring keyframe destinations, 52-56

    steps for iPhone, 56

    timing, 50-51

    UI, 56-57

keyframe destinations

    methods to, 46-49

    monitoring, 52-56

    path animation, 47

keypaths, KVC (key–value coding), 86

keywords, @synthesize, 93

KVC (key–value coding), 86

L

layerClass method, overriding, 172

layers

    adding animation to, 9

    adding list of animations to, 41-42

    adding to root layer, 34-35

alpha blending, 196-199

animation

    animating layer positions, 36-37

    animating versus setting layer properties, 37-38

    animation pacing, 9-10

    implicit layer animation and default timing function, 38-39

    visual stickiness, 39-40

CAEAGLLayer, 7

CAGradientLayer, 8, 168-171

CALayer, 5-6

    hit testing CALayer objects, 177-179

CAOpenGLLayer

    overview, 5-7, 131

    rendering multiple video channels, 138-148

    rendering video in, 131-138

    layer timing, 133-138

CAReplicatorLayer, 8

    adding ReplicatorView to window, 173-174

    creating ReplicatorView, 171-173

    properties, 171

CAScrollLayer, 7

CAShapeLayer, 8

    adding to layer tree, 161-163

    initializing, 161-163

    as layer mask, 165-167

    path stroke manipulations, 163-165

CATextLayer, 7

CATiledLayer, 7, 199-202

centering, 35

content, 63

deepest layer, 185

definition of, 5-6

Gaussian Blur Filter, 84

layer allocation considerations, 35-36

layer–backed views, 190

locking layer changes, 203

LZButtonLayer, 179-182

masks, CAShapeLayer as, 165-167

OpenGLVidGridLayer, 139-148

  –channelsReadyToDraw: function, 144

  –drawAllInRect: function, 146

  –drawChannel: function, 147-148

  implementation of drawing functions,
    143-144

  initialization code, 140-142

  initializing in AppDelegate, 142-143

  –readyToDrawNextFrame: function, 145

properties, 37-38

purpose of, 8

QCCompositionLayer

  adding to window, 153-154

QCCompositionLayer class, 7

QTCaptureLayer, 7, 123

  creating and displaying, 125-127

  current image, capturing, 127-129

  initializing capture session, 124-125

QTMovieLayer

  action methods, 112

  contentsRect, 122-123

  overlays, 118-119

  overview, 7, 111-112

  QTMovieLayer–based player, 112-118

  time codes, 119-121

removing animation from, 9

resizing, 31-32

rotating

  along one axis, 72-73

  along two axes, 73-74

  magnitude of rotation, 73

scaling, 10-11, 70-72

shake animation, 61

tiled layers, 199-202

transforms

  anchor points, 74-75

  in Cocoa Touch, 69

  combining, 76-79

  definition of, 69

  –rotate3DTransform:, 73-74

  –rotateTransform:, 72-73

  scale versus bounds, 79-80

  –scaleTransform:, 70-72

locking layer changes, 203

LZButton class, 181-182

LZButtonLayer class, 179-182

LZContentView class, 178

M

macro patches, 157

magnitude of rotation, 73

MainViewController class, 223-226

mask property, 21

masking fields, animating, 20-21

masks, CAShapeLayer as, 165-167

masksToBounds property, 21

methods

–acceptsFirstResponder method, 189

–actionForLayer:, 31

–action:, 225-226

–addAnimation:, 9

–addSublayer, 162

–animationDidStop:, 214

–applicationDidFinishLaunching:, 70, 76-77, 173, 213, 217

–autoplay method, 112

–awakeFromNib, 34, 113, 118-120, 126, 142-143, 153-154, 183-184, 200

–backgroundColorAnimation, 17

–buttonLayerHit, 184-185

–canDrawInCGLContext, 132-135, 159-160

–captureOutput:, 127

CATransform3DMakeRotation, 73-74

CATransform3DMakeScale, 72

–channelsReadyToDraw:, 144

–defaultActionForKey:, 102

–doItIn:, 11

–doTransition, 109

–drawAllInRect:, 146

–drawChannel:, 147-148

–drawInCGLContext, 132, 136-137, 159-160

–drawInContext:, 195

–drawLayer:, 201

–drawStar:, 213

–filters, 94-95

–getCurrentImage, 127-128

–getDotScreenImage:, 157

–gotoBeginning, 112

–gotoEnd, 112

–gotoNextSelectionPoint, 112

–gotoPosterFrame, 112

–gotoPreviousSelectionPoint, 112

–grabImage:, 128

–hitTest:, 179, 185

–(IBAction)action:(id)sender:, 77-79

–init, 181

–initCaptureSession, 124-125

–initVideoChannels, 140-142

–initWithFrame:, 172, 219

–initWithFrame:reuseIdentifier:, 197-199

kCAMediaTimingFunctionEaseInEaseOut, 39

–layerClass, 172

–mouseDown:, 185-187

–mouseEntered:, 187

–mouseExited:, 187

–mouseUp:, 186-188

–performSelectorOnMainThread:, 204

–play, 112

–readyToDrawNextFrame:, 145

–removeAnimation:, 9

–rotate3DTransform:, 73-74

–rotateTransform:, 72-73

–scaleTransform:, 70-72

–setAnimations:, 43

–setBounds:, 32, 109

–setCurrentTime:, 112

–setFillMode:, 40

–setFilters, 93

–setFrame:, 28-30

–setNeedsDisplay, 204

–setPosition, 4

–setRemovedOnCompletion:, 40

–setSelected:, 182

–setString:, 181

–setStrokeColor, 163

–setupVisualContext:, 135-136

–sliderMoved:, 115

–stepBackward, 112

–stepForward, 112

–stop, 112

–string:, 181

–throbAnimationDidStop:finished:context:, 221

–togglePlayback:, 117

–touchBegan:withEvent:, 219

–touchesCancelled:withEvent:, 220

–touchesEnded:withEvent:, 220-221

–touchesMoved:withEvent:, 222

–updateSlider:, 117, 121

–updateTimeStamp, 120

–valueForOutputKey:, 157

–viewDidLoad, 162-169

–zoom:, 201

Model–View–Controller (MVC) design pattern, 5

monitoring

animation progress, 52

keyframe destinations, 52-56

motion fields, animating, 17-18

mouse events

Color Changer sample application, 179

–awakeFromNib method, 183-184

–buttonLayerHit method, 184-185

–hitTest: method, 185

Interface Builder, 182

LZButtonLayer, 179-182

–mouseDown: method, 185-187

–mouseEntered: method, 187

–mouseExited: method, 187

–mouseUp: method, 186-188

hit testing CALayer objects, 177-179

mouseDown events, 89

overview, 177

–mouseDown: method, 185-187

–mouseEntered: method, 187

–mouseExited: method, 187

–mouseUp: method, 186-188

Move In transitions, 99

Movie Player with Overlay (QTMovieLayer–based player), 112-118

control buttons, 113-115

simple movie playback, 113

slider, 115

timer, 117-118

movies

adding overlays to, 118-119

adding time codes to, 119-121

Movie Player with Overlay (QTMovieLayer–based player), 112-118

control buttons, 113-115

simple movie playback, 113

slider, 115

timer, 117-118

multivideo streams, creating with Quartz Composer

compositions

adding filters to, 156

creating, 150-152

getting image data from, 155-156

input parameters, 152

passing parameters to, 154-155

obtaining current image in code, 157

overview, 149-150

QCCompositionLayer, 153-154

Xcode projects, creating, 152-153

multiple video channels, rendering, 138-139

OpenGLVidGridLayer, 139-148

−channelsReadyToDraw: function, 144

−drawAllInRect: function, 146

−drawChannel: function, 147-148

implementation of drawing functions, 143-144

initialization code, 140-142

initializing in AppDelegate, 142-143

−readyToDrawNextFrame: function, 145

VideoChannel, 139

VideoChannelController, 139

multithreaded animation, 202

locking layer changes, 203

threads and run loops, 204

with filters, 204

multithreading, 5

MVC (Model–View–Controller) design pattern, 5

N

nested transforms, 195

nondeletable applications, 57

NSAnimatablePropertyContainer, 28

NSAnimationContext object, 29-30

O

objects

animator proxy object, 28

binding in Star Label Animation application, 211, 213-214

CAAnimation, 9

NSAnimationContext, 29-30

offscreen rendering, 194

opacity property, 100

OpenGL layer. *See* CAOpenGLLayer

OpenGLVidGridLayer, 139-148

−channelsReadyToDraw: function, 144

−drawAllInRect: function, 146

−drawChannel: function, 147-148

−readyToDrawNextFrame: function, 145

implementation of drawing functions, 143-144

initialization code, 140-142

initializing in AppDelegate, 142-143

OS X, setting up Xcode projects for, 12-13

overlays, adding to movies, 118-119

overriding layerClass method, 172

P

pacing, 9-10

parameters, passing to Quartz Compositions, 154-155

path animation, 47

path stroke, manipulating with CAShapeLayer, 163-165

−performSelectorOnMainThread: method, 204

performance

    alpha blending, 196-199

    filters and shadows, 195

    hardware acceleration, 193-194

    multithreaded animation, 202

        with filters, 204

        locking layer changes, 203

        threads and run loops, 204

    nested transforms, 195

    offscreen rendering, 194

    overview, 193

    tiled layers, 199-202

    transition effects, 195

Photo Capture project

    capture session, initializing, 124-125

    current image, capturing, 127-129

    QTCaptureLayer, creating and displaying, 125-127

–play method, 112

positions of layers, animating, 36-37

positionUse property, 18

projects. *See also* **specific projects**

    application delegate class, 12, 33

    setting up Xcode projects for OS X, 12-13

    Xcode projects, creating, 33-34, 152-153

properties. *See* **specific properties**

Push transitions, 99

Q

QCCompositionLayer class, 7, 153-154

QCQuartzCompositionLayer class, 159-160

QTCaptureLayer, 123

    creating and displaying, 125-127

    current image, capturing, 127-129

    initializing capture session, 124-125

QTCaptureLayer class, 7

QTMovieLayer

    action methods, 112

    contentsRect, 122-123

    overlays, 118-119

    overview, 7, 111-112

    QTMovieLayer–based player, 112-118

        control buttons, 113-115

        simple movie playback, 113

        slider, 115

        timer, 117-118

    time codes, 119-121

Quartz Composer, creating multivideo streams with

    compositions

        adding filters to, 156

        creating, 150-152

        getting image data from, 155-156

        input parameters, 152

        passing parameters to, 154-155

    obtaining current image in code, 157

    and OpenGL, 159-160

    overview, 149-150

    QCCompositionLayer, 153-154

    Xcode projects, creating, 152-153

QuartzCore framework for Star Label Animation application, 211-214

 –animationDidStop: method, 214

 –applicationDidFinishLaunching: method, 213

 –drawStar: method, 213

 StarStepsAppDelegate interface, 212

QuickTime layers

 QTCaptureLayer, 123

  creating and displaying, 125-127

  current image, capturing, 127-129

  initializing capture session, 124-125

 QTMovieLayer

  action methods, 112

  contentsRect, 122-123

  overlays, 118-119

  overview, 111-112

  QTMovieLayer–based player, 112-118

  time codes, 119-121

QuickTime visual context, 135-136

R

random shaking, 61

–readyToDrawNextFrame: function, 145

Real–time Motion Graphics with Quartz Composer (Robinson and Buchwald), 149

receiving user input, 89-90

red background color, animating to green, 16-17

references, weak references, 180

reflection, applying with CAGradientLayer class, 168-171

–removeAnimation: method, 9

RemovedOnCompletion property (CABasicAnimation class), 40

rendering video

 in CAOpenGLLayer, 131-132

  advantages, 138

  –canDrawInCGLContext method, 132-135, 159-160

  display link callback signature, 133

  display links, 133

  –drawInCGLContext: method, 132, 136-137

  implementation of QuickTime visual context, 135-136

  layer timing, 133-138

 multiple video channels, 138-139

  OpenGLVidGridLayer, 139-148

  VideoChannel, 139

  VideoChannelController, 139

RepeatCount property (CABasicAnimation class), 41

RepeatDuration property (CABasicAnimation class), 41

ReplicatorView class

 adding to window, 173-174

 creating, 171-173

resizing

 layers, 31-32

 views, 30

 windows, 28-29

resolution independence, 164

Reveal transitions, 99

Ripple transition, 102-103

  AppDelegate implementation with delegation, 106-109

  AppDelegate implementation with encapsulation, 105-106

  RippleLayer interface, 104-105

RippleLayer interface, 104-105

root layers, adding animation layers to, 34-35

–rotate3DTransform:, 73-74

–rotateTransform:, 72-73

rotating layers

  along one axis, 72-73

  along two axes, 73-74

  magnitude of rotation, 73

  shake animation, 61

run loops, 204

S

–scaleTransform:, 70-72

scaling layers, 10-11, 70-72

selector methods, 54

–setAnimations: method, 43

–setBounds method, 32, 109

–setCurrentTime: method, 112

–setFillMode: method, 40

–setFilters method, 93

–setFrame: method

  view resizing, 30

  window resizing, 28-29

–setNeedsDisplay method, 204

–setPosition method, 4

–setRemovedOnCompletion: method, 40

–setSelected: method, 182

–setString: method, 181

–setStrokeColor method, 163

–setupVisualContext: method, 135-136

shadows, 195

shake animation, 57-61

  close box, adding, 61-62

  random shaking, 61

  rotation axis and layer geometry, 61

  starting/stopping, 64-65

shape layer. *See* CAShapeLayer

simplicity in design, 22

single keyframe animation, 66

–sliderMoved: method, 115

sliders, adding to Movie Player with Overlay project, 115

Speed property (CABasicAnimation class), 40

Star Label Animation application

  QuartzCore framework and object binding, 211-214

    –animationDidStop: method, 214

    –applicationDidFinishLaunching: method, 213

    –drawStar: method, 213

    StarStepsAppDelegate interface, 212

  setting up Xcode project, 209

  UIWindow, 210-211

  Xcode project setup, 209

StarStepsAppDelegate interface, 212

starting shake animation, 64-65

–stepBackward method, 112

–stepForward method, 112

stickiness (layer animation), 39-40

"sticky" effect, 91-92

–stop method, 112

stopping shake animation, 64-65

–string: method, 181

stroke, manipulating with CAShapeLayer, 163-165

@synthesize keyword, 93

T

–throbAnimationDidStop:finished:context: method, 221

tiled layers, 199-202

time codes, adding to movies, 119-121

TimeOffset property (CABasicAnimation class), 41

timing

default timing function, 38-39

keyframe animation, 50-51

monitoring keyframe destinations, 52-56

timers

adding to Movie Player with Overlay project, 117-118

selector methods for, 54

toggle functionality, 91

–togglePlayback: method, 117

touch system application

overview, 214-215

TouchableView, 218-223

header, 218

–initWithFrame: method, 219

–throbAnimationDidStop:finished:context: method, 221

–touchBegan:withEvent: method, 219

–touchesCancelled:withEvent: method, 220

–touchesEnded:withEvent: method, 220-221

–touchesMoved:withEvent: method, 222

TouchMeViewController, 216-218

Application Delegate's header, 217

Application Delegate's implementation, 217

TouchMeViewController.m implementation, 216

Xcode project setup, 215-216

TouchableView class, 218-223

header, 218

–initWithFrame: method, 219

–throbAnimationDidStop:finished:context: method, 221

–touchBegan:withEvent: method, 219

–touchesCancelled:withEvent: method, 220

–touchesEnded:withEvent: method, 220-221

–touchesMoved:withEvent: method, 222

–touchBegan:withEvent: method, 219

–touchesCancelled:withEvent: method, 220

–touchesEnded:withEvent: method, 220-221

–touchesMoved:withEvent: method, 222

TouchMeViewController class, 216-218

Application Delegate's header, 217

Application Delegate's implementation, 217

TouchMeViewController.m implementation, 216

transforms

anchor points, 74-75

combining, 76-79

definition of, 69

in Cocoa Touch, 69

nested transforms, 195

–rotate3DTransform:, 73-74

–rotateTransform:, 72-73

scale versus bounds, 79-80

–scaleTransform:, 70-72

transitions

filters

custom transitions, 101-108

default transitions, 98-100

performance issues, 195

tweening, 16, 45

24 frames per second (fps), 45

U

UI keyframe animation, 56-57

icon shake, 57-65

UIView, animations at UIView level

building application, 223

MainViewController, 223-226

UIWindow for Star Label Animation application, 210-211

–updateSlider: method, 117, 121

–updateTimeStamp method, 120

user interaction

keyboard events, 188-190

layer–backed views, 190

mouse events

Color Changer sample application, 179-188

hit testing CALayer objects, 177-179

overview, 177

user input, 23

receiving (filters), 89-90

V

–valueForOutputKey: method, 157

values animation, 49

video

rendering in CAOpenGLLayer, 131-132

advantages, 138

–canDrawInCGLContext method, 132-135, 159-160

display link callback signature, 133

display links, 133

–drawInCGLContext: method, 132, 136-137

implementation of QuickTime visual context, 135-136

layer timing, 133-138

rendering multiple video channels, 138-139

OpenGLVidGridLayer, 139-148

VideoChannel, 139

VideoChannelController, 139

VideoChannel, 139

VideoChannelController, 139

–viewDidLoad method, 162-169

views

layer–backed views, 190

LZContentView, 178

resizing, 30

TouchableView, 218-223

–initWithFrame: method, 219

–throbAnimationDidStop:finished:context: method, 221

–touchBegan:withEvent: method, 219

–touchesCancelled:withEvent: method, 220

–touchesEnded:withEvent: method, 220-221

–touchesMoved:withEvent:
    method, 222

header, 218

visibility fields, animating, 18

visual stickiness, 39-40

W-X-Y-Z

weak references, 180

windows, resizing, 28-29

Xcode projects
    creating, 33-34, 152-153
    setting up, 209
        for OS X, 12-13
        touch system application, 215-216

–zoom: method, 201

zPosition property, 18

Essential Resources for Mac/iPhone Developers

Cocoa Design Patterns
Eric M. Buck and
Donald A. Yacktman
ISBN-13: 978-0-321-53502-3

The iPhone™ Developer's Cookbook, Second Edition
Erica Sadun
ISBN-13: 978-0-321-65957-6

Cocoa® Programming for Mac® OS X, Third Edition
Aaron Hillegass
ISBN-13: 978-0-321-50361-9

iPhone® for Programmers
Paul Deitel,
Harvey Deitel,
Abbey Deitel, Eric Kern,
and Michael Morgano
ISBN-13: 978-0-137-05842-6

Developing Hybrid Applications for the iPhone
Lee S. Barney
ISBN-13: 978-0-321-60416-3

Programming in Objective-C 2.0
Stephen G. Kochan
ISBN-13: 978-0-321-56615-7

Cocoa® Programming Developer's Handbook
David Chisnall
ISBN-13: 978-0-321-63963-9

Addison Wesley

PRENTICE HALL

For more information and to read sample material, please visit informit.com/learnmac.

Safari Books Online

Titles are also available at safari.informit.com.

inform**IT****.com** THE TRUSTED TECHNOLOGY LEARNING SOURCE

 InformIT is a brand of Pearson and the online presence for the world's leading technology publishers. It's your source for reliable and qualified content and knowledge, providing access to the top brands, authors, and contributors from the tech community.

 Addison-Wesley **Cisco Press** EXAM**CRAM** **IBM** Press.   QUE PRENTICE HALL **SAMS** | Safari

LearnIT at InformIT

Looking for a book, eBook, or training video on a new technology? Seeking timely and relevant information and tutorials? Looking for expert opinions, advice, and tips? **InformIT has the solution.**

- Learn about new releases and special promotions by subscribing to a wide variety of newsletters. Visit **informit.com/newsletters**.

- Access FREE podcasts from experts at **informit.com/podcasts**.

- Read the latest author articles and sample chapters at **informit.com/articles**.

- Access thousands of books and videos in the Safari Books Online digital library at **safari.informit.com**.

- Get tips from expert blogs at **informit.com/blogs**.

Visit **informit.com/learn** to discover all the ways you can access the hottest technology content.

Are You Part of the **IT** Crowd?

Connect with Pearson authors and editors via RSS feeds, Facebook, Twitter, YouTube, and more! Visit **informit.com/socialconnect**.

inform**IT****.com** THE TRUSTED TECHNOLOGY LEARNING SOURCE PEARSON

 Addison-Wesley **Cisco Press** EXAM**CRAM** **IBM** Press. QUE PRENTICE HALL **SAMS** | Safari

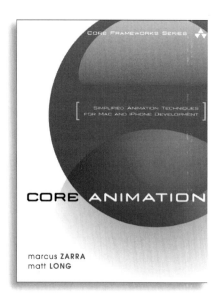

FREE Online Edition

Your purchase of **Core Animation** includes access to a free online edition for 45 days through the Safari Books Online subscription service. Nearly every Addison-Wesley Professional book is available online through Safari Books Online, along with more than 5,000 other technical books and videos from publishers such as Cisco Press, Exam Cram, IBM Press, O'Reilly, Prentice Hall, Que, and Sams.

SAFARI BOOKS ONLINE allows you to search for a specific answer, cut and paste code, download chapters, and stay current with emerging technologies.

Activate your FREE Online Edition at www.informit.com/safarifree

> **STEP 1:** Enter the coupon code: YPPLYFA.

> **STEP 2:** New Safari users, complete the brief registration form.
> Safari subscribers, just log in.

If you have difficulty registering on Safari or accessing the online edition, please e-mail customer-service@safaribooksonline.com